THE BUZZ ABOUT
LISA A. SHIEL'S BOOKS

BACKYARD BIGFOOT

*W*hether [you are a] novice or experienced researcher…*Backyard Bigfoot* is as informative as it is entertaining, and most especially recommended to the attention of those with an interest in human evolution, lost civilizations, UFOs, ancient artwork, metaphysical studies, and the legendary Sasquatch.
Midwest Book Review

*A*bsolutely one of the best types of investigative reporting I've seen as Shiel compiles so much information into this one little book that you will read [it] over and over again.…Whether you believe or not, you will enjoy the questions driven from this complete book of information.
Beverly Pechin, Reader Views

*W*ith the number of Bigfoot-related books available these days, I appreciate authors who try to push the envelope of this genre by investigating and discussing the most controversial aspects of this suprisingly complicated subject.…Lisa is to commended for her years of field observations, her thorough presentation of academic considerations, and her willingness to develop a coherent theory that unifies disparate academic and field matters. Lisa's book has everything I like to see in a Bigfoot book.
Tom Powell, Author of *The Locals: A Contemporary Investigation of the Bigfoot/Sasquatch Phenomenon*

*Y*ou may agree or not with her conclusions but you will be thoroughly entertained by the discussions.
Andrew Grgurich, *The Mining Journal* (Marquette, Mich.)

*R*eference-style books are fine; but if you are determined to go to the next level of your understanding and appreciation of the creature that is Bigfoot, listen to the witnesses. But when the author and the witness are one and the same, you are in for a real treat.
From the Foreword by Nick Redfern Author, *On The Trail Of The Saucer Spies*

THE BUZZ ABOUT
LISA A. SHIEL'S BOOKS

THE EVOLUTION CONSPIRACY

L isa Shiel is consistently convincing…that Evolutionary Scientists have defined "facts" and "theory" to suit themselves and in a way that any other scientific field (such as physics, mathematics, biochemistry, etc.) would find completely inappropriate.

Dr. Quinton R. Rogers, Distinguished Professor Emeritus
Dept. of Molecular Biosciences, School of Veterinary Medicine
University of California, Davis

T his gem of a book sheds light on the current status of evolution as a scientific theory.…The book is concise, lucid, and to the point. Although authoritative and well referenced, it is written in such a way as to be accessible to all levels of readers, from intelligent high school students to doctoral candidates at universities.

Michael A. Cremo, Author
Forbidden Archeology, Human Devolution, etc.

I n an era of learned helplessness and deference to authority, Lisa shows interested non-specialists can comprehend evolution and discover for themselves where scientific theory is strong and where it needs some additional work.

Tyler A. Kokjohn, PhD
Professor of Microbiology, Midwestern University

L isa Shiel makes the most difficult issues easy to comprehend. She explains the myriad of complex words, even providing the average Joe a glossary with useful definitions…This book is a delight because it encourages questioning and urges readers to think for themselves…Shiel reminds us that we can question, and we should.

Emily Decobert, BookPleasures.com

S cientifically rigorous and extensively researched…systematically dismantles the arguments that have long been the cornerstone of Darwinian hegemony in the biological sciences in workmanlike fashion, illustrating exactly what is wrong with the theory in a compelling and easy-to-understand text…A triumph of logic over dogma!

Timothy Birdnow
American Daily Review

FORBIDDEN BIGFOOT

Other Books by Lisa A. Shiel

Fiction

From Jacobsville Books

Confronting Sasquatch
Faces of Bigfoot [e-book]
Faces of Bigfoot 2 [e-book]
The Faces of Bigfoot Collection [e-book]

The Human Origins Series
The Hunt for Bigfoot (Book One)
Lord of the Dead (Book Two)
Relic of the Ancient Ones (Book Three)
Revenge of the Ancient Ones (Book Four)
Bigfoot Beginnings (Backstories, Vol. 1) [e-book]
The Bigfoot Effect (Backstories, Vol. 2) [e-book]
Traces of Bigfoot (Backstories, Vol. 1& 2) [e-book]
Bigfoot, Mummies, and Aliens: The Human Origins Series
    Collection (Books 1-4 with Backstories Vol. 1 & 2) [e-book]

Nonfiction

From Jacobsville Books

Creature of Controversy (Forbidden Bigfoot, Part One) [e-book]
Top Secret Sasquatch (Forbidden Bigfoot, Part Two) [e-book]
Backyard Phenomena (Forbidden Bigfoot, Part Three) [e-book]
The Evolution Conspiracy
Backyard Bigfoot

From The History Press

Forgotten Tales of Michigan's Upper Peninsula

From Trails Books

Strange Michigan (with Linda S. Godfrey)

FORBIDDEN BIGFOOT

exposing the controversial truth about Sasquatch, stick signs, UFOs, human origins, and the strange phenomena in our own backyards

✳

LISA A. SHIEL

Jacobsville Books
Lake Linden, Michigan

ISBN: 978-1-934631-54-6 (pbk., b&w)
ISBN: 978-1-934631-29-4 (pbk., color)
ISBN: 978-1-934631-41-6 (e-book: EPUB)

Manufactured in the United States.

Jacobsville Books
www.JacobsvilleBooks.com

Publisher's Cataloging-in-Publication Data

Names: Shiel, Lisa A.
Title: Forbidden Bigfoot : exposing the controversial truth about Sasquatch, stick signs, UFOs, human origins, and the strange phenomena in our own backyards / Lisa A. Shiel.
Description: First black & white edition. | Lake Linden, MI : Jacobsville Books, 2017. | Previously published in 2013 with a full color interior. | Includes bibliographical references and index.
Identifiers: ISBN 978-1-934631-54-6 (pbk., b&w) | ISBN 978-1-934631-29-4 (pbk., color) | ISBN 978-0-978-1-934631-41-6 (ebook)
Subjects: LCSH: Sasquatch. | Unidentified flying objects. | Cryptozoology. | DNA. | Fossil hominids. | BISAC: NATURE / Animals / Wildlife. | BODY, MIND & SPIRIT / Unexplained Phenomena. | BODY, MIND & SPIRIT / Ancient Mysteries & Controversial Knowledge.
Classification: LCC QL89.2.S2 S55 2017 (print) | LCC QL89.2.S2 (ebook) | DDC 001.9/44--dc23.

Contents

Preface

l didn't set out to become a Bigfoot researcher. For years I had been interested in Bigfoot and other strange topics, such as UFOs and alternative history. When I decided to write my first novel, *The Hunt for Bigfoot*, researching the topic of hairy, bipedal creatures was a natural first step.

I began my Bigfoot research the way many people do—I read every book I could find on the subject, watched documentaries, and visited websites. Soon, however, I began to wonder if the books, documentaries, and websites told the whole story. Something seemed to be missing. Virtually all of the sources I found advocated the theory that Bigfoot represents a type of giant ape, probably remnants of an ape called *Gigantopithecus*, known solely from fossils that date to no later than 300,000 years ago.

The giant ape theory raised questions in my mind. Why do eyewitnesses report un-apelike behavior, such as walking upright and running on two legs? What about evidence of stone tool use? Why do witnesses describe the creatures' faces as humanlike?

Thus began my career in Bigfoot research. After finishing my novel, I went on to write the nonfiction *Backyard Bigfoot*, with a significant portion of that book detailing my personal experiences. For several years, I ran a research group and actively collected sightings via a website. Though I still consider myself a Bigfoot researcher, I am first and foremost a writer. Maintaining a website and running a research group ate up precious time that I preferred to spend on writing books, both fiction and nonfiction, as well as magazine articles. As a consequence, I disbanded my research group and I no longer actively collect sightings.

Have I given up on Bigfoot? Absolutely not.

My desire to focus on writing is the main reason I've pulled back from official Bigfoot research (I use the word "official" in its very loosest sense here), but another reason plays a role as well. Bigfoot research is crazy!

Now before anyone gets riled up over my use of the C-word, let me explain. I don't mean that an interest in Bigfoot marks a person as insane. I mean that getting involved in Bigfoot research immerses you in a world of infighting, backstabbing, chicanery, and questionable behavior that may drive you to pull out your own hair. Cherry-picking data, censoring sightings, verbally abusing other researchers—all of this and more plagues the community of paranormal researchers in general, and Bigfoot researchers in particular.

Are all Bigfoot researchers guilty of these actions? Of course not. Because of my involvement with Bigfoot research, I've met many nice people, both researchers and witnesses. I've also encountered some people who are, to put it politely, misleading the public. They might edit sighting reports submitted by witnesses to remove anything that upsets their preconceived notions about Bigfoot. They might ridicule anyone who disagrees with those preconceived notions. They might fudge the data a bit or, at the very worst end of the spectrum, fabricate evidence to support their ideas or simply to get attention or bilk people out of money.

For this reason, much of Bigfoot research remains hidden from public view. Aspects of the Bigfoot phenomenon that are too controversial even for Bigfoot researchers to deal with rarely, if ever, get mentioned in TV documentaries or books about Bigfoot. Documentaries have gone the way of "reality TV," while most books about Bigfoot stick to rehashing the Patterson-Gimlin film or retelling the famous sightings.

When I wrote *Backyard Bigfoot*, I aimed to discuss topics rarely found in Bigfoot books (like the Bigfoot-UFO connection), along with my personal experiences with stick signs and mane braiding. I also critiqued the Giganto theory and connected evolution and human origins to the

Bigfoot phenomenon. Since the publication of *Backyard Bigfoot*, I've interviewed witnesses, developed new ideas that I explored on my blogs, interacted with other researchers, and continued to have personal experiences of the paranormal variety.

Enter *Forbidden Bigfoot*.

This book is the culmination of a decade of research into and experiences with the Bigfoot phenomenon. Once again, I aim to discuss controversial topics found in few, if any, Bigfoot books and to present evidence culled from my own original research. I will also do something that is practically verboten in Bigfoot research—I will theorize. And I'll explain why theories have, in their own right, become a controversial topic.

In Part One, I lay the groundwork with a discussion of the controversies within Bigfoot research, some secret and some well known, and how these arguments affect the current state of Bigfoot research. Part One also incorporates interviews I conducted with other Bigfoot researchers, who shared their candid opinions with me—and now with you. Part Two delves deep into the forbidden territory with discussions of UFOs and other high strangeness, theories galore (no matter how bizarre), and the facts about Bigfoot versus what we wish we knew about these creatures. Finally, in Part Three, I'll update my research into stick signs and mane braiding, complete with brand-new photos.

For reasons we'll explore in Part One, not every Bigfoot researcher capitalizes the word Bigfoot and not everyone calls these creatures Bigfoot. For the sake of consistency, and simplicity, I will generally refer to the creatures as Bigfoot (whether I mean one or several) and the term will be capitalized throughout this book. Also, the Bigfoot researchers I interviewed for this book often disagree with my opinions and conclusions about Bigfoot. The main body of the text is based on my thoughts and may or may not reflect the opinions of those interviewed. Their thoughts are included in sidebars or, when found in the main text, are clearly marked as quotes from a particular person. Everything else should be assumed to be my opinions.

When my thoughts disagree with those of the researchers quoted, doing so is not meant to denigrate the interviewees. I respect their opinions, and I'm grateful they agreed to share their thoughts in this book. Now...

Get ready to explore the forbidden territory in the Bigfoot woods.

As always, the hunt for truth never ends. Instead, it just gets weirder and weirder.

Acknowledgments

I offer my gratitude to the researchers who allowed me to interview them for this book. Their answers to my questions provide a no-holds-barred view of Bigfoot research heretofore available only to those folks interested enough to comb the Internet for hours upon hours, wading through forums and blog posts and web articles.

Want to know more about the researchers quoted in this book? Your wish is my command:

ERIC ALTMAN is a Bigfoot field investigator, the director of the Pennsylvania Bigfoot Society, a paranormal enthusiast, and an Internet talk show host/producer. In 1997, Eric began active field research into the Bigfoot phenomenon. In 1998, Eric joined the Pennsylvania Bigfoot Society, and in 2000, became the group's director. He has investigated over 250 Bigfoot cases and—along with his good friend and colleague, Sean Forker—developed the web-based talk show "Beyond The Edge Radio."

Eric's website: pabigfootsociety.com

MELISSA HOVEY, an Ohio-based researcher, is the president of the American Bigfoot Society (ABS). She runs the website "The Search for Bigfoot" and co-hosts the web-based radio shows "Let's Talk Bigfoot," "The Sasquatch Experience," and "The Grey Area." Since 2006, Melissa has explored the mystery of why false dermal ridges (lines similar to fingerprints) appear in some plaster casts of Bigfoot tracks. Melissa has also been featured on the History Channel's "MonsterQuest" series as part of an all-female Bigfoot expedition.

Melissa's website: americanbigfootsociety166.weebly.com

KATHY MOSKOWITZ STRAIN has a BA (1990) and an MA (1994) in anthropology from California State University, Bakersfield. Kathy is currently the Heritage Resource and Tribal Relations Programs Manager for the Stanislaus National Forest in California, where she is responsible for all archaeological, historical, and tribal resources. She is the author of *Giants, Cannibals & Monsters: Bigfoot in Native Culture*, published by Hancock House Publishers (2008).

NICK REDFERN is an author, lecturer, and journalist who writes about a wide range of unsolved mysteries, including Bigfoot, UFOs, and government conspiracies. He writes regularly for *UFO Magazine*, *Fate*, and *Fortean Times*. His books include *The Real Men In Black*, *There's Something in the Woods*, and *Memoirs of a Monster Hunter*. Nick has appeared on television shows such as the History Channel's "MonsterQuest" and the Syfy Channel's "Proof Positive."

Nick's website: nickredfern.com

THOM POWELL is an author, a science teacher with twenty-six years experience, an expert kayaker, and a whitewater river guide. He has written two Bigfoot-related books—*The Locals: A Contemporary Investigation of the Bigfoot/Sasquatch Phenomenon* and *Shady Neighbors*, which weaves some of his radical ideas about Bigfoot into a fictional story. Thom continues to be an avid outdoorsman, gardener, and writer, living with his family on a farm in rural Clackamas County, Oregon.

Thom's website: thomsquatch.com

REGAN LEE is a writer and researcher interested in the anomalous, as well as a witness to several UFO incidents. She writes for UFO Magazine and for numerous websites—including Binnall of America, UFO Digest, and several of her own blogs dedicated to paranormal subjects. She's currently working on two books, one about a Bigfoot sighting in her home state of Oregon and another about her personal UFO experiences.

Regan's website: reganleeufo.blogspot.com

Part One

Creature of Controversy

*It is not he who gains the exact point in dispute
who scores most in controversy—but he who has
shown the better temper.*

Samuel Butler

.

1
The Battle Zone

Bigfoot is a controversial topic in and of itself. Despite the fact that a lot of people believe in Bigfoot, or are at least interested in it, the media and mainstream scientists continue to scoff at the notion that an unrecognized species of hairy, bipedal creatures exists anywhere on earth. Although no scientific polls have been conducted concerning Bigfoot, a survey of visitors to the paranormal section of the About.com website found that 80% of respondents believed Bigfoot exists in some form. The highest percentage of respondents (38%) thought Bigfoot was neither a species of ape nor a bear, compared with 31% who agreed with the ape hypothesis.

Why do people believe in Bigfoot? I can't answer for all people, and I wouldn't want to, but I can present the reasons I believe.

Five Reasons Bigfoot Must Exist

Any researcher who understands the nature of the evidence must admit that the evidence for Bigfoot's existence remains anecdotal at worst and circumstantial at best. Eyewitnesses provide crucial clues, but eyewitness testimony alone will never convince the scientific establishment of

Bigfoot's existence. Yes, courts of law accept eyewitness testimony and circumstantial evidence, and juries often convict human beings of crimes based on these types of evidence. The key phrase here, however, is "human beings." Convicting a member of a known species—namely, human beings—of a crime is totally different than attempting to prove the existence of a species science rejects as pure myth. Yet those of us who believe in Bigfoot believe with good cause. Here are my top five reasons why Bigfoot must exist.

1. **Thousands of new species** are discovered every year, which suggests even more are still undiscovered. Arizona State University's International Institute for Species Exploration listed 19,232 new species identified in 2009 alone, including 41 new species of mammals (though most were rodents and bats). In the decade 2000-2009, scientists found 359 new living mammal species, including small primates. Scientists have also discovered new tribes of human beings, who have avoided contact with the rest of the world until now.

   Figure 1.1: After decades of searching, scientists finally tracked down the "highland mangabey," now officially known as *Lophocebus kipunji*. Tanzanian locals had told tales of the monkeys, but despite their small range of just 28 square miles, the species was not found until 2003 and not officially declared as a new species until 2005. Drawing by Zina Deretsky, National Science Foundation.

2. **Unexplored and/or uninhabited regions** still exist on our planet. The discovery of previously unknown tribes attests to this fact. Some people may believe no corner of this world is unexplored, but they would be wrong.

3. **Thousands of eyewitnesses** have reported seeing hairy, bipedal, nonhuman creatures in locations around the world.

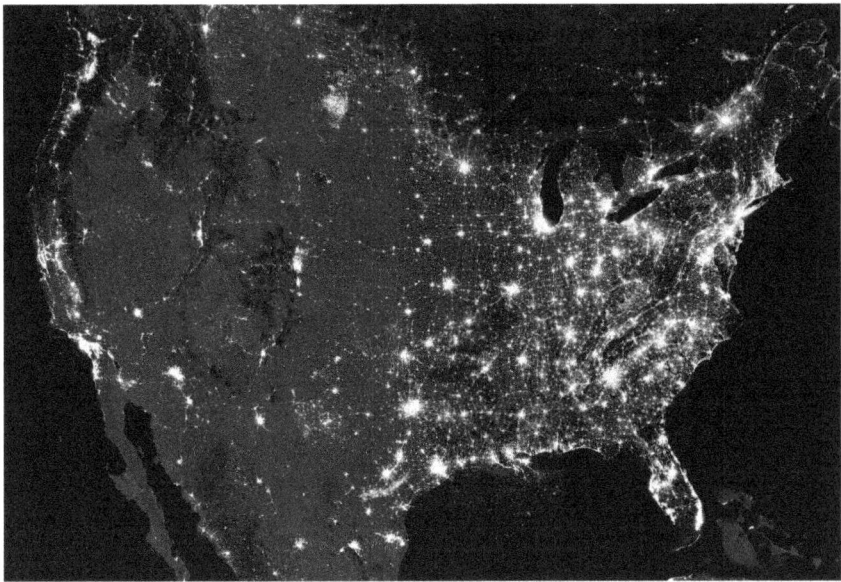

Figure 1.2: This nighttime view of the United States illustrates the coverage of city lights. Much of the western U.S. is blank, and Michigan's U.P. is barely even visible. Composite image courtesy of NASA Earth Observatory; image by Robert Simmon, using Suomi NPP VIIRS data provided courtesy of Chris Elvidge (NOAA National Geophysical Data Center).

The Uninhabited World

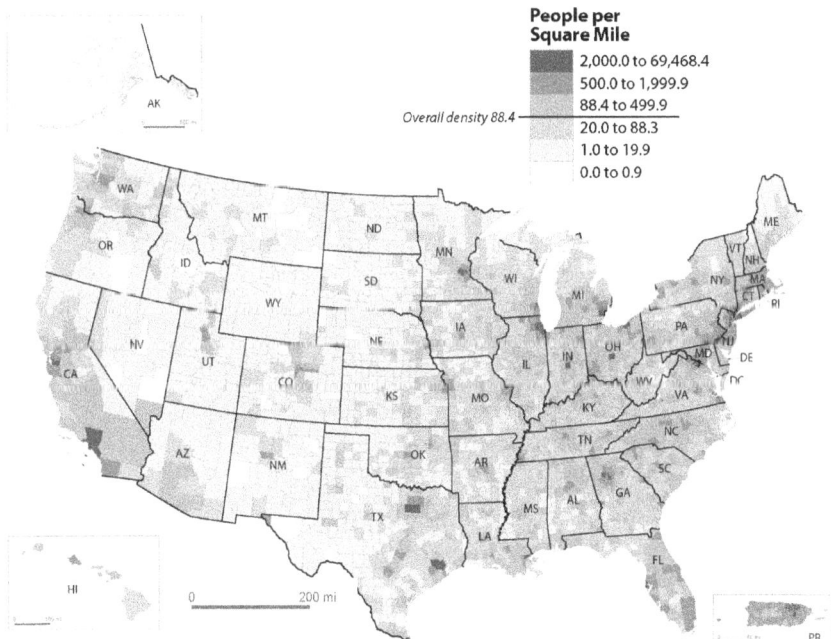

Figure 1.3: This map shows the average population per square mile for the United States, broken down by counties. Even in the U.S., many areas remain sparsely populated. Map courtesy of the U.S. Census Bureau, based on the 2010 Census Redistricting Data.

The witnesses run the gamut from cops to schoolteachers, and from scientists to lumberjacks. Sightings have been reported for hundreds, and perhaps thousands, of years.

4. **Thousands of footprints**, from single prints to long sequences of tracks, have turned up in every region where witnesses report sightings. Scientific analysis of the footprints has consistently demonstrated that they are not bear tracks or human footprints, but rather, the genuine traces of a scientifically unrecognized species.

5. **Neither hoaxing nor misidentification** can explain every footprint discovery and every eyewitness sighting reported throughout history, around the globe.

People who believe in Bigfoot clearly understand these reasons, and that's why they risk ridicule by accepting the existence of hairy, bipedal beings. With so much popular support, one might expect that a shared belief and shared ridicule might unite the people who research the Bigfoot phenomenon.

Think again.

Disunited Front

The scientific establishment denies Bigfoot exists, and no one has obtained the ultimate proof to convince scientists that such a species does indeed walk the planet. Within the Bigfoot research community, however, a surprising amount of controversy simmers and frequently boils over—though not because of arguments over whether the creatures exist. No, the tempers of Bigfoot researchers flare over everything from Bigfoot intelligence to the meanings of words. What follows is a necessarily incomplete list of topics sure to get the Bigfoot research kettle boiling:

The biggest controversy in Bigfoot research is...

The fact that people can't seem to agree and share information. For some reason, most people in this field seem to think that their opinion is the only opinion that matters and no one else can be right.

Eric Altman

- ⤷ Should the word Bigfoot be capitalized? Should Sasquatch be capitalized?
- ⤷ What is the plural of Bigfoot?

- Should we call them Bigfoot at all, or use an alternate term? What alternate term is preferable?

- Is Bigfoot paranormal? What does the word paranormal mean anyway? Can Bigfoot be both flesh-and-blood *and* paranormal?

- Is the term belief a dirty word? Should we shun it?

The biggest controversy in Bigfoot research is…

Everybody talks about the paranormal and then they talk about UFOs, but they lump the two together.

Melissa Hovey

- What does a Bigfoot look like? Is it humanlike, apelike, or something else?

- How smart are Bigfoot-type creatures? Are they more like humans or apes?

- Can a Bigfoot speak or communicate in a humanlike fashion?

- What *are* Bigfoot-type creatures? Are they hominids, humans, apes, aliens, or something else? What do all those words mean?

- How much do we really *know* about Bigfoot? What is the difference between knowing and believing?

- Do we have any hard evidence to prove Bigfoot's existence? What is hard evidence? What is proof? What is a fact?

- Will Bigfoot's existence ever be proven scientifically? What would it take to prove Bigfoot's existence?

- Should researchers kill a Bigfoot to prove the creatures exist? Can we prove it without killing one?

- Is it okay for Bigfoot researchers to censor the sightings submitted to them, to remove anything that goes against their preconceived notions?

- How big an effect does hoaxing have on Bigfoot research? What percentage of the sightings are credible? How do we decide if a sighting is credible?

The biggest controversy in Bigfoot research is…

"Kill" and "no kill."

Kathy Strain

- Are Bigfoot creatures descendents of *Gigantopithecus*? What was *Gigantopithecus* and did it look anything like Bigfoot?

- Should we believe a witness who claims to have had multiple encounters with Bigfoot-type beings? Should we believe a researcher who claims the same thing? Is there a double standard in Bigfoot research?

↬ Does Bigfoot share a connection with any other phenomena, such as UFOs?

The final question on the list, concerning a connection to other phenomena like UFOs, towers above all others as the most controversial topic in Bigfoot research. When phenomena cross boundaries—for instance, when a Bigfoot is seen with a UFO—the circumstance is often referred to as high strangeness. The person often credited with inventing the term high strangeness is J. Allen Hynek, a scientist who eventually became a UFO investigator, first with the Air Force's Project Blue Book and later as the founder of the Center for UFO Studies (CUFOS). Today, researchers apply the term high strangeness anytime another phenomenon dips its toes into their favorite arena of research. To UFO researchers, a Bigfoot is high strangeness when seen in conjunction with a UFO. To Bigfoot researchers, a UFO is high strangeness when seen in conjunction with a Bigfoot. Just about anything that falls outside the realm of what is acceptable to any particular researcher will qualify as high strangeness.

Another Bigfoot researcher might add topics to the above list. The biggest controversy of the moment changes regularly, but the topics in the list I've compiled are the most common sources of disagreement among Bigfoot researchers—although "disagreement" may be a bit of an understatement.

For some people, it's war.

> *The biggest controversy in Bigfoot research is...*
>
> The kill/no-kill and the so-called flesh-and-blood compared to a more high-strangeness kind of creature—the encounters with Bigfoot-type creatures that include things like UFOs and strange, paranormal events.
>
> *Regan Lee*

> *The biggest controversy in Bigfoot research is...*
>
> Without any doubt...why we haven't been able to catch Bigfoot or find a body or any hard evidence—which flies in the face, in my view, of any other animal that doesn't fall in the realm of cryptozoology.
>
> *Nick Redfern*

> *The biggest controversy in Bigfoot research is...*
>
> It doesn't exist, the evidence is fake, the government is hiding it, it's a conspiracy—and then of course, what does it all mean?
>
> *Thom Powell*

2
A War of Words

The battle over Bigfoot starts in an unexpected place—with
the word itself. The proliferation of websites and organizations named after
Bigfoot conceals a strange reality about Bigfoot research. Nearly every
aspect of the term Bigfoot holds within it the capability to trigger an all-
out war of words. And the skirmishes begin with the very first letter of
the word.

A Capital Offense

On a daily basis, millions of people unknowingly commit a heinous
crime. If you have ever written the word Bigfoot with a capital B then,
according to some Bigfoot researchers, you have breached the laws of
grammatical, cryptozoological, and political correctness. How can this
be so? According to some researchers, you have insulted the entire population of large, hairy bipedal creatures by insinuating only one such
creature exists. The crime was committed through the simple act of
capitalizing the word Bigfoot.

What difference does it make whether the word is capitalized or not?
According to *Merriam-Webster's Collegiate Dictionary, 11th ed.*, the word

Bigfoot may be written uncapitalized, but in common usage it's frequently capitalized. In other words, either way is correct. In library cataloging, my other field of expertise, Bigfoot is capitalized in book titles, even though other words generally are not. Library cataloging rules for capitalization are complex, but even the Library of Congress capitalizes Bigfoot.

On the word Bigfoot...

To capitalize a word (in my world) means it refers to "one" or "formal" and non-capitalized means "general group."...There is no one single Bigfoot, rather Bigfoot is a group representing many.

Kathy Strain

Library cataloging guidelines won't convince a cryptozoologist, though, and a dictionary definition rarely suffices in the world of Bigfoot research. When the topic of capitalization arises, someone will raise the objection that capitalizing the word gives the impression just one Bigfoot exists, rather than a population of the mysterious animals. (Many scientists would say this is a great reason to capitalize the word!) The argument lacks real merit, however, since we capitalize many words that refer to groups rather than individuals—such as American. The word American is always capitalized, whether it refers to one person ("an American") or a group ("American citizens"). Other words are sometimes capitalized and sometimes not. The word professor is usually lowercase, except when used as a title (e.g., Professor Smith). Names of Indian tribes, such as the Hopi, are capitalized—though no one claims the term Hopi refers to a solitary person.

On the word Bigfoot...

I use Sasquatch and Bigfoot interchangeably...I capitalize it. I just say Bigfoot—I might say something like "a family of Bigfoot" or "the witness saw two Bigfoot crossing the road."

Regan Lee

I prefer to capitalize the word Bigfoot, for two simple reasons. First, I see the word most commonly capitalized in everyday usage. Second, the word just looks funny when lowercased. It's a personal preference. None of the anti-capitalization proponents can offer a better reason for their viewpoint.

What should we conclude from all this? Despite what some Bigfoot researchers claim, the English language includes no law, grammatical or otherwise, about capitalizing the word Bigfoot. There's also no reason other than personal preference for embracing or eschewing capitalization. When it comes to the word Bigfoot, feel free to capitalize or not. I promise not to report you to the Bigfoot capitalization police.

What's Good for the Goose

So you've made a decision about whether to capitalize the word Bigfoot. Now the linguistic road ahead seems unobstructed—until your tire hits a nail, and you wind up crashed in the ditch. From whence did the nail come? The metal surprise probably originated with a Bigfoot researcher who heard you say "Bigfeet" or "Bigfoots."

What is the proper plural of Bigfoot?

As it turns out, no one can agree. If we go back to the *Merriam-Webster's Collegiate Dictionary*, we find out that according to the language experts the correct plural is either Bigfeet or Bigfoots. Many Bigfoot researchers would disagree. In fact, folks using either of those plural forms might find themselves on the receiving end of a tirade. The plural form should be Bigfoot, some people say, and as proof of this they point to words like moose and deer. The plural forms of these words are the same as the singular form: one moose, two moose; one deer, two deer. The trouble with comparing nouns is that inconsistencies plague the English language. Take moose and goose, for example, two words spelled similarly. The plural of moose is moose, but the plural of goose is geese. Likewise, the plural of grouse is grouse or grouses but the plural of mouse is mice.

An argument against using Bigfoot

On the word Bigfoot...

Whatever you feel comfortable calling it works. I've had people say that for multiple Bigfoot it should be called Bigfoot and leave it at that, or Bigfeet. It doesn't matter. I try not to worry about the smaller, silly stuff.

Eric Altman

On the word Bigfoot...

I just call it Bigfoot....People take this stuff so seriously sometimes, and oftentimes it's not even about things that really matter....It blows me away what some people will find as being the most important topic, and it really has nothing to do with what we're trying to do....When I find this animal, I'm going to name it Melissa's animal and just tick off everybody.

Melissa Hovey

as the plural and singular has arisen, though. Some folks say it's too confusing and, as with capitalizing the word, may give the impression that only one Bigfoot creature exists in the world. Is the general public so easily confused? In my experience, most people understand that when you talk about Bigfoot, whether or not you capitalize the word and whatever plural form you use, you're talking about more than one individual. If I say "Bigfoot live in various environments around the world," most folks will understand I mean the term Bigfoot to refer to a group rather than one animal. Only debunkers use the term Bigfoot to imply that just one creature exists, and therefore Bigfoot is a myth.

How then can we know what plural form to use for Bigfoot? As I said, the dictionary advises us to use Bigfeet or Bigfoots. I generally say Bigfoot, whether I mean one or many. Why do I go against the dictionary? It's personal preference, pure and simple. Bigfeet sounds silly to me, and Bigfoots strikes me as awkward. So

Figure 2.1: One moose, two moose. Photo by Ryan Hagerty/U.S. Fish & Wildlife Service.

while in general I defer to the dictionary, in this particular case I depart from standard usage. However, I reserve the right to change my mind at any time without advance notice.

What word should you use when referring to more than one hairy, humanoid creature? In the grand scheme of things, it makes no difference. Use whichever plural form you like.

Figure 2.2: One goose, but two geese. Photo by Donna Dewhurst/U.S. Fish & Wildlife Service.

A Bigfoot by Any Other Name

Just when we think we've figured out how to spell Bigfoot, we run head-first into another brick wall of controversy. Should we even call these creatures Bigfoot?

Some Bigfoot researchers spend an inordinate amount of time discussing, and often arguing over, what to call these creatures. Names bandied about include the well-known alternative term of Sasquatch, as well as lesser-known terms such as forest giants. Besides being a waste of time, such arguments make researchers look petty. What's in a name anyway?

Certain people contend the name Bigfoot is insulting to the hairy, bipedal creatures to whom it refers. Although I've seen the term forest giant used on e-mail discussion lists, these creatures don't live solely in the forest. Besides, Bigfoot-type creatures in Florida are known as skunk apes, a name that hardly flatters the creatures. Should we rename the Florida creatures swamp giants? That won't work either, though, because not all of them are giants. Invoking the term giant might insult shorter creatures, just as the term Bigfoot supposedly insults these hairy humanoids by referring to their feet as, um…not small.

> ## On the word Bigfoot…
>
> I call them Bigfoot.…People are smart enough to recognize that you're not really talking about just one running around here, there, or everywhere. You might have an English professor who says technically that's not correct to say this in a sentence.… When you get down that path, you're heading into obsessive-compulsive disorder territory.
>
> **Nick Redfern**

Figure 2.3: What should we call Bigfoot? Well, this one answers to John Skidmore. John was the mascot at the 2011 Bigfoot Bash in Comins, Michigan. Photo by Lisa A. Shiel.

I've heard people use the term squatch, a contraction of Sasquatch. Squatch sounds a lot like squat, which might seem insulting too. Even with the term Sasquatch, we run into a problem. Sasquatch is derived from a word in the Salish language spoken by certain tribes in the Pacific Northwest. Perhaps Bigfoot of different regions find it insulting when we refer to them by a name specific to one region.

The term Bigfoot seems to be the most widely recognized among the general public. Everyone knows what you mean when you talk about Bigfoot. But with so many terms to choose from, each of us faces a decision. What should we call these creatures? Ignore the petty arguments and make up your own mind.

3
The Semantics of Sasquatch

The English language can be confusing. With at least 30% of the language borrowed from French, and the remainder a mishmash of Germanic- and Latin-based terms, with minor influences from other languages, even native speakers can have trouble sorting out the intricacies. But what does semantics have to do with Bigfoot research?

Semantics is the study of meaning, specifically of words within languages. We might accuse someone of "arguing semantics" without realizing what the phrase actually means. To argue semantics is to debate the minutiae of what a word means, from its literal definition to its common usage in everyday discussions. The ultimate goal of semantics is to weed out the misuses and develop a clearer understanding of the language, thereby improving human communication.

As I go through the semantic controversies raging within Bigfoot research, I'll provide you with the information needed to make up your own mind about the genuine importance of each issue. Buckle up, there may be turbulence ahead.

Beyond the Normal

What is the most reviled word in Bigfoot research? Well, the word paranormal certainly inspires the most vociferous debates. A related term, supernatural, can rile up folks in the Bigfoot research community almost as much as the word paranormal.

"Don't call Bigfoot paranormal!" the rant goes. "It's a flesh-and-blood animal, not some supernatural boogeyman."

Yet what do the words paranormal and supernatural really mean? Paranormal means simply that science cannot as yet explain it because the phenomenon is so rare that cannot be replicated for scientific verification. Despite what some researchers claim, no one can guarantee you'll see a Bigfoot if you go into the woods with a Bigfoot researcher. No one has captured a live Bigfoot or found a dead one. Claims have surfaced, but as of this book's publication, none has proven true.

Paranormal means...

Something outside the normal.
Eric Altman

Paranormal means...

As far as this animal is concerned, I'd say when people try to attribute abilities such as jumping through wormholes to get from place to place or being able to disappear in the blink of an eye, it's those types of things.
Melissa Hovey

Paranormal means...

I wonder if I know anymore. I think it's just a term we use to quickly define something we can't explain.
Regan Lee

Given the evidence currently available, can science explain Bigfoot? A hairy, bipedal creature wandering the backcountry of our world does defy accepted science. Their very existence makes Bigfoot scientifically unexplainable and, therefore, paranormal. I consider Bigfoot very much flesh-and-blood animals, yet they are also paranormal; one does not preclude the other.

Paranormal and supernatural are in effect synonyms. Supernatural means a phenomenon departs from the normal, seeming to go beyond the natural laws as we know them. How can a flesh-and-blood animal transcend natural laws? One little word in the definition of supernatural leaves the door open for Bigfoot. The word is "seems." Something supernatural *seems* to transcend nature's laws. Seeming to transcend nature and actually doing it are two different things. Bigfoot does indeed seem to exist beyond the laws of nature. These creatures apparently live in numerous locations around the world yet humans only see them on rare occasions. Mountain lions are rarely seen in the wild, but we have examples of them in zoos. No Bigfoot live in any zoo anywhere in the world.

The meat of the definition states that a supernatural event or being departs from what is usual or normal. A hairy, bipedal creature definitely departs from the normal. The best we can do is guess wildly about how many Bigfoot live in any particular area, because we have no evidence of how the species survives. Do they have a large enough population to procreate without detrimental inbreeding? What do they eat? Where do they sleep? We don't know the answers to any of these questions. Bigfoot appear to survive without a large population, an obvious food source, or a place to lay their heads down; therefore, they appear to defy natural laws.

The nature of Bigfoot, coupled with the state of our knowledge of these creatures, satisfies the definitions of supernatural and paranormal. The extreme elusiveness

Paranormal means...

To me, it means "out of bounds of the known."

Kathy Strain

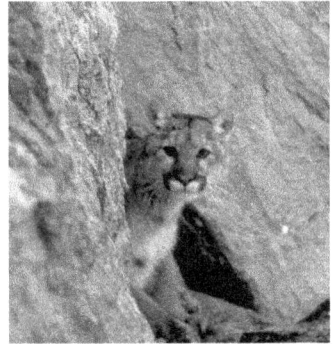

Figure 3.1: Mountain lions (top) and bobcats (bottom) are less elusive than Bigfoot. Top photo by Larry Moats/U.S. Fish & Wildlife Service; bottom photo by Lisa A. Shiel.

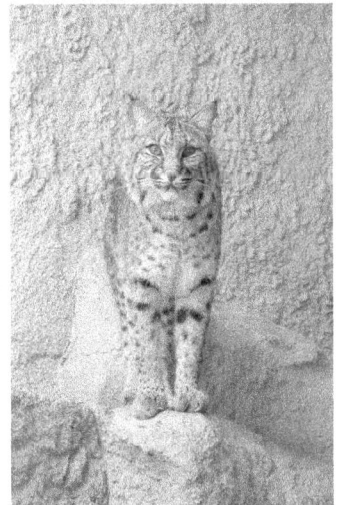

Paranormal means...

[It's] like a catchall term for something that we don't really understand. What I personally believe is that there is something about Bigfoot that makes it elusive and that takes it away from just the realm of a normal flesh-and-blood animal.

Nick Redfern

Paranormal means...

My ax to grind is to try to get people to not recoil in horror from the paranormal and let it be understood as the frontier of what we know. Today's paranormal is tomorrow's scientific understanding.

Thom Powell

of Bigfoot, which seems to defy logic, by itself qualifies these animals as both supernatural and paranormal.

The Nature of Belief

Within the ranks of paranormal researchers, especially in UFO and Bigfoot research, a particular viewpoint predominates. Many Bigfoot researchers declare that they don't believe in Bigfoot, and they may even go so far as to say they believe in nothing. They say belief has no place in Bigfoot research. To use the word belief or believe, they proclaim, implies that people interested in Bigfoot or UFOs are akin to religious wackos. But do the words belief and believe always suggest blind faith?

Figure 3.2: Is Bigfoot a flesh-and-blood creature or something otherwordly? The answer may not be a simple either/or choice.

Bigfoot could be...

	Flesh and Blood	Paranormal
Eric Altman	✓	✓
Melissa Hovey	✓	
Regan Lee	✓	✓
Nick Redfern	✓	✓
Lisa A. Shiel	✓	✓
Kathy Strain	✓	

I think the creature is a flesh-and-blood animal, but I think it has attributes that we're not familiar with and that are not recognized. Right now Bigfoot is an anomaly in itself.

Eric Altman

As far as I know, there is no other animal on this planet that has the capabilities ascribed by some [to Bigfoot]. I believe, if this animal is out there, it is "flesh and blood."

Melissa Hovey

In some people's worldview, a thing that can be both [paranormal and flesh and blood] just cannot be, but I don't have a problem with that. It's pretty obvious to me...there are a lot of things in our world that cannot be explained so easily and readily.

Regan Lee

I'm more inclined to go with the idea that it's either quasi-physical, or it's elusive not because it's metaphysical but it's elusive because it literally dips in and out of our reality.

Nick Redfern

Believing, Semantically

In reality, few words have one meaning and one meaning alone. The English language is rife with semantic gray areas, shades of meaning that native speakers learn from birth how to distinguish. Belief can refer to faith, as of the religious variety. But belief also means to be convinced that something is true or real after scrutinizing the evidence for and against it. Therefore if someone believes in Bigfoot, it simply means that person accepts Bigfoot exists as a real thing (whether as an animal or something else). There's nothing wrong with becoming convinced, based on the available evidence, that a being or phenomenon is real. Besides, if we don't think UFOs or Bigfoot are real, or at least might be real, then why investigate the sightings?

In essence, belief happens when we examine the evidence for a phenomenon and become convinced of its genuineness. There's nothing silly or unscientific about belief. To believe simply means to form an opinion. Without opinions, without belief, science would never advance. Truth begins as a question, followed up by the gathering and examination of evidence, and culminating in an informed opinion—i.e., a belief.

On the surface, believing in nothing seems logical, even smart. Believing in nothing lets Bigfoot researchers avoid the traps set by hoaxers. Doesn't it?

Shunning belief might spare researchers from the embarrassment of getting taken in by a hoax. Yet this idea presumes that people who subscribe to the nonbelief theory are smarter and less gullible than those who don't subscribe to the theory. If someone says

On belief...

It's not so much a belief thing, because belief is more set up for religion. It's more about being convinced that there's something out there or not. At this point we really don't know what's going on—we don't know what this creature is or where it's from. We don't know much about it other than what people are experiencing.

Eric Altman

On belief...

In certain respects, the use of the word belief does imply faith. I don't have faith in anything—I either trust it or I don't....To me, it doesn't have anything to do with belief right now, because we cannot prove that this animal is out there....People seem to think that to be a Bigfoot researcher you have to either be a total 100% believer or be skeptical. I run right down the middle, because I don't know. I have not seen one.

Melissa Hovey

"I believe in Bigfoot," then according to the nonbelief theory, that person is a nincompoop. Obviously, the researcher in question has abandoned reason in favor of faith.

Nonbelief advocates would instead say they don't "believe" anything but are "convinced" Bigfoot exists. What they fail to realize, however, is that the two statements are synonymous. To believe in Bigfoot means to be convinced it exists.

In paranormal research, we have no proof and no incontestable evidence. We must say we "believe" a certain piece of evidence is genuine or a certain witness is truthful. We can prove nothing. We know almost nothing. We have only our beliefs—our informed opinions—on which to base our research.

Blind belief is a separate issue. Belief demands an examination of evidence; so-called blind belief stems from refusing to see the evidence (skeptics often engage in this behavior). Religious belief relies on faith in the absence of evidence. Believing evidence, believing witnesses, believing a theory—those situations rely on knowledge, experience, and analysis of the evidence.

If Bigfoot researchers want to believe in nothing, they have that right. Ridiculing or reviling those who do believe, though, makes the person doing the ridiculing seem petty. Neither side in the debate over belief is smarter, less gullible, or more erudite than the other. After all, even nonbelief advocates unwittingly believe. They've simply chosen to believe in nonbelief.

When it comes to paranormal phenomena, belief has everything to do with it—whether "it" is Bigfoot, UFOs, ghosts, or leprechauns. Everyone must believe something about each of these topics. Belief need not refer to religious zealotry or blind faith. To believe means to form an opinion after examining evidence. Conversely, to believe nothing means to have no opinions. Why bother discussing an issue about which you have no opinions?

Debunkers and the media like to call us believers, hoping to make us feel stupid so we'll shut up about all this paranormal stuff. If we understand the true meaning of the word believe, then we can easily pop the debunkers' balloon by agreeing with them. An insult only wields power when we react negatively to it.

I believe in both UFOs and Bigfoot, and I'm not ashamed to say so. Maybe the Bigfoot research community wouldn't be so fractured if more of its members dared to believe in something—or at least decided to stop battling against the words belief and believe.

On belief...

I said to someone once, I don't believe in my toaster. I know toasters exist. I use them. But I don't believe in it, as if it's a god or an entity you believe in and that you go pray to....I don't believe in Bigfoot, but I believe Bigfoot exists. It's just a semantic head game we can entertain ourselves with. At the end of the day, it doesn't really matter.

Regan Lee

Believing vs. Knowing

Now that we've explored the nuances of the words belief and believe, another question arises. Is there a difference between believing and knowing?

If we omit the religious form of belief, then we are left with the basic type of belief where the word simply means to be convinced. After studying Bigfoot and UFOs for many years, I believe both are real phenomena that mainstream science cannot explain within the confines of accepted theories about how the world and the universe at large work. Do I know Bigfoot are hominids and UFOs are extraterrestrial? No. I believe they are, but I can't prove it. To believe means to be convinced, whereas to know means to be certain. Without ultimate proof, which may never come, I can't claim to know much of anything about Bigfoot, UFOs, or any other paranormal phenomenon.

Only witnesses who have seen a Bigfoot face to face know they're real. Those witnesses cannot know, however, exactly what Bigfoot is or that the creature they saw is the same type of creature others have seen. Bigfoot has given us few facts and no conclusive evidence.

In everyday usage, does it really matter which word we use? Probably not. But I strive for accuracy in the words I choose, therefore I will talk about believing in—and not knowing the truth of—Bigfoot and UFOs.

The Trouble with Names

What is Bigfoot? This question inspires plenty of debate and, truth is, nobody has enough evidence to answer it definitively. Words such as ape and hominid get bandied about like verbal footballs. Hardly anyone seems to really understand what these words mean. Chapter 11 includes a brief overview of taxonomy, the discipline that deals with cataloging living things and organizing them into a sort of family tree. In a moment, we'll see why taxonomy is relevant to the discussion of Bigfoot.

Now, let's explore the semantics of apes and humans to see what secrets we can uncover.

Of Apes and Ape-Men

Some researchers call Bigfoot an ape, and a few refer to Bigfoot as an ape-man. But what is an ape-man, or for that matter, an ape? The answer isn't as obvious as it may seem. The term ape-man would seem to refer to an ape who walks upright like a man. The term often gets used in this manner. But an ape-man is really a primate with characteristics that place it between our species, *Homo sapiens*, and the great apes. The great apes belong to a family known as Pongidae, a group that includes chimpanzees, gorillas, and orangutans but not humans or the pre-human hominids (such as *Homo erectus*). Therefore, ape-man means an animal that exhibits traits of both apes and humans without belonging to either group. The prehuman hominids fall into this category.

Figure 3.3: Gorillas, like this one, are primates but not ape-men or hominids. Photo by Lisa A. Shiel.

The above definition of ape-man tells us two things: 1) an ape-man is neither an ape nor a human, and 2) the fossil hominids are considered ape-men. This definition leaves us with another question, however. What is an ape?

An ape is a nonhuman, tailless primate. Humans are primates but we are not apes. In recent years, some scientists have tried to lump the great apes into the human category—the family Hominidae—based on the genetic similarities between humans and apes. The most famous example is chimpanzees, with whom we share about 98% of our DNA. The push to turn apes into humans, or conversely humans into apes, has received far-from-unanimous support. Most scientists still list the great apes in a separate family, distinct from humans and the fossil hominids.

So, what have we learned? Humans are primates. We are not apes, however, nor are we ape-men. Bigfoot might represent a new kind of ape-man or hominid, or perhaps even an ape. The latter seems the least likely scenario, given the definition of the term ape and the traits exhibited by living apes.

The H Words

Hominoid. Hominid. Human. Most people don't understand the difference between these three words. All three refer to primates—a group that includes a broad array of mammals both living and extinct, from humans to monkeys. In fact, a primate is simply any member of the order Primate, a taxonomic category applied to animals that share certain characteristics. So to what primates do the terms hominoid, hominid, and human apply?

The order Primates embraces the superfamily Hominoidea, as well as the family Hominidae and the genus *Homo*. Any creature that belongs to the superfamily Hominoidea is known as a hominoid. The hominoids include humans, apes, gibbons, and their fossil relatives such as *Proconsul* and *Australopithecus*. *Homo erectus* and the Neanderthals are also hominoids.

The term hominids, however, is distinct from the term hominoid. Only members of the family Hominidae, one step below the superfamily Hominoidea, qualify as hominids. Thus, all hominids are also hominoids, but not all hominoids qualify as hominids. At this point, it becomes clear that scientists need to broaden their horizons when it comes to naming taxonomic groups! Giving a superfamily and a family names that are virtually identical serves only to confuse the lay public.

What separates a hominid from other hominoids? Hominids are bipedal, for one. The family Hominidae includes human beings and the fossil creatures deemed to be our closest, albeit extinct, ancestors. The fossil hominids include the genus *Australopithecus* as well as every member of the genus *Homo*. As mentioned earlier, some scientists have tried to cram the great apes into the hominid family, but that viewpoint remains a fringe element within anthropology. The mainstream viewpoint says that apes do not qualify as human. Yet do the ancient hominids qualify as humans?

We might assume that the word human consistently alludes to members of the species *Homo sapiens*. Thus, when reading an article about stone tools found under the waters of the North Sea, we might presume that the "humans" blamed for dumping the tools there belong to our own species. Yet what seems logical is often not, at least when it comes to anthropology.

Everyone from the news media to scientists themselves tosses about the word "human" with all the care of children playing with a Nerf ball. Sometimes the word means *Homo sapiens*, and sometimes it doesn't. Because scientists assume humans evolved from the ancient hominids, such as *Homo erectus*, they feel free to label those ancient hominid species as "human" too. Most actual humans, however, tend to think of humanity as a *Homo-sapiens*-only club.

The 11th edition of *Merriam-Webster's Collegiate Dictionary* defines human rather loosely, identifying humans as nothing more than bipedal primates who are also hominids. Princeton's WordNet describes a human as any species belonging to the family Hominidae, whether living or extinct, who walks upright and exhibits "superior" intelligence and speech capabilities. Nobody wants to offend either the fossil hominids or the great apes by telling them they're not humans. So when we hear the word human, we must ask a question. How can we know whether the person using the term means an actual human being or an ancient, somewhat-apelike species that walked upright and from whom we supposedly evolved?

Any dictionary, like any science textbook, assumes the fossil species that scientists label human ancestors have all gone extinct. The standard definition also assumes that humans descended from the ancient hominids. However, as I discussed in my previous book *Backyard Bigfoot*, this may not be the case. Bigfoot of today may represent the true children of the ancient hominids, which would make Bigfoot both hominids and hominoids. Because I believe Bigfoot and other similar creatures represent descendants of the ancient hominids, I sometimes refer to Bigfoot as hairy hominids.

Depending on each person's notions about Bigfoot ancestry, they might call the creatures hominoids, apes, primates, aliens, or humans. Once we understand the real meaning of the words, however, we can at least phrase our opinions more accurately.

4
Bigfootology

Most people want the respect of their peers, validation for their hard work, and approval from the community they live in or the people with whom they work. But people who engage in a field of research that's scoffed at, like Bigfoot or UFOs, must accept that the scientific establishment will not lavish praise on them. In spite of the debunkers and naysayers, paranormal researchers set out on their mission to learn and explore these often-mocked subjects. They go into it knowing what they will face.

Why then do so many paranormal researchers bemoan the lack of respect given to their research? They all but beg scientists to give them a big hug, welcoming them into the scientific establishment. We need scientists to accept our research as valid, these people say. Why can't they like us? Scientists say Bigfoot research is not science, even when it's called cryptozoology. Bigfoot researchers proclaim they use scientific techniques to document the evidence, which surely merits at least grudging approval from the scientific establishment. Who's right?

Do we have any facts about Bigfoot? Before we can answer that question, we must determine what a fact really is, both in lay terms and in scientific usage. We must also define the terms theory and scientific method, and figure out how scientists actually apply those terms, as opposed to how they like us to presume they use them. First, though, another term needs defining.

What is science?

Science, Defined

As we go through life, most of us develop basic misconceptions about the nature of science—specifically, that science is a quest for ultimate truth and that scientific laws are immutable. Neither is true. Science is simply a way of studying natural phenomena by asking questions and seeking plausible answers through the development of hypotheses and theories and the collection of evidence. Rarely, if ever, does science provide absolute certainty. A theory is accepted when the evidence for it convinces enough scientists so that the idea becomes widely acknowledged as the most likely answer.

Where do our misconceptions about science originate? Perhaps it begins with the best-known aspect of science—the scientific method.

The Myth of a Method

In school we learn that scientists follow a process called the scientific method to study nature, mathematics, and even the human mind. The number of steps in the method varies depending on the specific textbook consulted. In general, though, the method involves a series of steps for every phenomenon:

1. Pose a question or identify a problem.
2. Form a hypothesis (educated guess) based on the observed evidence.
3. Conduct an experiment, properly controlled, to test the hypothesis.
4. Reach conclusions (a theory) based on the evidence.
    a) If the data supports the theory, move on to step 5.
    b) If the data contradicts the theory, return to step 1.
5. Share those conclusions with other scientists.

The steps sound a bit like the instructions on a shampoo bottle telling us to lather, rinse, and repeat. As taught to schoolchildren, the steps in the scientific method sound about as exciting and innovative as shampooing hair. The method as outlined comforts us, lulling us into believing scientists follow set procedures that enable them to induce, deduce, and elucidate all the mysteries of the universe with pure objectivity. In reality, not every scientist uses the steps listed above or engages in purely objective inquiry. No one can shed every bias lurking in the human subconscious. On *Star Trek*, even the ever-logical Vulcans succumbed to emotion and bias on occasion.

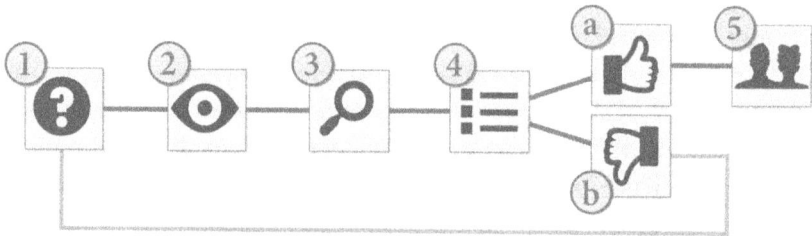

Figure 4.1: The scientific method sounds like a straight-forward prescription for advancement, but things are not what they seem. Chart by Lisa A. Shiel.

Rather than acting as a legal code, the scientific method really serves as a guideline to promote both objectivity and professionalism. Police don't arrest scientists who stray from the method. In some disciplines, the strict scientific method cannot be applied at all, or cannot be applied rigorously, due to the nature of the phenomena studied. The textbook method also makes no mention of creativity, a key factor in many scientific discoveries.

So what is the scientific method? The key to understanding how science really works lies in understanding the concepts of theory and hypothesis.

A Hypothesis about Theories

Wouldn't it be grand to live in a world where every word has one meaning, a single indisputable definition? Nobody would misuse words or argue about the connotations. Of course, a world free of linguistic shades would also rob us of puns and double entendres.

Most people think of science as a world unto itself where the residents have shed all bias and self-involvement in favor of pure scientific advancement. In this perfect place, words have clear meanings that everyone understands. Even if the average dummy who lives outside of Science Land misunderstands scientific jargon, surely those brainy folks with letters after their names do understand. Scientists, however, are no different than anybody else. They get confused too.

Take the words theory and hypothesis. The layman's definition of a theory is an idea someone dreams up with or without evidence, such as a conspiracy theory. A hypothesis should be an educated guess. In science, a hypothesis ought to be conjecture based on observations; a theory, then, should be a deduction based on the gathering and testing of evidence, the next step after forming a hypothesis. A true scientific theory should have a solid foundation in fact, account for the available evidence, be consistent and logical, produce testable predictions, and be falsifiable. The steps in the scientific method dictate this.

In the fantasy land where scientists use the steps prescribed by the textbook scientific method in precise order, theories flow from hypotheses in a rational, linear process. In the reality land where most of us live, the actual methods used by scientists involve the human elements of creativity, fallibility, and prejudice. Without a creative spark to light our minds, science could never advance. If we needed only to follow the textbook method to achieve scientific breakthroughs, then any ten-year-old could crank out a unified theory of physics.

In everyday science, a hypothesis amounts to an educated guess, a tentative explanation in need of testing or further study. A theory is an explanation that accounts for all the facts observed; a theory, ultimately, must survive repeated tests and rigorous study. A theory must also be falsifiable, meaning that the scientist can collect and test evidence to determine the accuracy or fallacy of his theory. In the real world, many scientific theories cannot be tested. Examples include the Big Bang theory in astronomy and string theory in physics. The Big Bang happened billions of years ago and therefore cannot be witnessed, although astronomers can recognize its aftereffects. We certainly wouldn't want to repeat the Big Bang either! Strings, if they indeed exist, are too small for the most advanced equipment to detect. Since no one can test either theory via observation or practical experimentation, both rely on interpretation of data. Neither theory is falsifiable at present.

In the books written for laymen, many scientists use the terms theory and hypothesis interchangeably, and then in the next sentence bemoan the average person's misuse of the terms. Because few scientists actually use the mythical method schoolchildren learn, the distinction between theory and hypothesis blurs. Once a proposal reaches the theory level, a scientist should have more data to back it up—in theory. In reality, many scientific projects ignore the scientific method.

But surely science has given us cold, hard facts. Hasn't it? What seems like a yes or no question proves far more complicated. What is a fact?

Figure 4.2: The Big Bang created the universe, but proving the Big Bang theory is incredibly difficult, if we follow the strict scientific method. Image by NASA, ESA, and the Hubble Heritage Team [STScI/AURA]/J. Green, University of Colorado, Boulder.

Just the Facts

In certain disciplines, such as physics, experiments can prove or disprove a theory. Drop an egg to see the effects of gravity. In other disciplines, like anthropology, the kind of experimentation required by the scientific method becomes impossible. How does one test the theory that *Australopithecus*, a type of extinct hominid, walked upright? With no complete skeletons of the genus to study and no living examples to observe, anthropologists can perform neither experimentation nor observation, two key elements of the scientific method.

Some scientists have devised computer models to test the theory. Models remain limited by the parameters entered into them, which are restricted by the scant evidence available to programmers. The major component in the majority of anthropological, archaeological, and paleontological theories is conjecture.

Even a loosened scientific method includes some basic principles. A scientist should at the very least observe phenomena, hypothesize about what he sees, then examine evidence to test the hypothesis and solidify a theory. The facts observed will bring up questions the scientist strives to answer.

This process requires facts. But what is a fact? In science, nobody knows anything with absolute certainty and no fact becomes immutable; nevertheless, a scientific fact ought to satisfy a few fundamental criteria. Facts should consist of confirmed observations that have already undergone in-depth investigation, so that the data becomes accepted as real and accurate. That the earth revolves around the sun stands as a fact. We have observed this phenomenon as it happens and verified our observations. An eagle's ability to fly is a fact too, as anyone who observes eagles can testify.

A fact is merely a confirmed observation, or information drawn from those observations. How does an observation become confirmed? The answer depends on each person's viewpoint. Scientists would say that if an idea has survived repeated and rigorous testing, then it qualifies as a confirmed fact. However, as discussed earlier, scientific theories often cannot be tested. The practical answer to the question is that an idea becomes a fact when it has received widespread approval from scientists.

The Science of Bigfoot

What have we learned so far? The scientific method is a guideline, not a strict framework. A hypothesis is an educated guess based on observations, a theory is a hypothesis that has been borne out by the evidence collected and analyzed, and a fact is a confirmed observation that's often the result of a theory.

In everyday life, however, a fact is often nothing more than something a person observes to be true—whether or not scientists accept the phenomenon as a fact. I have seen UFOs, and I consider their existence a fact. What they are, I can't say for certain. Some UFOs may be extraterrestrial in origin, while others may originate closer to home, but neither notion qualifies as a fact. Scientists would say the existence of UFOs is not a fact either. To me, it is. Facts can be subjective. This is why a fact can also be defined as information believed to represent objective reality.

Mostly, an idea qualifies as a fact when someone speaks about it in an authoritative voice. Bigfoot researchers who scoff at the Bigfoot-UFO connection like to use this tactic. These researchers will speak authoritatively, as if they know everything about Bigfoot and therefore can tell us, without doubt, that no connection exists between Bigfoot and UFOs. Yet I can speak with just as much authority about the plausibility of the Bigfoot-UFO connection. Have we both stated facts? No, neither of us has offered facts. We proffered evidence which led each of us to a different conclusion. Until I witness a Bigfoot stepping out of a UFO, the connection will remain hypothetical. Until someone presents conclusive, scientific proof that Bigfoot is nothing but an ape, no one on the other side of the argument can say with absolute certainty that no connection exists between Bigfoot and UFOs.

To say a fact is information believed to represent objective reality means that evidence has been presented which may prove the reality of some event or phenomenon. If I attend a conference and show a footprint cast to the audience, I have presented that cast as objective reality. However, I proved only that the cast is real. We can all touch it and see that I have not fooled everyone with a holographic projection. Yet the cast alone cannot prove that the track it represents belonged to a Bigfoot, or that the track belongs to any real animal. The cast certainly cannot prove what Bigfoot is or even that Bigfoot is a real animal rather than a myth. Even if I can demonstrate I did not fake the cast itself, I have still failed to present evidence of what created the footprint that I cast. The reality of the cast becomes a fact. The source of the footprint remains speculative.

Bigfoot has given us next to nothing in the way of facts. It's a fact that witnesses from all over the world have reported seeing hair-covered, bipedal creatures. It's a fact that Bigfoot researchers argue a lot. Little else about these mysterious creatures qualifies as a fact. Whether Bigfoot research qualifies as science depends on whom we ask. Most scientists would say no. Most Bigfoot researchers would probably say yes. Though science is simply a process of inquiry, evidence collection, and the formation of hypotheses and theories, in the real world scientists themselves have the final say in answering the question of what qualifies as science. Until universities grant degrees in Bigfootology (or cryptozoology), the study of these mysterious creatures will remain outside the domain of mainstream science.

Now that we know the truth about science and facts, we can explore another controversy in Bigfoot research—the debate over theories.

5

The Bigfoot Theory

Anyone who picks up a book about Bigfoot will find lots of sightings, and lots of photos of Bigfoot researchers, but very little of one ingredient—theories. An awful lot of Bigfoot researchers pride themselves on their dogmatic refusal to consider any theory about the nature of Bigfoot. I like to call this attitude the No-Theories Theory. Some researchers cite the lack of conclusive evidence as a reason to shun theorizing, while others claim it's more scientific to simply gather data without reaching even tentative conclusions. On the surface, these statements sound reasonable, and perhaps noble. Don't bias the data by formulating theories, just gather the evidence.

But if we accept this rationale, then we must ask ourselves a question—why?

The Hunt for a Purpose

Why talk to witnesses if we have no interest in examining the data, forming hypotheses, and debating the merits of those hypotheses? Proponents of the No-Theories Theory collect sightings, toss the information into a database, and forget about it. Maybe they run some software that spits out a few statistics about the average height or weight of Bigfoot, or the possible geographic distribution of the species. Maybe the statistics show Bigfoot prefer to scare hikers on Tuesdays between the hours of 9 AM and 11 AM. What does it all mean? Proponents of the No-Theories Theory will simply look at the statistics and shrug.

As discussed in Chapter 2, Bigfooters don't like to admit they believe in Bigfoot. At most, they will say they're convinced Bigfoot is a real animal. If we can't admit to something as basic as believing these creatures exist, then it makes sense to avoid developing ideas about what they might be and how they might fit into the grand scheme of life. But the No-Theories Theory leads to an unavoidable and vital question.

On theories…

People form theories and opinions about everything all the time—that is human nature. It would be nice if opinions/theories fell within known behavior/abilities of all living things, but so be it. What I don't like is speculation on people's motives or making up "facts" to suit your opinion. The entire nature of science is to form opinions/hypotheses and then test them. That's what we do!

Kathy Strain

What is the point of Bigfoot research?

For the No-Theories Theory crowd, the answer seems to be that they want nothing more than to collect data and file it away in the hopes that one day the scientific establishment will come knocking on their door and beg for the chance to see that data. For me, the answer is that I want to understand these creatures as best I can given the evidence available at this time. To accomplish this goal requires hypothesizing and theorizing. I may change my mind about my theories later on, or adjust them based on new evidence.

The problem with trying to please the scientific establishment is that they don't want to be pleased. They want Bigfoot to remain a myth. It's easier to ignore Bigfoot than to look at the data and attempt to fit it into their preconceived notions about the natural world. Mainstream scientists have a vested interest in scoffing at Bigfoot and other paranormal phenomena.

We all must decide for ourselves what we want to get out of studying Bigfoot, whether our research entails full-scale expeditions or just reading about and analyzing the available evidence. No research method is more valid than the others. Choose a method, and choose a goal. But remember, if acceptance from the scientific establishment at large is the only goal, then we may be setting ourselves up for failure.

The Bigfoot Method

Bigfoot researchers and ufologists alike love the No-Theories Theory. They will even go so far as to chastise folks for using the word theory. A theory, they say, must adhere to the scientific method. It must begin as a hypothesis, advance to the theory stage via rigorous testing and evidence collection, and then perhaps one day become a law. Sounds good, right? As we learned in Chapter 4, however, many scientific theories don't adhere to this strict version of the scientific method. Those theories usually lack the capability of being tested, often because the phenomenon in question cannot be repeated or cannot be observed; hence, the theory isn't falsifiable.

Take evolution, for instance. How does one prove evolution doesn't happen? Evolution happens so gradually, in such tiny increments, that we cannot observe it happening. No scientist has repeated the evolution of eyes, or the modifications that led to zebras having stripes. Evolutionists hypothesize some changes, such as the evolution of eyes, happened independently at several different times in different lineages, yet their conjecture has no concrete evidence to support it. As far as anyone can tell, such events happen once and every change evolutionists assume happened is unique. Given

Figure 5.1: Evolutionists have never recreated, or believably explained, the evolution of zebra stripes. Photo by Walt Shiel.

that evolution fails the tests for observability and repeatability, it certainly fails the final test of falsifiability. Nobody can confirm an invisible, singular phenomenon.

We can, however, observe that life-forms adapt to their environments. For life to have evolved from that first cell into everything alive today requires more than the simple adaptations we can witness, however; life's evolution requires that one kind of living thing metamorphose into a completely different kind of living thing. Evolution requires the creation of new species. Of course, scientists can't agree on what a species is, so even if it were possible to witness the transformation, we wouldn't know for sure we had seen it.

Now look at string theory, which states that everything in the universe consists of particles called strings which are so small not even the most advanced equipment on earth can detect them. How can we prove or disprove the existence of something nobody can see? The evidence for string theory lies in complicated math, not practical experiments. String theory isn't falsifiable or observable, yet scientists refer to it as a theory, not a hypothesis. Evolution is not be reproducible, observable, or falsifiable— yet scientists frequently refer to evolution as both a fact and a theory.

Given what we've learned about the true nature of science, can we use the scientific method to study the paranormal? We can apply scientific techniques (in the way we collect evidence) and scientific processes (such as DNA analysis), but as with string theory and evolution, we cannot follow the strict scientific method. Why not? Let's take a look at the issues:

> **Testability.** The scientific method requires testing, and we cannot test a phenomenon that occurs sporadically, without warning, in varied locations.
> **Observability.** Unlike string theory and evolution, Bigfoot is hypothetically observable. Unfortunately, we can't summon

---

On theories...

If you're seriously discussing the topic, you have your own opinion one way or the other. You just don't want to tell people what it is...."We have better things to do with our time" is the biggest argument I hear for not caring. If you don't have an opinion one way or the other, then why are you even talking about it?

Melissa Hovey

up a Bigfoot whenever we choose or accurately predict where and when one will make an appearance. Some people claim they can do this, yet they have never produced irrefutable evidence to support their claims.

⚫ **Repeatability.** Because we can't predict Bigfoot sightings, the phenomenon is not repeatable in the scientific sense. A handful of witnesses claim to have ongoing encounters with Bigfoot, but hard evidence is lacking in these cases. The Bigfoot phenomenon remains rare and, therefore, unrepeatable.

⚫ **Falsifiability.** Although scientists would say the lack of evidence proves Bigfoot doesn't exist, the truth is that we can neither prove nor disprove Bigfoot's existence. The evidence is circumstantial and often subjective.

When it comes to Bigfoot, we're better off forgetting the scientific method. Since a number of scientific theories ignore the method too, we're in good company. Most paranormal phenomena fail to meet the four requirements listed above. One particular branch of the paranormal, however, has achieved a measure of success in satisfying the requirements. Laboratory experiments, conducted by credentialed scientists, have produced interesting results concerning psychic phenomena such as telepathy. Many Bigfoot researchers like to think that cryptozoology, and especially the study of Bigfoot, is far more scientific than the study of psychic phenomena. Yet Bigfoot research has yet to produce the kinds of repeatable, testable results that studies of psychic phenomena have generated.

When it comes to Bigfoot, our theories continue to be untestable, unrepeatable, and unfalsifiable. Does this mean we should avoid forming theories about the paranormal?

On theories...

If you're studying this scientifically, that's how you come to a conclusion. You have to have a hypothesis, then you test the hypothesis, and then you come up with a conclusion. If people aren't willing to do that, then they're not really looking at it scientifically. If you're just going to collect information about it, what is that information going to do if it's not analyzed and if you don't come up with your own opinions on it?

Eric Altman

A Daring Approach

Some people will chastise anyone who uses the word theory in relation to the paranormal. A theory and a hypothesis are different, they say. Yet scientists will use the two words interchangeably—even after castigating dumb laymen for failing to grasp the difference. In reality, a theory is simply a hypothesis that's supported by evidence. What constitutes evidence depends on your point of view.

On theories…

When it comes to Bigfoot, we have to be open-minded but not credulously too open-minded. As long as we do that, we stand a chance of looking for the answers. Don't write off one theory at the expense of promoting another. It may be that both theories have some merit to them, but in a way we don't understand yet.

Nick Redfern

Debunkers love to quote Carl Sagan's statement that extraordinary claims require extraordinary evidence. So if I plop a dead Bigfoot on a scientist's desk, that wouldn't suffice because a type specimen (a body) is ordinary evidence used to prove the existence of new species. What extraordinary evidence would I need to prove Bigfoot's existence?

A theory is nothing more than an explanation for a natural phenomenon, based on the available evidence. What does all of this mean for paranormal research?

Go ahead and theorize!

We can't apply the scientific method to the paranormal, but neither can we apply it to a lot of theories accepted by science as true. We have evidence for paranormal phenomena, in some cases more evidence than scientists have for mainstream scientific theories.

Examine the evidence. Observe. Think. Form opinions. And, above all, dare to theorize.

6

The Researchers Speak

A discussion of the controversies in Bigfoot research could go on for a thousand pages. The controversies I've chosen to focus on are, naturally, the ones that interest me the most. Of course, I've saved my favorite controversy—the paranormal connection—for Part Two, to give it the in-depth treatment that it deserves. I'd like to end Part One by letting the researchers I interviewed speak for themselves.

In the previous chapters, I've included brief, pertinent quotes from each of the interviewees. Now, I present a selection of their lengthier comments on some of the other controversies in the field of Bigfoot research. Enjoy!

Should we kill a Bigfoot to prove they exist?

⊖

Eric Altman

My group is considered a no-kill group. We try to do passive study through audio-video recording, but I don't get involved in the killing of the creature. I don't advocate it. I go out in the field and try to document evidence and cast whatever I can when I'm out.

I used to be all about the serious documentation and trying to prove it exists, but after the last five or six years I've gotten to the point now where I just want to go out and see one for myself and I want to enjoy myself out in the woods. The information or data that I collect I'm happy to share with those who want to hear it and want to see it. Other than that, I could care less whether these things are proven to exist or not. I just want to experience one for myself.

↭

Melissa Hovey

What a scientist is going to tell you is what they can get from the necropsy of the animal, from the study of it. That'll tell scientists that it was alive at one point. But I've told people this before—you go ahead and you shoot your one animal and take it in there [to a scientist]. Say it's a male. The scientist is going to turn around and say this specific specimen only tells me about a male. I'm going to need a female, because we have no idea what the differences are between the two. I need you to go out and get me a female now.

So Joe Hunter goes out and bags himself a female and brings it in to the scientist. The scientist says this is really great. We have a male and female now to study, but we don't really know anything about babies. I need you to go out there and bag me a baby. If people really think that this is going to stop with one animal, they've lost their minds, because that's not what science is about. The initial bringing in of the first body will tell scientists that, yes, this animal existed. Then they could also say you may have just killed the only one in existence. How do we know? We need you to go back out.

That's bad, but as much as it's bad, I know that it's a scientific necessity because they need proof. They need hard evidence. They need something they can see, touch, and feel. I'm just not willing to give them that much.

↶↷

Regan Lee

I think the only thing that's going to satisfy a lot of Bigfoot researchers in the world, including scientists, is a dead body or a captured body. I have mixed feelings about that, because if it's not strictly flesh and blood, how could that happen? I don't think it can happen, because Bigfoot transcends the physical. It's not just a giant ape running around.

Figure 6.1: Bigfoot have proven hard to catch and even to kill. Witnesses have reported shooting at, and hitting, a Bigfoot only to have it run away or vanish in a flash of light. Maybe they wear bulletproof vests! Artwork by Kerrie Shiel.

Let's pretend that it is only flesh and blood. The idea that anyone would even consider going out there with the sole purpose in mind to kill one is just appalling to me. I just can't understand that concept, though I understand the reasoning behind it. This is a huge argument. I've been involved in discussions around this idea. It makes no sense to me. On the other hand, I think people are wasting their time going out there [to kill or capture a Bigfoot], so let them have at it because it's never going to happen. It isn't a flesh-and-blood creature. It can't be caught.

Science will never seriously entertain that Bigfoot could be anything other than flesh and blood, so they're going to be on this never-resolved quest to find a body, because that can't happen. But of course, they think that it could happen—or rather, if it did happen, that it would be the proof they need. It's this endless loop.

⤻
Nick Redfern

If Bigfoot has a flesh-and-blood quality to it, and if the only way to prove it exists is to kill one, then as much as it pains me to say it, I think we should. The ideal scenario would be to find a living Bigfoot, tag it, tranquilize it, and have the entire proceedings filmed—not by the local Bigfoot group, but by a mainstream TV news company with three or four people of academic scientific background there. The best scenario of all would be simply that we stumble across a dead body. We wouldn't be relying on a bit of DNA and we wouldn't have to kill one. We would have a corpse. Now of course, corpses don't last long in the woods.

This is why I don't rule out the idea that Bigfoot has flesh-and-blood qualities. A lot of big animals, when they die in the woods, don't last long. Nature takes care of them. So you've got to be in the right place at the right time. In that respect, it's going to be a challenge to stumble across a dead body. That's going to be the most amazing of all coincidences, to go looking in a large area of forest on the day it dies and before it starts to get destroyed and eaten by all the other animals.

If Bigfoot has flesh-and-blood qualities, the chances of stumbling across a dead one are very high. I think we might have a hell of a time catching and tagging one. So I think unfortunately, if it's flesh-and-blood, the only way it's going to be proven is if somebody kills one. Would it be as much of a vindication for cryptozoology as it would be a tragedy? Yes, it would. I don't see anything heartwarming about killing a Bigfoot to prove it exists. In scientific terms, will it take a body, however we get ahold of it? Yes, I think it will take a body.

⤻
Kathy Strain

As a scientist, I can't be emotional about the issue. We can't protect the species as a whole without following standard scientific protocols. I don't love the idea of losing pieces of history (like buildings or artifacts), but sometimes it's necessary in order to save other pieces of history that are more important to the greater good.

What might Bigfoot be?

Eric Altman

I honestly don't know. I used to think it was an undiscovered primate, or some type of relic hominid maybe, a close ancestor of ours. Anymore, I just don't know. The longer I've been in this, I have more questions than I do answers.

Melissa Hovey

I think it's an animal. I think it's a nonhuman primate. Even if they were able to get DNA samples from it that said it was closer to human than chimpanzees, it still doesn't make it human.

There are very specific things that define humans from non-human primates, and I just don't think that this animal is ever going to reach that level. It could be very close to human, but then the question becomes, in order to cross that hurdle, does it have some of the same things that humans have, like the ability to reason and think. That's an incredible hurdle to overcome. Could there be something that's still out there that could be the missing link between the human and the nonhuman primate? It's possible.

Thom Powell

The basic competing scenarios are ape, human ancestor, missing link. Extant Indian tribe is one that probably isn't treated very thoroughly but should be. Then there are people who say that it's super-powerful, that it's more capable than we are at what it does and so therefore we can't really justify characterizing it as in any way less powerful than we are, or less capable or smart. The more I stay with it, personally, the more I gravitate toward that position. They're really smart. They're not just primitive man.

The ape scenario is completely out of the question. I understand why people want to stay with that. It's certainly the most palatable suggestion. This is probably the only point of view that has a ghost of a chance of being accepted by the scientific community. Everything is geared toward what the scientific community will accept, and I don't blame people who are trying to get the evidence looked at for going in that direction. It's probably prudent. I don't think it's consistent with what we're getting in the field.

<e>

Nick Redfern

I veer between different theories, and maybe there's an overlap. I look at the tulpa angle with a lot of interest. Perhaps the human love and fascination with strange, spooky locations and legendary creatures has spawned tulpa-style versions—a tulpa being where the human mind can construct something within its depths to such a powerful extent that it gives birth to a mind-monster that can be externalized and that has a quasi-self-aware existence of its own. That's why it's so elusive. The tulpa can only exist in high states of human emotion, so in other words, maybe they appear for people purely to provoke high states of fear and then feed on it, and then vanish into this strange twilight semi-reality.

The other theory that I think is an interesting one is the idea that Bigfoot could be a denizen of other dimensions. Things like quantum physics today are allowing for the existence of multiple dimensions, even if we don't necessarily understand fully the concept of what they are. Physics does allow for the idea of other realms.

Of course, a big challenge is that most people in cryptozoology don't want to hear this. Many people are very much anti the idea that there's anything strange about Bigfoot other than it being a strange type of ape. When you start talking about portals, tulpas, other realms, Bigfoot having ESP, or things like this, then most cryptozoologists shy away or roll their eyes. It's a big tragedy, because I've always been of the opinion that whatever these things, we should address all the evidence. To write off certain data because it doesn't fit with the preconceived view that you've got isn't just wrong, it's actually hindering the search.

Can Bigfoot be habituated (domesticated)?

↜↝

Eric Altman

Anything's possible at this point. I think it is possible that there are people who have a relationship or some kind of communication with these creatures, whether they're feeding these animals like a pet or they have a rapport with these animals, where the animal recognizes that they're not a threat. It feels comfortable enough to continually come around. I think there may be more of those cases than we actually know about. There have been some well-documented cases of habituation that have been brought to the public eye. Unfortunately, those people were met with ridicule and they quickly stopped talking about it. I'm not aware of any [cases] myself right now, but it's definitely a possibility.

↜↝

Melissa Hovey

I think that it's possible. If this animal has a home range, like most other animals do in the world, it would seem plausible to me that there would be one if not more families in this country who have been able to do this. But then the question becomes, if you don't have photographs of what you're habituating, is it Bigfoot or is it a bear.

↜↝

Regan Lee

I suppose a lot of it has to do with the intent of the humans involved. I would imagine to the Bigfoot, it's their choice and they know what they're doing. If we're talking about something that transcends flesh and blood, there's a lot more going on there. I think it could be a very profound thing to happen.

⌇

Thom Powell

It's pretty much axiomatic that if someone has a buddy-buddy relationship with local Sasquatches, they also understand the Sasquatches want it to be kept on the down low. If somebody has the whole habituation thing going on, they're generally not talking. The ones that do talk are rare.

My feeling is that at this point the most valuable thing is a researcher who has a very informed perspective from years of doing it, kind of like the crop circle and extraterrestrial folks. They pretty much understand that one more person who saw a flying saucer isn't going to add to the knowledge. Even the person who has had some sort of contact is not going to add to what they already know. What you have to do is assimilate everything as a researcher, from all of these sources, and then work your own experiments and try to establish communication yourself. It can be done. It is being done. You're going to learn a ton, but don't even think about going on TV and telling people what you know. You're going to look like a fool when you open your mouth and say I know it's Sasquatch because they told me.

⌇

Nick Redfern

I won't call these [claims of habituation] rogue cases, because that's like smearing the witness, but I would use the term rogue case in the sense that they're few and far between. You do seem to have evidence of Bigfoot living in one area and taking an interest in the family involved to where they get closer and closer, allegedly interacting. There are stories of ESP-type encounters.

First, I have to say that I've never actually investigated one of those cases, although I've read a lot about them. There's absolutely no doubt those types of stories are controversial. I do sometimes wonder if people were more open to these phenomena, like Bigfoot, maybe they'd have some of these more profound experiences. Maybe these entities pick up on it, and that's why certain people who live in certain locations have repeated experiences, because the phenomenon becomes more comfortable interacting with them.

I think there could be something to that. The main reason is not because I've investigated cases like this, but because I've seen it happen in the UFO subject. I've been benevolently manipulated to link up with certain people or go to certain areas to learn and understand more about the phenomenon. If Bigfoot is somehow connected with all this, then it would make sense for it to happen in that realm as well.

Is it wrong to make money off Bigfoot by selling books, memberships in organizations, etc.?

↭

Eric Altman

There are people who feel that way. I don't know why they do. If you're able to sell books and people want to read about it, why shouldn't you be able to sell books? That's your decision to do so. I'm not going to knock anybody for doing it.

On the other side, there are people who are deliberately trying to exploit these creatures for profit. This is a business to them. They want to get the holy grail so they can make money off of it. I can't tell somebody what to do and what not to do. It's not my place. But if I can sell a couple T-shirts at a Bigfoot conference to cover my gas to go to a conference, or if I'm speaking at an event and somebody wants to offer me fifty bucks to speak, I'll take it. I'm not going to turn it down. But I've honestly spent more of my own money in this subject for the last thirty years than I have made money.

Melissa Hovey

That's about the only thing people in this research can really agree upon, and it's about somebody else's business...

Stay out of other people's business. Buy the book, don't buy the book. Donate to the organization or don't. I have no problem with groups or individuals who ask for donations. I have a problem when they use bad evidence to try to make money. But in the end it's going to be your name and possible fraud charges you're going to have to deal with.

Other scientists get funding for research for other topics. I don't see why there's such a stigma attached to the Bigfoot researcher that asks for donations, because this is an expensive pursuit. I'm focused on trying to get this research solved, not how or where or when people decide to publish a book or do something to try to make money. That's really nobody's business but their own.

Figure 6.2: Bigfoot researchers argue about whether it's wrong to make money off of their research, but no one has asked the Bigfoot what they think! Artwork by Kerrie Shiel.

Regan Lee

People have to earn a living and if you write a book, I don't care what it's about, why shouldn't you be paid for that? There's absolutely nothing wrong with that. I don't understand this criticism of people who write books on what are called fringe subjects—UFOs, Bigfoot,

Loch Ness, whatever it may be. Oh, they're making money off this book. I hope they are!

We all know you don't make a whole lot of money anyway. It gets back to intent—if you're pure of heart and you really want to share your research and your voice. Nobody's making other people pay. I belong to a forum where I pay a few dollars a month because I believe in supporting that person and that research. It's my choice.

If you're some yahoo who takes a troupe of people out to go look for Bigfoot—it's a big expedition and you've got all this equipment clanking around—that annoys me for a lot of reasons. We can make comparisons to some of the ghost hunting things. I have mixed feelings about that. But generally speaking, with researchers who write books and publish the books, there is absolutely nothing wrong with that as long as the person's being honest. Whether you agree with them or not, if they're being honest and putting their research out there, no one's making you buy the book.

⤏

Thom Powell

You'll get help from them [the Bigfoot] as long as it's not utterly monetary. I would say that you can work it to your benefit, especially for creative purposes. As far as writing and so forth, I think that they do want their message out and so if you're trying to just advance the message, it's fine with them.

⤏

Nick Redfern

If you're in it for the right reasons, to share information and get it out and because you think you've got a good story to tell and you're not ripping people off, then I don't see what the problem is. Nobody complains if somebody writes a book about the history of the Middle Eastern conflict or a biography of Winston Churchill. But if you write a book about Bigfoot, that's wrong. For some weird reason, which I actually don't understand, if you either write books or do lectures and earn money from speaking about paranormal phenomena, you're somehow the equivalent of a used car salesman. Part of it comes down to petty jealousies. Somebody wants to write a book but they can't get published, and they flat out don't like it when somebody else does.

There's this misconception that when Nick Redfern writes books it's just for the money. But where's the money? I've actually had this where people think that when you write a book about UFOs or Bigfoot, you're living in the Hollywood Hills and driving around with a Ferrari and you've got a Lamborghini for Sundays. Most publishers don't pay advances. You just get a royalty payment, say twelve months after publication.

Your books might sell eight hundred or a thousand copies. If you get a royalty payment of one and a half dollars per book, every twelve months you get one and a half grand. Don't get me wrong, I'm not complaining, because I understand the nature of the field I'm working in. I'm grateful that a publisher wants to publish something that I want to put out, and that there are one and a half thousand people that might want to buy the book. The idea that people would write books about Bigfoot to make money is ridiculous.

Could I earn a full-time living, or even a half-time living, writing about Bigfoot? No, there's just no way. That doesn't stop me doing it, because I have a passion for it. That passion overrides the thinking that if I write about this, it's going to earn $50,000. The reality is none of my books ever earned $50,000 and I've written twenty books. I would've stopped by now if that was the motivation.

⤺

Kathy Strain

I'm an archaeologist by profession. I "buy" membership into various organizations. I pay to attend conferences and special fieldtrips. I buy archaeology books, t-shirts, etc. Biologists, botanists, and other professionals can say the same thing. Since this is the standard, why would Bigfoot be an exception?

If it cost me money to get X-Y-Z evidence, I have the right to expect television programs (who are also making money) to pay for those rights. As for expeditions, I have never charged but I usually go out with friends and organizational members.

Final Words

While talking to Eric Altman, I asked him what he would like the general public to know about Bigfoot researchers, given all the controversies and arguments. The public sees a lot of hype about hoaxes, and hype for reality TV shows related to Bigfoot—not mention the ridicule from the mass media that pervades public discussions of Bigfoot. So I wondered what an experienced researcher like Eric would say if he could address the public at large. His response to my question provides a nice closing to this section of the book.

Eric Altman

What I would like to pass on to the general public is that we're not crazy people looking for the Easter Bunny or Santa Claus. This is something that has been around for hundreds of years. It's ongoing. The majority of people doing the research want answers. We want to know if it's real or not. We want to know if there's legitimacy to this or not. Like with any other mystery, we want answers. We spend our money. We spend time away from our loved ones and families to try to find out the answers. I think we're foolish as human beings not to always want to know more. We want to know the answers to these questions. That's what we're about. That's what we're looking for, to try to find the answers.

Part Two

Top Secret Sasquatch

*For strange effects and extraordinary combinations
we must go to life itself, which is always far more
daring than any effort of the imagination.*

Arthur Conan Doyle

7
The Paranormal Picture

Everyone knows at least one know-it-all, a person who thinks he knows everything about everything and lets no facts get in the way of his certainty. Know-it-alls are different than people who express a strong opinion, bolster it with facts, and stand firm whether dissenters like it or not. Know-it-alls behave as if they know everything about subjects that a) they have no concrete knowledge of; b) they think are silly; or, c) no one can know about with any degree of certainty.

Take, for instance, Bigfoot research.

The debunkers would fall into categories A and B. They know nothing about the subject and won't deign to learn because they consider it ridiculous. Yet Bigfoot research harbors another group of know-it-alls who possibly do more damage than all the debunkers lumped together.

Bigfoot researchers.

I've heard too many researchers make the following statements, or similar ones:

- ↔ We know a lot about Bigfoot.
- ↔ We know how Bigfoot behave.
- ↔ Bigfoot cannot be related to UFOs or other weird things.

These statements have no foundation in facts. Based on the evidence available, no one can know much of anything about Bigfoot, other than that witnesses report sightings. To proclaim that Bigfoot cannot be related to UFOs or other strangeness flies in the face of the sightings data, which includes some very strange encounters.

The evidence—mainly anecdotal—proves nothing, though it suggests much. What do we actually know about Bigfoot? Just three things:

- Legends around the world tell of hairy humanoids.
- Thousands of witnesses worldwide claim to have encountered hairy humanoids.
- People have found thousands of humanoid-yet-not-human footprints in locales around the globe.

That's it. We can and should theorize, infer, and conclude based on the evidence available. Yet we must keep in mind the unavoidable truth. We know next to nothing about these creatures. Why then do so many researchers proclaim that no connection can possibly exist between Bigfoot and other phenomena? Because the evidence points to something far stranger than what the average researcher's comfort zone will accommodate.

But ignoring the evidence will never make it disappear. Only when we examine all the data, and dare to see the big picture drawn by that data, will we ever hope to understand the Bigfoot mystery.

Figure 7.1: Note the hairy body of the German wild man shown in this fifteenth-century engraving. Legends of hairy humanoids date back thousands of years. Image courtesy of the National Gallery of Art, Washington.

Self-Imposed Limits

In both the Bigfoot and the UFO fields, researchers often paint themselves into a corner. They cover up the underlying phenomena until all they can see is the tiny circle beneath their feet that encompasses their chosen topic (Bigfoot or UFOs). Paint creates no real barrier, though, which means people can step outside their little circles if they choose to do so. Too often they recoil at the suggestion. Fear of getting their shoes dirty prevents such folks from exploring the wider world inside their minds, forcing them to hide out in the tiny space delimited by their comfort zone. They have erected self-imposed limits on what is possible.

Look at UFOs the learn about Bigfoot? Bah!

Research fairies to learn about UFOs? Humbug!

Bring all three together to gain a deeper understanding of the paranormal world? Balderdash!

Before we can examine the bigger picture, of course, we must first admit that UFOs and cryptozoological beasties are all paranormal. The first hurdle to big-picture research comes from fear of that one word, which I discussed in Part One. Fear of the word paranormal makes people stretch to unbelievable lengths to pretend their chosen specialties don't fit the definition of that word.

Mainstream science refuses to accept ufology or cryptozoology as science. Both disciplines encompass phenomena unrecognized, and ignored, by science. UFOs seem to defy the laws of nature as we know them, in the way they move and appear/disappear at will. Cryptids defy the laws of biology by existing in places they shouldn't and resisting all attempts to capture or document them scientifically. Could a giant ape-like creature hide in the woods? Could a huge serpent (or relict dinosaur) inhabit either Loch Ness or Lake Champlain? Could alien craft flit about in the skies, undetected? No way to all three, science tells us.

Yet even if we cross onto the threshold of the comfort zone by admitting our cherished phenomena qualify as paranormal, we still must take a leap to cross beyond the threshold into the wider world of the paranormal. Once we overcome the self-imposed limits that prevent us from exploring all possibilities, and accept that Bigfoot and UFOs are each paranormal, we can begin our big-picture research.

Then, and only then, might we answer the #1 most forbidden question in Bigfoot research. Does something connect all paranormal phenomena?

Crossing Over

Too many researchers in ufology and cryptozoology live in abject fear of the word paranormal and in denial of that fear. Yet even if we cross onto that threshold, admitting our cherished phenomena qualify as paranormal, we still must tiptoe further outside our comfort zone to cross the threshold into the larger world beyond.

Why do so many researchers fear crossing the threshold? The reasons are probably as individual as the researchers themselves. Some despise anything "strange," preferring to make believe that UFOs or Bigfoot or Nessie represent explainable, natural phenomena that would cease to baffle us if scientists would just take the research seriously. Others jealously cling to their specialties, not wanting anyone else to trespass on "their" territory. Most probably suffer from a common ailment, which I call experience bias.

How much do our personal experiences limit our worldview?

Figure 7.2: One camp of Bigfoot researchers wants to keep their creature away from UFOs and other high strangeness. But not even a big wall can prevent the two from crossing over anytime they want. Artwork by Kerrie Shiel.

Experience Bias

The refrain goes like this: *If it hasn't happened to me, I don't believe it can happen!* This belief lies at the core of experience bias, and at the core of why so many paranormal researchers refuse to look at the big picture in paranormal research. Strangely, these same people usually can believe in one specific phenomenon—Bigfoot or UFOs, for instance—without any personal experiences in that area (they've never had a sighting), but they cannot venture outside their specialties because of experience bias.

Bigfoot and UFOs? Bah! I've never seen them together, so neither could you.
Fairies and UFOs? Puh-leez! I ain't never seen no fairies, so they can't exist.

Experience bias seems like a natural part of the human brain. Overcoming experience bias, therefore, takes some effort. When someone tells a story that seems outrageous—such as "I saw a half man, half snake creature"—we feel that knee-jerk reaction to denounce the idea as poppycock. We've never seen a man-snake, or even heard of such a thing. And yet... how do we know man-snakes are bunk if we shut our eyes to the evidence?

Other Bigfoot researchers have told me that they only investigate "credible" sightings. What is the basis for determining the credibility of a sighting? Often, researchers use a single criterion. If something about the sighting doesn't fit with what the researcher already believes about Bigfoot, then the sighting is not credible. Any sighting involving high strangeness and Bigfoot automatically goes into the dumper because the researcher thinks stuff like that just *can't* happen. In other words, such events lie outside the experience of the researcher in question. The criterion for credibility revolves around the experience bias of the researcher.

The human mind has an incredible ability to ignore events and information that throw into question deeply ingrained beliefs. The belief that Bigfoot is an undiscovered primate, and nothing more, must be questioned if Bigfoot has a connection to UFOs or other high strangeness. Hence, any researcher who subscribes to the theory about Bigfoot must summarily reject any evidence concerning high strangeness.

Forbidden Connections

When I first researched the Bigfoot phenomenon, for my novel *The Hunt for Bigfoot*, I knew nothing about the UFO connection. My research led me to read about the sightings involving Bigfoot and UFOs, and the idea intrigued me. As I researched UFOs, I discovered connections with ancient history and fairy lore. The deeper I delved into paranormal phenomena, the more connections I uncovered. My vision, once clouded by experience bias, cleared until I could see around me an astounding variety of phenomena that defy rational explanation, contradict scientific "fact," and taunt us with their inscrutability.

Call it another dimension, the shadow world, the spirit realm, whatever you like. The reality remains. An unseen puppet master twirls his invisible strings around us.

Connections abound. Fairies cavort with hairy, bipedal beings. UFOs watch over the hairy, bipedal beings we call Bigfoot. Fairy lights—UFOs—accompany the fairies and their hairy pals. Bigfoot and UFOs exhibit seeming telepathy in their communication with witnesses. In fairy lore, fairies are sometimes viewed as spirits of the dead and witnesses have seen their deceased relatives in the company of fairies. Ghosts, fairies, Bigfoot, UFOs—all can appear and disappear at will.

When we pull back the twin veils of fear and experience bias, when we open our eyes at last, we can see the big picture. A world of paranormal wonders awaits.

8
The Invisible World

All paranormal phenomena are connected. I can't prove this statement. But when you study the paranormal for very long, strange things start to pop out at you. Paranormal phenomena often cluster in certain areas, or around certain individuals. Bigfoot, UFOs, ghosts, fairies...the lines between them begin to blur. The phenomena also share traits in common:

- ↭ The ability to appear/disappear at will.
- ↭ A tendency to abduct humans;.
- ↭ The belief by experiencers that the phenomenon will impart some great wisdom to them.
- ↭ A long, worldwide history of legends and sightings.
- ↭ An elusive quality that makes scientific study of the phenomenon impossible.

The list could go on and on. I also see another aspect common to all the phenomena—they seem to come from "elsewhere."

In fairy lore, this other realm is called Fairyland. In ufology, people call it another dimension or another planet. In Bigfoot research, we might call it "the deep woods." In all cases, this "other place" seems out of reach of humans. We cannot find it. We may try to track a Bigfoot back to wherever it goes when it's not frightening backpackers, but we invariably fail. Some people have claimed to find Bigfoot nests or favorite places where the creatures hang out, but none of these claims has produced solid evidence to support the contention. The Bigfoot simply go "elsewhere."

Back in the seventeenth century, the Reverend Robert Kirk dubbed this land the Secret Commonwealth (also the title of his book on the subject). Three centuries later W.Y. Evans-Wentz, a chronicler of fairy lore, referred to this place as the Invisible World. Evans-Wentz described our world, the Visible World, as "immersed like an island in an unexplored ocean." The ocean is the Invisible World—the world of the paranormal.

What might we learn if we could touch that world?

Parallel Realms

What precisely is the Invisible World? To Evans-Wentz, the Invisible World was the land of fairies, pixies (known as piskies in Cornwall), and

Figure 8.1: Might the deep woods, like these in Michigan's Keweenaw Peninsula, represent one aspect of the the other realm once known as fairyland? Photo by Lisa A. Shiel.

elves. It's the "otherworld" that exists in tandem with our own, what we might today call a parallel universe or another dimension. Evans-Wentz saw a connection between the fairy folk and ghosts. If he'd known about Bigfoot and UFOs, he may well have drawn a connection between those phenomena and Fairyland, aka the Invisible World, as well. Today, the realm of the paranormal encompasses myriad phenomena, from Bigfoot to UFOs to ESP and even fairies. The Invisible World described by Evans-Wentz can now be extended to include countless phenomena that haunt the margins of our perception. These phenomena remain elusive, difficult to document, and impossible to prove, despite centuries of trying.

In Evans-Wentz's day, neither the terms Bigfoot and UFO nor the disciplines of cryptozoology and ufology existed. Strange lights or craft in the sky were known as fairy lights, or airships, or some other term that made sense in the witnesses' cultural frame of reference. Hairy, humanoid beings were called by many names, including wild man, and they also make guest appearances in fairy lore under various pseudonyms. Fairies, like our Bigfoot, were associated with strange lights and supernatural occurrences such as telepathy. Evans-Wentz listed seven types of phenomena associated with fairies that science could explain. I reproduce here the exact terminology used by Evans-Wentz:

1. Collective hallucinations and veridical hallucinations.
2. Objects moving without contact.
3. Raps and noises called "supernatural."
4. Telepathy.
5. Seership and visions.
6. Dream and trance states manifesting supernormal knowledge.
7. "Mediumship" or "spirit-possession."

Veridical means genuine or real. The modern definition of a veridical hallucination is a vision that matches with reality but occurs through some means other than the normal visual process, a means that scientists do not as yet understand. In Evans-Wentz's day, a veridical hallucination meant a vision that coincided with a real event in another place or that conveyed some knowledge the viewer could not have possessed. Most often, a discussion of veridical hallucinations centered on a living person who saw an apparition of a loved one who, it later turned out, died or experienced some crisis at the exact time the apparition occurred.

Unlike a typical hallucination, a veridical hallucination cannot exist without an external stimulus—namely, the coincident but distant event of which the experiencer had no knowledge at the time of the apparition. In the early twentieth century, veridical hallucinations were thought to be a type of telepathy. Psychical researchers of the time recounted experiments in which a living person induced, via telepathy, someone else in a distant location to have a vision of the experimenter. These experiments led researchers to conclude that telepathy—which, as we'll explore later, has been scientifically documented in recent years—may seem like a hallucination when it is actually the genuine transmission of thoughts from one person another.

Most of the phenomena in Evans-Wentz's list are reported in modern times as part of UFO and/or Bigfoot sightings. We also find them in the annals of ghost research, a discipline that was well known in Evans-Wentz's time (and thus led to his conclusion that ghosts and fairies are connected). The similarities between phenomena reported in UFO/Bigfoot encounters and those associated with fairies and ghosts leads to a forbidden question. Could all these phenomena be connected? Do they all belong to the Invisible World?

Let's compare some of the items from the Evans-Wentz list with the phenomena reported by Bigfoot witnesses.

Hallucinations and Telepathy

How on earth can ghost-like apparitions have any parallel in Bigfoot research? As already explained, a veridical hallucination refers to a psychic event or an image created by the mind, the origins of which cannot be explained by conventional visual processes. A collective hallucination is simply a hallucination experienced simultaneously by more than one individual.

In his book, Evans-Wentz related what he considered to be the best example of a collective hallucination. One of the folks he interviewed, the Reverend Canon Kewley, told Evans-Wentz about an event which happened one evening while the Reverend, his sister, and their coachman made their way down a road. All three witnesses saw the same thing: a crowd blocking the road ahead, about thirty or forty yards away. The road was so packed with people that the witnesses could not see past the crowd. As the witnesses drew closer to the throng, however, the vision faded into nothing. Even their horse had reacted to the sight, leading the Reverend to believe it was more than a mere figment of the human mind.

How does any of this relate to Bigfoot? The annals of Bigfoot sightings include cases where people experienced what felt like telepathic contact, messages or feelings transmitted to them from an outside source, during a sighting. Witnesses have also reported seeing Bigfoot disappear right in front of them, often in a flash of light. In a few sightings, the witness describes a Bigfoot creature that seemed semi-transparent. These sightings are not widespread, but they do occur and they suggest that the just-an-animal theory falls short of explaining the full phenomenon. Could these disappearing and invisible Bigfoot be a form of veridical hallucination, similar to those described by Evans-Wentz?

When I say hallucination, I don't mean a delusion brought on by mental derangement or drug use. That's the modern definition. The phenomena reported by Evans-Wentz and others might best be termed extrasensory perception (ESP). What at first appears to be a hallucination may turn out to contain some truth or information

Figure 8.2: This image, taken from the cover of my novel *The Hunt for Bigfoot*, depicts an event similar to what eyewitnesses have reported— Bigfoot disappearing in flashes of light. Artwork by Kerrie Shiel.

that the experiencer could not have known at the time of the ESP experience. Though Evans-Wentz separates hallucinations and telepathy, the two terms may in fact describe the same or closely related phenomena.

ESP experiences that manifest as visions may be nonphysical, but does that mean they're unreal? Nonphysical phenomena may indeed have the ability to manipulate or affect the world in a real way, making such phenomena not mere delusions or figments of the imagination. For instance, a mysterious light may seem illusory because the witness's hand goes right through it, but the light can also burn the grass or cause objects to move.

Electricity has no physical form that we can hold in our hands, yet it affects the world in numerous ways. The human eye can't see electromagnetic radiation, but we feel its effects. We cook our food with microwaves, a type of electromagnetic radiation.

Raps and Noises

This may seem to have no bearing on Bigfoot research, but in fact, it does. Both witnesses and researchers report hearing knocks, whoops, screams, and other sounds that they attribute to Bigfoot. Evans-Wentz calls the sounds associated with fairy beings "raps and noises called 'supernatural'." The word supernatural refers to phenomena which *seem* to be beyond anything in the natural world.

The Bigfoot witnesses and researchers who report hearing raps, knocks, whoops, and other sounds do not see the creature making the sound. I've heard whooping cries and knocking noises, but I never saw what made the sound. I believe the noises were Bigfoot related because of the other activity in the same area (stick signs, footprints, mane braiding). Perhaps the noises attributed to fairies were really caused by Bigfoot-type creatures. Hairy beings, of varying sizes, often appear in fairy lore. Take, for instance, the *nains*—dwarves with a coat of black hair on their bodies. Fairy lore also spoke of hairy creatures known as *fions*, who accompanied the fairies on their sojourns into the world of humans.

Like Bigfoot, fairies were thought to cause rapping or knocking sounds. Pixies often got blamed for mysterious knocking sounds and, interestingly, also for trees shaking. Bigfoot are also said to shake trees, as well cars and buildings. Both pixies and Bigfoot also get fingered as the culprits when something bangs on the outside walls of houses. A variant of the

Figure 8.3: Legends tell of fairy-type beings known as knockers who alerted miners to rich veins. Perhaps knockers helped out the miners in the Quincy Mine (shown above), a now-defunct copper mine in Michigan. Photo by Lisa A. Shiel.

pixies, known as knockers, would create rapping noises in mines to alert the miners of where to find a rich vein of whatever metal they sought, and also to warn the miners of danger. The similarities in the types of noises attributed to Bigfoot and to fairy beings hints at a deeper truth about the nature of both phenomena.

The UFO Correlation

Though not included in Evans-Wentz's list of unexplained phenomena associated with fairy beings, another attribute deserves mentioning here. Mysterious lights (aka UFOs) form another link in the chain that connects Bigfoot and the Invisible World.

In Brittany, folks knew about the *fions*, hairy dwarves who came out at night with the fairies. They had black eyes and carried small torches. The fairies themselves were associated with UFOs called fairy lights, which witnesses often saw dancing above the hills. Early in the twentieth century in Ireland, a young girl watched white fairy lights soar in formation above the hill fort of Crillaun toward another hill fort. She and her friends had seen the lights on other occasions too.

Legends of hairy dwarves persisted in the Poitou region of France up until the late nineteenth century. Here, the creatures were called *farfadets*, and in their description echoed that of the *fions*. The dark-colored *farfedets* slept in caves during the day, emerging at night to taunt farm folk. In the 1850s, several women watched in fear as a group of *farfadets* pulled a "chariot" uphill toward them. The "chariot" then flew up into the sky and vanished from sight.

Fairies may be seen dancing in a circle of light, which emanates from no visible source, or they may step out of an orb-like light. One particular light associated with fairies was known as the death candle. It appeared as a glowing light with a bluish tint that often danced about or rolled in the air. In one encounter with a fairy, a man looked out the window of his home to see a fairy woman prancing about in his field. The woman, dressed in white, carried some kind of light that she swung to and fro. This incident echoes a 1973 sighting in Pennsylvania, where two girls saw a Bigfoot carrying a glowing orb.

Sightings involving glowing orbs and Bigfoot, though rare, do exist in the annals of paranormal research. The synchronicity of Bigfoot and glowing orbs—when they appear in the same area but not at the same time—seems even more prevalent than sightings of the two together.

Witnesses have also seen Bigfoot in association with other kinds of UFOs, including saucer-shaped craft. In 1974, William Bosak saw a disk-shaped craft while driving to his home near Frederic, Wisconsin. The UFO was shrouded in mist and sported a windshield of sorts, in the form of a curved window. Through the window, Bosak could see a hairy hominid. He studied the creature for several seconds, until fear overcame him and he sped away.

In April 1977, two witnesses reportedly saw a cigar-shaped UFO hover low to the ground in the woods of Mason County, Washington. What they described as a purple elevator then lowered from the bottom of the craft and a hairy, bipedal creature exited the UFO. The creature carried a wood plank, which it then lugged off into the woods. Shortly thereafter, the creature returned to reenter the craft, which then zipped off into the sky. That same year near Snohomish, Washington, Steven Unzelman encountered two humanlike beings who came out of an egg-shaped craft that descended from above. Unzelman also noticed a Bigfoot-type creature nearby, to whom the other beings signaled. The Bigfoot then departed with the other beings in their UFO.

A more recent case from July 4, 1996, occurred near Fayetteville, Arkansas. A witness reported that he and several friends left a holiday gathering to walk in the woods near his home. A bright light up ahead attracted their attention. Worried someone was shooting off fireworks inside the woods, they moved toward the light. Through a break in the trees, they saw three triangular UFOs hovering in the woods, each pointing beams of light downward from its three corners. Three creatures, whom the witnesses took for the pilots of the UFOs, stood outside the craft talking to each other. The creatures were tall and covered with hair. The creatures sniffed at the air for a moment, then retreated into their craft.

Here's another interesting point about UFOs and fairies. The two phenomena share an affinity for water. UFOs have been seen descending into and rising out of bodies of water. Often called USOs, short for Unidentified Submersible Objects, these mysterious craft pop up in sighting reports around the world. Some witnesses have even watched UFOs draw water out of lakes. Fairies and their ilk also seem to like the water. The fairy goddess Aine lived in a lake, and her son lived in an underwater castle. Water fairies were believed to inhabit certain rivers and lakes in Ireland, such as Lough Gur in County Limerick, whose waters legends say conceal an entrance to the fairy realm.

The Algonquian Indians of North America preserve similar beliefs about fairy-like beings and their connection to water. Legends tell of the *May-may-gway-shi*, beings who live in and around water. The caves of Burnt Bluff, along the shores of Lake Michigan, contain a type of rock art called pictographs, which are painted onto the rock using red ocher. The Algonquian legends associate the *May-may-gway-shi* with similar pictographs found at other locations, which archaeologists date to the pre-columbian era, into which the Burnt Bluff pictographs fall. The Burnt Bluff pictographs depict humanoid figures with barrel chests, wide shoulders, and almost no neck. The images resemble similar figures found in ancient rock art from the Four

Figure 8.4: This pictograph, known as the Spider Man, is found at Burnt Bluff in Michigan's Upper Peninsula. Might it represent a Bigfoot? Drawing by Lisa A. Shiel.

Figure 8.5: Lough Gur, an Irish lake, is said to be inhabited by fairies. About 980 feet away from the lake lies this stone circle, an ancient and mysterious monument. Image © iStockPhoto.com/Peter Zelei.

Corners region of the U.S. The figures all resemble Bigfoot far more than humans.

The Trickster Connection

Another correlation between Bigfoot, UFOs, and fairies also deserves mentioning. All three phenomena seem to involve a trickster element. The notion of tricksters harkens back to ancient mythology, where tricksters were gods who broke all the rules, flouting the cultural dictums of both god and man. They blithely crossed the boundaries of the physical world, and harassed humans and gods alike. They sometimes acted in a malicious manner, but other times their actions might seem only playful. Tricksters often played tricks in order to get food.

A strong trickster element runs through fairy lore. The changeling phenomenon, where fairies were believed to abduct infants and re-place them with fairy children, is essentially a trickster occurrence. One tale tells of a man who, while out riding one night, found a baby alongside the road. He took it home, but when he offered the child to his wife he found it had turned into a block of wood. Fairies were heard outside the house chastising the man for falling for their trick. The knockers mentioned earlier played tricks on miners, often distracting them from discovering a big lode. Fairies might also play rather innocuous tricks on people who neglected to show them the proper respect, for instance by appearing less than grateful for gifts the fairies left for them. Fairies might punish the humans by overturning pots or tangling the manes of horses.

Figure 8.6: Mane braiding is a phenomenon that has been reported around the world, often in conjunction with Bigfoot. This intricate, distinctly unnatural braid showed up in my horse's mane overnight back in May 2005. Photo by Lisa A. Shiel.

This last trick, tangling or braiding horses' manes, also appears in the annals of Bigfoot activity. In areas around the world—including Russia and South America—people believe that Bigfoot braid the manes of horses, and in some cases witnesses have seen the Bigfoot doing this. I wrote about mane braiding extensively in my previous book, *Backyard Bigfoot*. Though I have yet to witness a Bigfoot braiding the mane of one of my horses, I have repeatedly found intricate plaits in their manes that most certainly did not occur naturally. I've also found stick signs, another type of Bigfoot activity, in front of the horse barn.

"Stick signs" refers to small sticks laid out in geometric and distinctly unnatural formations. These signs turn up along trails in the woods and out in open fields, and they appear overnight. As documented in *Backyard Bigfoot*, I found numerous examples of stick signs both in Texas and in Michigan. They occur in the same areas where I found possible Bigfoot footprints, heard as-yet-unidentified whooping calls, and discovered mane braids. Stick signs also play into the trickster element of paranormal phenomena. Whoever or whatever leaves them prefers to remain unseen, dropping their little signs in the woods or even in my yard. In one case, I found two stick signs in the woods—an H shape and a pair of parallel sticks. I collected the sticks and deposited them in a pile in a small flatbed trailer outside my house. The next morning, I found the sticks rearranged, inside the flatbed trailer, into the configurations in which I'd found them in the woods.

Like the fairies, Bigfoot have also been reported to leave gifts, especially food. UFO occupants have also presented humans with gifts, such as in the 1961 case of Joe Simonton. The Wisconsin man reported that after a flying saucer landed on his farm, he saw three men inside it. Using gestures, one of the men indicated to Simonton they needed water, and so Simonton fill the jug for them. In return, one of the UFO occupants gave him three pancakes. Later, Simonton would give the cookies to the Air Force, which sent them off for analysis. The contents of the pancakes were rather ordinary, mainly wheat, but strangely they contained no salt. The case remains unsolved.

This case is but one example of the trickster element in UFO sightings. A similar vein runs through Bigfoot sightings in fairy lore. If something connects these phenomena, then why do most people seem ignorant of, or at least unconcerned with, the implications of this link? The blame may lie with our civilized ways.

The Civilizing Influence

If all paranormal phenomena are connected, then perhaps they do originate from and retreat back into the Invisible World described by Evans-Wentz in his book *The Fairy Faith in Celtic Countries*. Since the Industrial Revolution, we humans have divorced ourselves from the natural world. Writing in the early twentieth century, Evans-Wentz already recognized this fact. Urban dwellers no longer understood country folk, and no longer felt an innate connection to the land. The unnatural, such as machines and crowded cities, replaced the natural. In this new world, Evans-Wentz saw the fairy lore being squeezed out of existence. Rural folk who believed in such things were ridiculed by the more "civilized" city folk.

We suffer this problem now more than ever. Many people, particularly scientists, expect every natural phenomenon to have an explanation that fits within both the scope of everyday experiences and the narrow definition of what the scientific establishment deems possible. Perhaps this expectation explains why so many Bigfoot researchers must shove the phenomenon into the narrow box labeled "giant ape" or, at best, "unknown primate." If we place Bigfoot into the context of the Invisible World, with fairies and glowing orbs, what then? We have no concept of that would mean.

Figure 8.7: Science still cannot explain everything—like the moving rocks of Racetrack Playa in California's Death Valley. These rocks move on their own, and scientists don't know why or how. No one has ever witnessed the rocks moving, but they leave visible trails that often zigzag and make ninety-degree turns. The obvious explanations (wind, earthquakes, etc.) have been ruled out, leaving a true natural mystery. Photo courtesy of NASA/GSFC/Cynthia Cheung.

We must expand our horizons beyond the city limits. Get back to our folk roots. Remember the stories and myths and beliefs that shaped humanity's past, to inform our future.

Then, and only then, we might find the Invisible World has indeed become visible.

The True Nature of the Paranormal

We've just explored what the Invisible World is and why modern people have so much trouble with the notion. We've also explored the possibility that Bigfoot, UFOs, and fairies are all connected by this Invisible World—the paranormal world that exists everywhere around us but that we cannot or will not see. Bigfoot, as a paranormal phenomenon, would then share the Invisible World with fairies and UFOs and everything else the so-called civilized world pooh-poohs.

Why should we consider this idea? Let's recap the similarities between Bigfoot, UFOs, and fairies:

1. Bigfoot and fairies have both been associated with UFOs, and vice versa.
2. Telepathy has been reported in conjunction with all three phenomena.
3. Strange noises are often associated with all three.
4. Fairies, UFOs, and Bigfoot each seem to possess the ability to appear and disappear at will.
5. Cultures that preserve legends of Bigfoot-type creatures also recount legends of fairies, UFOs, and other denizens of the Invisible World.
6. Like Bigfoot and UFO occupants, fairies reportedly abduct humans on occasion.

Bigfoot also share another connection to fairies. Both classes of beings apparently like to braid the manes of horses. I've experienced the mane braiding phenomenon myself. I wrote about it in my previous book *Backyard Bigfoot* and I update my research into these phenoemena in Part Three of this book.

Now let's consider some other facts about Bigfoot that suggest these creatures represent more than an undiscovered species of primate:

1. We cannot demonstrate that Bigfoot exist in enough numbers to support a population.

2. Witnesses have reported seeing Bigfoot vanish in puffs of smoke or flashes of light.
3. A rash of Bigfoot sightings will occur in an area then fade away, as if the creatures simply disappeared.
4. People have reported finding Bigfoot tracks that start and/or end abruptly with no explanation as to why (no change in soil conditions, etc.).
5. The harder we try to document the Bigfoot phenomenon, the more it seems to slip away from us.

What does all of this mean? The very nature of the Bigfoot phenomenon is telling us to look beyond the everyday, beyond what science accepts as possible, into the world of the unexplained—into the Invisible World.

The world of the supernatural.

Supernatural Sasquatch

What is the supernatural? A paranormal phenomenon is supernatural by its very nature because it is rare and unusual, it seems to defy natural laws, and it remains unrecognized by mainstream science—and therefore poorly understood by scientists who refuse to examine the phenomenon. Supernatural and paranormal serve as synonyms of one another, which means that Bigfoot and UFOs exist as both paranormal and supernatural phenomena.

In the world of Bigfoot research, and in UFO research, the above statement is heresy. Bigfoot researchers and ufologists each separately cry that their favorite phenomenon is neither paranormal nor supernatural and it's most definitely not related to any other phenomena. Their cries fulfill no other purpose than to give them a sore throat. When we understand that the word paranormal refers to anything that is rare or unusual and not recognized by science, we see clearly that the term applies to both Bigfoot and UFOs. If Bigfoot and UFOs weren't rare, we could take scientists out to a field and show them a UFO or drag them into the woods to introduce them to some Bigfoot. A rare phenomenon defies our attempts to document it scientifically because we cannot predict when it will occur.

If science recognized Bigfoot or UFOs, we wouldn't need any of the myriad organizations that specialize in studying these creatures in the hopes of proving to scientists they exist. Every child would learn about Bigfoot and UFOs in school, the National Science Foundation would award grants to UFO and Bigfoot researchers, and the government would declare Bigfoot an endangered species (whether or not it should be one).

Few researchers who investigate topics like fairies or ghosts would freak out if somebody called their research paranormal or supernatural. Yet Bigfoot and UFO researchers will react to that word with the kind of knee jerk that could break a bystander's jawbone. As we've seen so far, both Bigfoot and UFOs share a lot in common with the beings and phenomena described in fairy lore. If folks expended half as much energy on actual research as they do on battling words like paranormal and supernatural, who knows what we might learn about both phenomena.

Bigfoot. UFOs. Crop circles. Phantom black cats. Lake monsters. Fairies. The shadow of a greater mystery envelops these phenomena. What people of the past called fairies, we might today call by another name.

Aliens.

Whether they hail from another planet, another dimension, or the hidden spaces in this world, the beings who pilot UFOs and the beings known as fairies and Bigfoot definitely qualify as alien. They are strange and different from anything else on earth. They don't belong.

And perhaps, neither do we.

9
The Ethics of Bigfoot

How far will researchers go to hide the truth? Browsing the website of a Bigfoot or UFO group usually reveals a database of sightings that have been reported to that group. What won't show up on most of those sites?

Sightings that cross the boundaries between the two disciplines.

A visitor to those sites would conclude that no Bigfoot-UFO sightings get reported. An awful lot of ufologists and cryptozoologists cringe from poking one toe into the forbidden territory where Bigfoot, UFOs, and other phenomena merge. As we've seen in the previous chapters, however, paranormal phenomena often cross those boundaries without regard for the wishes of researchers.

Crossing the Line

In his book *The Locals*, Thom Powell reveals how sightings that mention high strangeness were thrown out by the Bigfoot group that he joined. High strangeness events include UFOs sighted with hairy humanoids, a Bigfoot vanishing into thin air at the end of the sighting, or anything else beyond a Bigfoot traipsing past a witness. Witnesses who claim to have had repeated encounters with Bigfoot fall under the same umbrella as high strangeness cases, meaning few researchers will believe them.

Numerous cases of high strangeness exist, though finding them requires reading many books, some of them hard to find and some that superficially seem to have no connection to Bigfoot. Take, for instance, the book *Hunt for the Skinwalker*. It's not the kind of fare most Bigfoot researchers would consume, yet it contains bizarre and fascinating information about Bigfoot-related phenomena on a ranch in Utah. The authors, journalist George Knapp and scientist Colm Kelleher, discuss the crossover problem as it relates to their research at that ranch. On the property, nicknamed the Skinwalker Ranch, residents experienced varied and numerous paranormal events—from glowing orbs to cattle mutilations to Bigfoot encounters, all of which often overlapped one another. Years earlier, a ranch in Colorado served as the stage for similar events, which included sightings of Bigfoot and UFOs together.

How many cryptozoologists read books with titles like *Hunt for the Skinwalker*? What about *Dimensions*? In his book of that title, UFO researcher and astrophysicist Jacques Vallee wrote about hairy beings associated with UFOs. Would very many Bigfooters pick up the book *The Fairy Faith in Celtic Countries*, and if they did, would they believe any of what they read or just dismiss it as fantasy and superstition?

Books that deal with the crossover problem often get labeled "sensationalist" or "fringe." Yet the number of books that have dealt with the topic testify to the widespread nature of the phenomenon of crossover cases. Even the books that don't call the creatures Bigfoot, but refer to them as hairy humanoids or use some other term, get labeled irrelevant. Hairy creatures seen with UFOs have no relation to the hairy creatures seen by Bigfoot witnesses.

We all know the old saying if it walks like a duck and quacks like a duck...

A handful of researchers will acknowledge that crossover cases exist. While they prefer to file them away in the Weird & Inexplicable folder, they do recognize that paranormal sightings occur. At least the researchers who take that attitude aren't feeding the sighting reports to their paper shredders; however, they are squirreling away those sightings where no one can see them. How can anyone accurately gauge the frequency of high strangeness cases when the data is concealed in someone's file cabinet?

Praying for Credibility

I've run across more than one Bigfoot website where the sighting report form includes a statement saying flat out that if the witness is reporting a sighting that involves high strangeness, don't report it to them because they won't believe it anyway. The more-polite (or perhaps less-rude) researchers might suggest the witness report their sighting a UFO website instead. Either way, the witness may be left feeling a bit offput. The researchers defend their attitudes by saying that, after all, Bigfoot are giant apes and have nothing to do with that silly UFO stuff. Those researchers also like to say that sticking to the so-called flesh-and-blood cases improves their credibility.

Last I checked, science still had not accepted the existence of Bigfoot—nor had the majority of scientists stopped snickering at the

Figure 9.1: If this were the temple of credibility, Bigfoot researchers would line up for miles waiting to get inside. But would the gods be pleased with their behavior? Fortunately, this is just the Nashville Parthenon in Tennessee, a faithful replica of the Greek temple dedicated to the goddess Athena. Photo by Lisa A. Shiel.

notion of hairy, nonhuman bipeds living in the woods. Disregarding strange sightings has failed to impress the scientific community.

What about the witnesses? Has the number of sightings reported each year increased due to the enhanced credibility brought on by tossing out data? It's difficult to gauge this as well, since Bigfoot sightings get reported to so many websites spread out across the Internet. Browsing the most popular site for Bigfoot research, however, suggests an unfavorable trend. The sightings database maintained by the Bigfoot Field Researchers Organization (BFRO) shows that the number of clear, high-quality sightings (as opposed to vague glimpses, strange sounds, and other phenomena) has decreased substantially since the 1960s. Thanks to TV reality shows like *MonsterQuest* and *Finding Bigfoot*, more people are reporting their new and old experiences, but the quality of the data collected has diminished. People now report more vague sightings—as well as a larger number of "vocalization" or "wood knock" experiences, where they hear a strange scream or knocking sound, and instances of rocks thrown at witnesses. For the state of Washington, the top state for Bigfoot sighting reports, the BFRO database shows that 55% of the reports involve vague encounters; of the sightings that took place since 2000, fully 67% involve lesser-quality reports.

Regardless of whether the number of sightings being *reported* has gone down over the past five decades, the *quality* of the sightings reported clearly has plummeted. The popularity of reality shows about Bigfoot and cryptozoology may spur more folks to fill out an online report form, but the experiences they report are vague and often do not involve an actual sighting. The timeframe in which reports have gotten less informative also coincides with the timeframe when the *Gigantopithecus* theory emerged and gained prominence among Bigfooters who subscribe to the "flesh-and-blood" theory.

Many researchers essentially tell long-term and high-strangeness witnesses to buzz off, a tactic that would seem to have paid off in the wrong way. Could other factors have influenced the decrease in sightings reported? Of course. A change in the behavior of Bigfoot, media ridicule of the subject, and a changing social climate could all play into the issue. But we can no longer pretend that the bad attitudes of many researchers haven't also affected the situation.

And science has a thing or two to teach us about bad attitudes.

The Science of Fudge

No one will ever find credibility by stepping over a trash heap of inconvenient sightings. Yet, in an unexpected and perhaps undesirable way, Bigfoot researchers may be emulating scientists—albeit unintentionally.

Science is often portrayed as a bastion of unbiased, rational thought that produces unsullied results from the hard work of scientists we can trust. Standards and oversight weed out the few bad seeds who would corrupt the system. Unfortunately, this view of science is idealized and naïve, and fails to account for a serious problem in the scientific community.

A shocking number of scientists apparently see nothing wrong with fudging, massaging, or outright fabricating data.

For a 2009 report in the journal *PLoS One*, Daniele Fanelli of the University of Edinburgh compiled and analyzed the results of twenty-one surveys of scientists. The surveys questioned participants about their feelings concerning scientific misconduct. Fanelli boiled down the types of misconduct into three main categories common to all the surveys:

1. **Fabrication**—making it up out of thin air.
2. **Falsification**—manipulating or distorting the data.
3. **Plagiarism**—stealing someone else's work.

Falsification turns out to be the most disturbing category, because it often drifts into gray areas. The English language includes many euphemisms for this type of behavior—cooking, mining, fudging, cherry-picking. Yet all these behaviors distort the outcome of scientific research and, like a common cold, branch out to infect the research of other scientists who may not even realize the original result was falsified.

According to Fanelli's analysis, about 2% of scientists admitted to outright fabricating data, and another one third fessed up to other forms of misconduct, including deleting data because their gut feelings told them to do so. Most shockingly, 86% of scientists said they witnessed other scientists engaging in various types of misconduct. Over the eleven-year time span represented by the included surveys, statistics show a decrease in the number of scientists willing to admit to committing misconduct themselves but no decrease in the number of scientists who report witnessing the misconduct of others. This points to one of two possibilities. Either scientists are less willing to admit their misdeeds, even anonymously, or their ideas about what constitutes misconduct have narrowed over the years. Scientists no longer consider scientific misconduct to include activities known by deceptively innocuous terms such as fudging and cherry-picking.

Another study examined the reasons for retracting papers published in scientific journals. A retracted paper is one that's already been published, and therefore already disseminated to the scientific community at large, but the journal or author(s) later decided to rescind their work. The 2012 study included 2,047 papers (all published after 1977, when the first retraction took place) and found four reasons for retractions—error, duplicate publication, plagiarism, and fraud or suspected fraud. Fraud and plagiarism far outnumbered the two more innocuous reasons, accounting for 53.2% of the retracted papers; fraud alone accounted for 43.4%. And between 1975 and 2011 the number of papers retracted due to fraud or plagiarism skyrocketed, jumping to almost ten times the 1975 level. Perhaps even more disturbingly, some articles whose authors are suspected of fraud never get retracted—even when there is enough evidence of fraud for the Office of Research Integrity (ORI) to find them guilty.

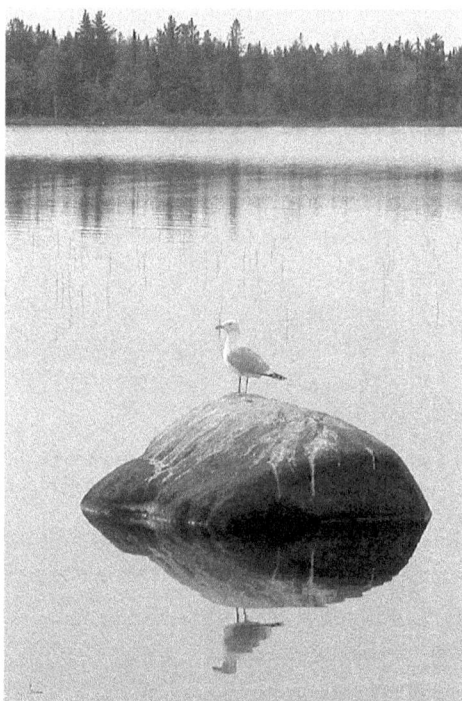

Figure 9.2: Ethical misconduct is treacherous territory, for scientists and Bigfoot researchers alike. It's hard to get off that rock once you jump onto it! Photo by Lisa A. Shiel.

ORI is a branch of the U.S. Department of Health and Human Services that handles allegations of misconduct and metes out punishment, such as being barred from receiving federal grants for research or federal contracts (known as debarment). ORI's list of cases currently undergoing administrative action includes forty-four entries. Of those cases, six have resulted in a retracted paper. Eighteen of the scientists in question have been debarred, three for life. All of this data points to one unsettling fact: misconduct in the scientific community has become a far more serious problem than most people know.

In the area of misconduct, scientists share a lot in common with some Bigfoot researchers. If the data doesn't suit their preconceived notions, they nudge it, fudge it, or just plain erase it. But do we really want to emulate the bad behavior of scientists?

Of course, Bigfoot researchers who dump undesirable data often declare that any witness who claims to have experienced anything other than a so-called flesh-and-blood sighting must be crazy, mistaken, or lying. They feel justified in ignoring the sighting. They may even feel they've protected the integrity of the sightings data and of their research.

In scientific parlance, this type of behavior is known as falsifying data—and it's a bad thing. A truly scientific researcher will accept data as it comes, in the absence of any evidence of tampering, and go from there. That's the definition of unbiased.

But misconduct isn't the only problem affecting Bigfoot research.

The C Factor

We've seen how misunderstandings about the meaning of the word paranormal can lead researchers to wage a futile battle against the word. Another word can also trigger a cascade of conniptions among Bigfoot researchers. The word is "crazy."

Many researchers seem to have a phobia about evidence that contradicts their long-held beliefs. Why is this so? Does fear of the C word compel researchers to censor sightings?

Some Bigfoot researchers have tried to recruit credentialed scientists into their ranks, with moderate success. University scientists need to worry about things like tenure and professional credibility. Dipping their toes into Bigfoot research exposes them to the derision of their fellow scientists, even if they stick to the unknown-primate hypothesis. It's no surprise then that these scientists shun high-strangeness cases. Those types of sightings will certainly earn them an extra helping of ridicule and, the reasoning goes, trash the credibility of their Bigfoot research. Non-scientists involved in Bigfoot research adopt the same mentality. Only by cherry-picking their data can they achieve any level of credibility with the scientific community and avoid the C word.

If I came across a sighting that totally invalidated all my precious little theories, what would I do? First of all, my theories aren't that precious to me. But I handle boat-rocking cases the same way I handle any other case. I'd investigate it, assess the reliability of the witness, and then compare what I'd learned with what I knew already. Perhaps I'd need to change my theories. That would be fine with me. Learning is the goal and the thrill of any research.

I say that I handle boat-rocking cases this way because I've already encountered one such case. A few years ago, a witness reported to me her experience with missing time. Missing time refers to an instance where the witness feels as if no time has passed, but discovers that a significant period of time has elapsed. In ufology, missing time is a well-known aspect of the UFO phenomenon. I've experienced my own case of missing time in association with a UFO encounter, as described in my previous book

Figure 9.3: Some folks would love it if Bigfoot research were a stone boat firmly cemented in the ground, with no high strangeness cases to rock it. Unfortunately for them, this is only the USS Kearsarge memorial in Michigan's Upper Peninsula. Photo by Lisa A. Shiel.

Backyard Bigfoot. Yet in the case reported to me, the witness experienced the missing time after apparently striking a Bigfoot with her car. I had never heard of missing time in conjunction with a Bigfoot encounter. When the witness shared her experience with me, I needed to consider the story for awhile before I could really accept that it was possible. The witness seemed quite believable, and she had previously shared with me what might be termed "normal" Bigfoot encounters.

I finally realized that, since evidence does exist pointing to a connection between Bigfoot and UFOs, it should come as no surprise that missing time might also occur in Bigfoot sightings. I can't prove that it did happen to the witness in question, but then we can't "prove" any Bigfoot sighting is true. Even corroborating evidence, such as footprints or even photographic evidence, falls short of proving scientifically that these creatures exist. It also falls short of proving the veracity and accuracy of events witnesses report experiencing.

Bigfoot research relies on one simple premise, whether we like it or not. We must decide whether we believe the physical evidence and the witness testimony. I decided to accept the word of the witness who shared with me her story of missing time and Bigfoot. Doing so forced me to reevaluate my ideas about Bigfoot. If I ever receive a report of a Bigfoot living with a band of gorillas or a troop of chimpanzees, I might have to rethink my stance on the just-an-ape theory. Until then, I stand firm in my beliefs because I based them on the available evidence—the uncensored evidence.

Many Bigfoot researchers, and even many UFO researchers, would probably chuck the missing-time Bigfoot encounter into the waste basket if it came across their desks. It's not credible, they might say. If asked why they dismiss it as not credible, they will probably reply that such an incident is simply not possible. Why isn't it possible? Because things like that just can't happen in relation to Bigfoot. Why not? Because it's not possible. Round and round we go, trapped on a carousel of illogic, spinning at high velocity. The direct, and honest, answer would be to say "I threw away the sighting because I'm not comfortable with strange cases that might force me to question my preconceived ideas."

Researchers who do look into the strange cases often get labeled crazy—by other Bigfoot researchers. Since everyone involved in Bigfoot research gets labeled crazy by the debunkers and the so-called skeptical scientists, it seems odd that Bigfoot researchers themselves might exhibit a similar intolerance. It's also shortsighted. None of us knows what Bigfoot is, though we each have our own ideas about it. If evidence emerges that provides conclusive proof of the Bigfoot-UFO connection, all the Bigfoot researchers who ridiculed the very notion and struggled so hard to censor the sightings might feel rather stupid. If the "flesh-and-blood" camp finally acquires conclusive proof for their theory, anyone who ridiculed or dismissed out of hand that theory might also feel rather stupid.

We would all do well to remember a few relevant points:

- ↭ Involvement in Bigfoot research attracts ridicule no matter what approach is taken, unless it's the debunking approach. Adopting the it's-a-primate-and-nothing-but-a-primate-with-no-connection-to-any-other-phenomena approach offers no protection from ridicule or the "crazy" label.
- ↭ Numerous degreed scientists are involved in research into UFOs, psychic phenomena, and other paranormal phenomena. Fear of professional repercussions is often cited as the top reason for tossing out unusual sightings. The reasoning sounds valid, until we examine it more closely. The scientists involved in other areas of paranormal research manage to weather the ridicule squalls. Clearly, they decided paranormal phenomena deserve scientific study and that engaging in such research is worth the risk to their careers—or else they'd already earned tenure!
- ↭ Manipulating the data to present the picture we want the world to see may bond Bigfoot researchers to scientists, but is this a link we really want to cultivate? Data manipulation may be widespread in the scientific community, but in the long run we would do better to emulate the behavior of ethical scientists.
- ↭ Finally, we come to the most important point of all. No one gets an accurate picture of any phenomenon by censoring the data to suit their preconceived ideas. Only by daring to see the whole phenomenon can we hope to gain an accurate understanding of it.

Researchers may wish to ignore unusual sightings because those sightings interfere with the just-an-ape theory. Scientists serve as the scapegoat for Bigfoot researchers who want to ignore crossover sightings where the Bigfoot phenomenon intersects with other phenomena. I have one response to this mentality.

Wake up!

The Bigfoot phenomenon is paranormal, with or without the high strangeness, and Bigfoot research will always attract ridicule. Whether these creatures represent nothing more than undiscovered primates or they share a link with other phenomena, their very nature makes them paranormal. Have the integrity to admit crossover sightings happen. Adopt an ethical standard of research wherein strange sightings are not discarded by default, but are at least kept in the Weird & Inexplicable drawer. Anyone who intends to collect sighting reports—of any cryptozoological creature or unexplained phenomenon—must have the integrity to acknowledge and investigate every sighting report received.

Nothing says you have to believe every one of them. But if the sole reason for discarding a sighting is that it "can't happen" with Bigfoot, ask yourself a question. Why can't it happen?

Then, answer honestly.

The Secret Society of Sasquatch

So we've cleared the credibility hurdle, which we now realize is nothing more than a speed bump. The path ahead seems clear. We're heading into the weird woods, but we feel ready to explore the strange side of Sasquatch wherever it lurks.

Whoa there, pard'ner. Who said you could enter these woods? You ain't no real Bigfoot researcher, pal, so scram.

Okay, I haven't heard anyone use those exact words. But I have come across instances where certain people are dismissed as being not "real" Bigfoot researchers or not "credible" Bigfoot researchers. What qualifications does a person need to undertake Bigfoot research?

Figure 9.4: Some Bigfoot researchers seem to revel in secrecy, as if Bigfoot research were a classified government project—like the B-2 stealth bomber. U.S. Air Force photo by Bobbie Garcia.

In the real world, none. Behind the imaginary walls of the Bigfoot research community, the answer varies. Most explanations of what constitutes a "real" Bigfoot researcher center on a single, unscientific premise.

Cronyism.

Sasquatch Snobbery

In other words, the answer to the question of who are the real Bigfoot researchers is "only me and my buddies!" Virtually every branch of paranormal research has splintered into cliques that let nobody breach their inner circle. In most cases, the inner circle consists of people with lots of money to blow on fancy equipment, marketing, buying each other's merchandise, paying for memberships in each other's organizations, and purchasing slots on each other's expeditions. Everyone in these cliques wants to have his own Internet radio show or podcast, episodes of which feature—surprise, surprise—the host's buddies. The insiders play musical podcast chairs, switching back and forth so often we can practically hear the chairs scraping on the virtual floor.

The secret society within each field of paranormal research ignores all outsiders and locks out those individuals whom the members deem unworthy. How do you know you're a member of a paranormal secret society? Well, if you have to ask then you aren't. How does someone become a member? Learn how to lick the boots of snobs and, eventually perhaps, they will grant you admission.

Advice for the insiders: If you've got piles of spare money lying around and you just love gadgets, go forth and spend. Have fun hanging out with your pals online and in the forest. Jet off to Bangladesh to study the legendary creatures purportedly living there. And remember to jangle your keys to the inner circle in front of everyone else, so they know you belong and they don't.

Advice for the rest of us: Should we feel inadequate? Shall we give up on exploring the paranormal because we lack the gadgets, the funds, and the keys to the paranormal country club? No.

What should we do? Whatever we want. The exclusionary, and often obnoxious, tactics of the inner circle can get you down. *I'll never be one of them*, you may think, *so why bother trying?* Instead of giving up on Bigfoot research, try changing your goal. Forget about fitting in with the elitists.

Instead of bemoaning your outsider status, embrace it. Remember, being an outsider means not having to abide by the insider's rules. Conduct research in a manner the insiders look down their noses at—i.e., refuse to chuck those pesky high-strangeness sightings, consider options other than the just-an-ape hypothesis, read about hairy beings who cavort with fairies, talk about the possibility of Bigfoot telepathy.

Maybe after conducting your research, you'll decide Bigfoot really is just an ape after all. At least you'll have reached the conclusion based on examination of all the available evidence, including the stuff the insider's group ridicules. That's the truly scientific way of approaching the Bigfoot phenomenon, and indeed all paranormal phenomena.

The Outer Circle

The insider group within Bigfoot research ignores the rest of us, writing us off as wackos or reprobates. We are the outer circle to their inner circle. What should we do?

The better question is why do anything. If our theories or methods go against what the insiders have deemed appropriate, so what? Ridicule has become the most potent weapon aimed at non-insiders. The inner circles within paranormal research use ridicule against the outer circle equally as often as debunkers use it against the insiders!

Why do paranormal researchers employ a debunker's favorite weapon against people in their own field of study? Because it works. If someone outside the inner circle dares to espouse a theory the cronies don't like, or if that someone presents evidence they'd rather nobody saw, they need a way to shut up that person. With most people, ridicule works like magic. Call the person crazy and—poof!—she will be silenced. Nobody likes to be made fun of, especially by well-known insiders. Imagine how a physicist might feel if Stephen Hawking mocked him publicly, calling him a fraud, a flake, or a total nutjob?

But ridicule is nothing more than a misdirection tactic.

The Illusion of Power

Magicians—or illusionists, as they prefer to be called these days—often rely on misdirection to create the sense of magic. The magician will draw the audience's attention away from himself at the critical moment so they won't notice how the trick is accomplished. A card shark might also use misdirection to secretly pull a card from his sleeves while drawing his opponent's attention elsewhere.

Debunkers long ago realized the power of misdirection, and many Bigfoot researchers seem to have taken a lesson or two from the debunkers. Today Bigfoot researchers use misdirection deftly in their attempts to silence other researchers, or anyone interested in the Bigfoot phenomena, who dares to disagree with their viewpoint. These researchers don't pull cards out of their sleeves or rabbits out of hats. Instead they use ridicule, intimidation, baiting, and countless other tactics to draw attention away from the real issue—the evidence.

Why? Because the arguments for excluding data are too weak to survive a debate.

Ridicule is the most powerful weapon in any debunker's arsenal, and the "anti-paranormal" Bigfooters have become debunkers in their own right. They sling words like wacko, crazy, stupid, ignorant, impossible, and worse at anyone who dares to suggest we should not discard high-strangeness Bigfoot sightings. Many people will clam up in the face of such attacks, which is precisely what the attackers desire. These linguistic attacks, however, serve as nothing more than clever and sometimes amusing misdirection designed to take pressure off the attackers. No need to discuss the evidence when they've got everyone defending themselves from personal attacks. As a bonus, anyone who isn't on the defensive has been humiliated into silence.

How should you handle ridicule? Ignore it. The attacker's balloon will swiftly deflate if we fail to light the fire needed to fill it with hot air.

When it comes to misdirection, though, the anti-paranormalists have other weapons at their discretion. Another favorite tactic is baiting. This diversion tactic has two sides:

1. *Baiting as harassment.* The attacker keeps coming after someone with personal attacks and/or vague comments that the person is wrong about "everything." This type of baiting is designed to elicit anger. React with anger, and the attacker will use that reaction to label the target a "hothead." Personal attacks, or ridicule, often provoke the desired response quicker than the second form of baiting.

2. *Baiting as trickery.* The attacker hammers the target with endless demands that the person provide long, detailed treatises in response

to vague complaints. Baiting someone with endless demands has one goal—wasting the other person's time. Too many people who disagree with the insider's group fall for this trick, spending countless hours in vain attempts to satisfy the evidentiary requirements of the anti-paranormalists. Trouble is, no matter how many vague complaints the target addresses or how many lines of evidence the target proffers, the attacker will always come back with another demand *but no counterarguments.*

How should we handle baiting? As with ridicule, the best response is to ignore it. Anyone who partakes in paranormal research must learn to ignore petty attacks. The inner circle will try to shut out and shut up anyone from the outer circle. When confronted with such attacks, try this exercise. Imagine an invisible shield, à la *Star Trek*, surrounds you. Watch the verbal missiles bounce off your shield, hurtling back toward your attacker. Instead of blowing up your attacker, the missile spews icky green slime all over him. Now, isn't that more fun than getting angry?

Remember, no one has a degree in ufology or cryptozoology or whatever-ology. Nothing makes one person more qualified than another

Figure 9.5: If we respond to baiting by debunkers, we are crawling right inside their cleverly laid traps. Photo by Tess McBride/U.S. Fish & Wildlife Service.

to study any paranormal phenomenon. Scientists may bring specific expertise to the field, but their credentials do not make them any more qualified to pontificate about Bigfoot. Membership in a particular group, such as the inner circle, does not make certain individuals more worthy than anyone else. The fact is, everyone involved in Bigfoot research operates with the same disadvantages—namely, the circumstantial and inconclusive nature of the evidence. Denying that fact inevitably leads to illogical assumptions and unethical behavior. What's the solution?

Stop fighting the truth. Deal with it. Work with it.

And most important of all, have fun!

10
The Nature of the Evidence

Many researchers proclaim that their main goal is to prove Bigfoot is a real, physical animal. Occasionally someone will announce, usually with great fanfare, that they have indisputable "proof" of Bigfoot's existence and identity. But what constitutes proof? The answer depends on which group we try to convince.

Proof is a compilation of evidence that, when examined, convinces the examiner of some truth represented by the evidence. However, proof can be quite subjective. Evidence that convinces one person may not convince another. Someone inclined to accept the existence of crypto-zoological creatures will consider circumstantial evidence, like footprints and eyewitness accounts, to be totally convincing. A scientist, however, will hold out for more. Therefore, footprints and eyewitness testimony serve as proof for the layman but not for the scientist.

Two different people might look at a footprint and reach two different conclusions. Even two scientists may reach disparate conclusions based on identical evidence. One may see dermal ridges and decide this proves the footprint was not faked; another may see the ridges as artifacts of the casting process. Each individual can present evidence to support the differing conclusions. For the first person, the footprint becomes proof of an unrecognized bipedal primate; for the other, the footprint remains inconclusive at best.

We could apply this to the Bigfoot-UFO connection too. I look at the evidence for a connection and find it convincing, therefore the evidence becomes proof for me. A researcher from the just-an-ape camp would look at the same evidence and denounce it as worthless, spurious nonsense. For this person, the evidence stays exactly that—evidence. Proof emerges out of evidence only when enough evidence accumulates to convince someone.

Evidence in Context

The just-an-ape folks imply, or outright say, that the evidence for their theory about Bigfoot is stronger, more believable, and more scientific than the evidence for the Bigfoot-UFO connection.

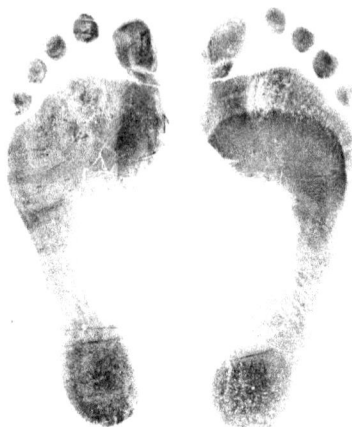

Figure 10.1: Dermal ridges appear in human footprints and fingerprints. They're one way authorities can identify perpetrators, and they've also been touted as proof of Bigfoot's existence. Photo © iStockPhoto.com/UnderGroundArts.

They might say that footprint evidence is good enough for a court of law and this clearly means footprints are solid, nearly irrefutable evidence. The trouble with this analogy lies in the context of the evidence.

In a court of law, footprint evidence is presented to show that a human being was present at a particular location. The scientific community accepts that human beings exist. We would be hard-pressed to find anyone who denies that human beings exist. The footprint evidence may prove that a certain person stepped in a certain patch of mud, but this is only possible because everyone agrees human beings are real animals.

The existence of Bigfoot remains a controversial topic, with a large number of people refusing to accept the reality of these creatures. Therefore, the footprint evidence must be able to prove not only that a Bigfoot stepped in a particular patch of mud, but also that the Bigfoot in question is a real animal. That's why footprint evidence, in the case of Bigfoot, fails to qualify as proof—at least to the scientific community. I doubt a court of law would accept the evidence as proof of Bigfoot's existence either.

What about videos and photos of supposed Bigfoot? Often a video or photo will be touted as the "ultimate proof" that Bigfoot exists. But can photographic or video evidence prove once and for all the reality of Bigfoot?

Once again, it depends on who we want to convince. Even the clearest video will never satisfy the scientific community that Bigfoot are real. If a piece of film could prove Bigfoot exist, then the 1967 Patterson-Gimlin film should've sealed the deal and garnered Bigfoot a spot in biology textbooks. No footage since has measured up to the Patterson-Gimlin film in terms of quality. Yet the Patterson film failed to end the debate. Among those of us already interested in the Bigfoot phenomenon, footage like the Patterson-Gimlin film offers convincing evidence and perhaps even proof that Bigfoot is not a hoax or a delusion, but a genuine animal. To skeptics, film footage proves nothing.

Since 1967, the technology to manipulate photos and videos has advanced at light speed. We can't believe what we see anymore. If film footage couldn't prove anything in 1967, then it surely won't prove anything today. Downloading grainy, low-resolution videos of a figure peeking out from behind trees can provide entertainment or, at best, an intriguing clue. But videos and photos will never prove the reality of Bigfoot. The next time someone announces they have "ultimate proof" in the form of a video, go ahead and take a peek at the footage. Just don't expect earth-shattering revelations.

The best videos and photos serve as evidence—never proof.

Elusive Clues

How elusive are Bigfoot? Why are they elusive? What does it mean to be elusive? The term elusive refers to something that avoids detection and/or capture. The word can also indicate something that stymies our attempts to understand it. Some Bigfoot researchers claim Bigfoot and other cryptids aren't really elusive. We simply haven't proven yet they exist, and hence, can't determine what they are.

To support the not-really-elusive theory, proponents will often point to so-called cryptids that eventually attained the status of a scientifically recognized species. The most-touted example is the coelacanth, a honking-big fish. Scientists used to think the coelacanth went extinct 65 million years ago, around the same time as the dinosaurs. Then in 1938, a live specimen was discovered in the Indian Ocean off the coast of Africa. The problem with touting the coelacanth as a prime example of a cryptozoology success story is that the coelacanth was never a cryptid in the first place. Scientists knew full well the creature had existed in the past. No living examples turned up until 1938, but the creature was never unknown to science.

A better example might be the platypus, one of the strangest-looking mammals. The platypus has a duck-like bill, feet reminiscent of an otter, and a beaver-like tale. Males of the species have venomous spurs on their back legs. Given these bizarre features, it's hardly surprising that when faced with the first specimen of this creature, Australian scientists dismissed it as a hoax. Later, after examining more specimens, the scientific community recognized the platypus as a genuine animal. Still, the platypus was discovered in 1799, long before cryptozoologists came

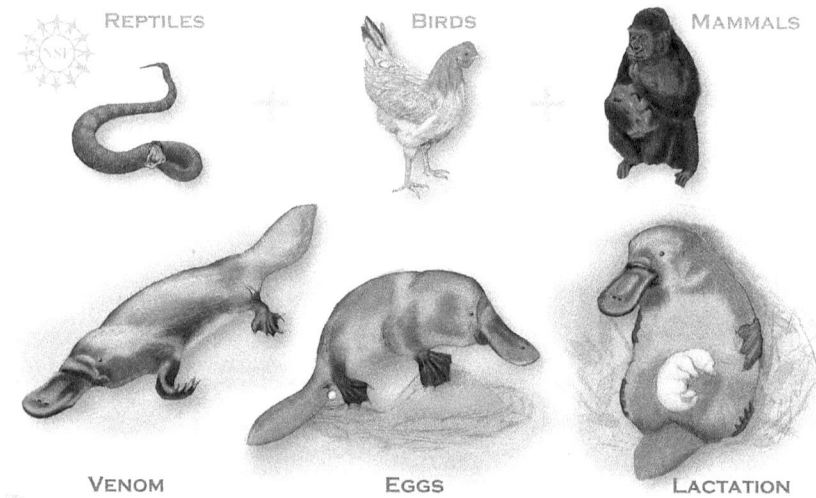

Figure 10.2: This illustration shows the strange genetic links between the platypus, reptiles, and mammals. Male platypuses are venomous, thanks to poison spurs on their back feet, and females lay eggs but also lactate. Despite this confusing mix of traits, the platypus is considered a mammal. Artwork by Zina Deretsky, National Science Foundation.

onto the scene. Unlike modern cryptids, the platypus lacks both a background in legend— save for a mention in the creation mythology of Australian aborigines—and a history of sightings prior to its discovery. The same is true of most "discovered" cryptids.

This brings up a question then. What is a cryptid? Put simply, a cryptid is any creature studied by cryptozoologists. So what is a cryptozoologist?

Word Games

It seems like a growing number of people enjoy branding themselves as cryptozoologists. The term sounds scientific and implies that the person has earned a degree in some branch of science, or at least acquired some training or professional experience in applying scientific methods. But what does the word cryptozoologist actually mean?

The term cryptozoology was coined in the late 1960s. The prefix "crypto" means literally "hidden" or "covered" and zoologist means someone who studies animals. Literally, then, a cryptozoologist is someone who studies hidden animals. In common usage, the term refers to those folks who devote their time and energy to hunting for and studying animals that scientists dismiss as mere legends. Of course, the prefix "crypto" can also mean secret or occult. I rather doubt cryptozoologists want to be called occultists!

Though zoology is a branch of biology, cryptozoology is a field of study. No universities offer degrees in cryptozoology and the scientific establishment disavows any kinship with cryptozoology. Tacking a prefix onto the name of a branch of science does not create a new scientific discipline. The individual responsible for first joining the two parts has coined a new word, which can serve as shorthand for a complicated array of research topics. But cryptozoology is still a field of study, not a science. Cryptozoologists are nonscientific researchers (nonscientific and unscientific are not the same), unless they also have degrees in zoology or biology or some other scientific discipline.

A handful of scientists have chosen to get involved in cryptozoology; however, their involvement does not elevate cryptozoology to the status of science. Their involvement may bolster the credibility of certain aspects of Bigfoot research, and we should thank these brave scientists for dipping their toes in the very cold waters of paranormal research. Yet cryptozoologists need no degrees, no certification, no internships, no particular work experience. The field requires nothing more than a willingness to explore scoffed-at areas of research, and a thick skin to deal with the debunkers.

Anyone can lay claim to the title of cryptozoologist. Anyone who studies legendary animals is a cryptozoologist. Now that we understand what a cryptozoologist is, we can explore what a cryptid is. The unrecognized animals dismissed as hoaxes or myths by the scientific establishment are cryptids. Since a cryptid is a "hidden" or "secret" animal, this means we have trouble seeing and finding them—the very definition of elusive.

This is why, despite decades of field research, Bigfoot and other cryptids remained "undiscovered." Hard evidence, and indeed the creatures themselves, hide just beyond our grasp.

The Fallacy of Field Expeditions

In some disciplines, full-fledged field expeditions net great results. Take archaeology, for instance. A good expedition can dig up (literally) massive amounts of evidence, from pottery sherds to human remains. The littlest things help shed light on a previously unknown or poorly understood culture. With all the well-funded expeditions that continue to search for Bigfoot, shouldn't we have ultimate proof of the creature's existence at any moment?

Some groups expend a staggering amount of money and time jetting out to the location of a recent sighting, or to an area that has a history of frequent sightings. Countless Bigfoot researchers have done this already, over the course of the past fifty years. None of these expeditions has returned with anything more than photos or casts of footprints, or perhaps a grainy photo of *something* in the woods. Even modern expeditions equipped with thermal-sensing cameras fail to capture more than vague images. Most of these expeditions consist of a passel of people tromping into the "woods," usually a state park close to a highway and comfortable lodging for the participants.

Suppose we know of an area where numerous sightings have occurred in the past. Shouldn't our expedition see a Bigfoot too? The odds are stacked sky-high against it. We still have hordes of participants tromping through the woods with cameras and radios and flashlights and sundry other pieces of technology. Animals do not like this. Such an expedition would be unlikely to see a deer, much less a Bigfoot.

Figure 10.3: If tromping through the woods is really the best way to find Bigfoot, then why haven't field expeditions produced definitive proof? Photo by Lisa A. Shiel.

Recently, a new type of Bigfoot expedition project was announced. A group of researchers, including anthropologist Jeff Meldrum of Idaho State University, have begun fundraising for their Falcon Project. This effort will employ a 45-foot unmanned dirigible equipped with the latest thermal (heat-sensing) imaging and high-definition video equipment. The idea is, apparently, to fly the dirigible over certain areas at certain times to watch for Bigfoot. This is an interesting idea, but seems just as unlikely to produce real, scientifically acceptable results as any traditional expedition. Even if a video is captured, and it shows something bipedal walking through the forest below, this won't prove what that something is. Skeptics can still claim it's nothing more than a guy in a monkey suit.

Now, let me set the record straight here. I'm not saying field research is pointless, but anyone taking part in an expedition —whether the boots-on-the-ground kind or an unmanned aerial vehicle—must set the right goal. If you want to have a fun adventure, and possibly find some footprints or hear a strange scream, go for it. But to search for proof that

Bigfoot exists—to attempt to trick a Bigfoot into getting his picture taken, or fool one into stepping into a vat of mud where he'll leave a footprint, or whatever other tricks a person might dream up—that's just plain silly. You're setting yourself up for failure. Even when these tactics succeed, the evidence obtained is circumstantial at best. Spending a lot of money on equipment, and charging participants wads of dough to take part in the expedition, guarantees nothing except a nice chunk of cash in the wallets of the expedition's organizers.

Bloated expeditions. Made-up terms. Cryptid "discoveries" that aren't. These are the secrets many Bigfoot researchers, and many cryptozoologists in general, prefer to keep hidden from the general public. Bigfoot researchers harbor other secrets, though, that did more than anything else to damage the credibility of their research. Bigfoot researchers, it turns out, don't know as much as they think.

Or at least, they don't know as much as they want everyone else to think they know.

The Abracadabra Method

Here's yet another commonality between Bigfoot researchers and UFO researchers. They like to conjure statistics out of nothing, like magicians who pull rabbits or doves out of their hats. Unlike magicians, however, these researchers don't have a hidden method for pulling off this trick. Their statistics don't stem from data hidden up their sleeves or concealed in a secret compartment. They simply make up the numbers from nothing.

According to these researchers, the best method for deriving statistics about UFOs or Bigfoot is to pick a number at random—say, eighty—then use the number in a sentence like this: eighty percent of Bigfoot sightings are misidentifications or hoaxes. Even more prevalent than the magically derived statistics are the vague blanket statements. A researcher might say that "most" or "the majority of" Bigfoot sightings are misidentifications or hoaxes. Neither statement has any basis in facts. Yet when a researcher speaks in an authoritative voice, quoting official-sounding statistics, we can't help but assume that person has solid evidence to back up the statement.

Why don't percentages quoted by researchers have a factual basis? Countless websites gather sighting reports from witnesses, and countless books detail more sightings. Surely we can glean statistics from this data.

The proliferation is the problem. With so many websites collecting sightings, no one could possibly search through all of them. Add to the mix an unknown number of researchers who collect sightings but have no website, as well as an unknown number of sightings that go unreported, and the problem is compounded exponentially. It's also become clear to me that an awful lot of Bigfoot researchers don't bother to read books about the subject and they only browse the websites of their friends. How then can anyone claim to have accurate statistics about anything to do with Bigfoot? The best any of us can do is offer our opinions based on the information and evidence we have personally examined.

How many Bigfoot sightings are hoaxes or misidentifications? Any one researcher can comment on what percentage of the sightings that he has

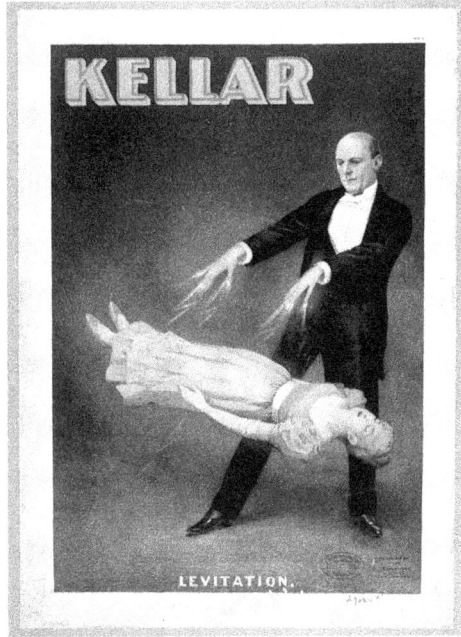

Figure 10.4: Like nineteenth-century magicians performing mind-boggling feats, some Bigfoot researchers like to pull statistics out of thin air as if by magic. Image courtesy of Library of Congress, Prints & Photographs Division, LC-USZC4-8001.

personally investigated turned out to be hoaxes or misidentifications. No single researcher has examined every sighting report or spoken to every witness. Why then do they feel the need to downplay the frequency and validity of Bigfoot sightings?

Two factors may explain this behavior. First, the Bigfoot researchers who quote imaginary statistics are also the researchers who most desperately want to achieve scientific acceptance, not just for Bigfoot, but also for themselves. They hope that quoting statistics gives an air of formality and certainty to the subject. Dismissing the majority of sightings, and consequently downplaying the frequency of sightings, ought to demonstrate how reasonable and scientific researchers are. That's what they hope, at least. Unfortunately, the scientific establishment remains unconvinced by made-up statistics and unimpressed by the feigned reasonableness of Bigfoot researchers.

The second factor also springs from the desire to seem both reasonable and scientific. Oftentimes when researchers from the just-an-ape camp receive a high strangeness sighting, they immediately dismiss it as a hoax, either perpetrated intentionally or arising from a delusional mind. The sighting report in question probably goes into the waste basket, but the researchers can add another check mark in the "hoaxes/misidentifications" category in their files. Without ever having investigated the sighting, and probably without ever having spoken to the witness, the researchers have inflated their statistics.

Was the sighting really a hoax? Was the witness really a fruitcake? The researchers can't *know* because they did no research. Yet the researchers who engage in this type of behavior talk about it as if cherry-picking the data in this manner makes them more scientific and reasonable. After all, those pesky little sightings of Bigfoot and UFOs can't be credible because such things can't happen. Scientists won't take Bigfoot research seriously unless those sightings go in the dumper.

When it comes to dumping undesirable data, 73% of Bigfoot researchers feel it's the right thing to do. Where did that statistic come from? I made it up myself.

But hey, that's how we do it in paranormal research. Right?

In Search of a Better Method

Every researcher—whether devoted to Bigfoot, UFOs, or something else—wants to appear to know everything about the subject. In fact, a lot of researchers downplay certain aspects of the research in order to appear more godlike in their knowledge and expertise. The truth often lies far from the idealized image promoted by these individuals and groups.

To wipe the fog from our glasses and see a clear picture of the Bigfoot phenomenon, we must first come to grips with five uncomfortable facts:

1. All the evidence concerning Bigfoot is circumstantial or anecdotal.
2. DNA taken from items such as samples of hair or feces will never prove Bigfoot's existence.

3. Whether ape or hominid or something else, Bigfoot *are* paranormal.
4. More than sixty years of field expeditions have netted no irrefutable evidence.
5. We are no closer to solving the mystery today than we were fifty years ago.

We could expand #4 to say field expeditions represent a silly waste of money and effort. So-called expeditions are in reality Bigfoot-themed vacations. Expeditions never have and never will bring back "ultimate proof." That sort of proof is more elusive than hard evidence, the search for which seems like an attainable goal. Yet both hard, scientific evidence and "ultimate proof" have proved as elusive as the beasts themselves.

Bigfoot research should have one goal—research. To learn, to explore, and to seek out evidence are the only attainable goals. To make proof the primary objective serves no purpose other than to guarantee failure. Making scientific acceptance the goal will also assure failure.

Does this mean we should stop gathering evidence? Of course not. We simply need to understand the fundamental truths about this field of research. Then, and only then, can we set achievable goals for ourselves. The first goal should be to develop a new method of conducting Bigfoot research, because the current methods are dismal failures.

Forget large-scale expeditions. To get involved in Bigfoot research, a person doesn't need to spend a lot of money or travel the globe. Get to know your own backyard, or at least an area close to your home. The less traffic the area gets, the better. Keep an eye out for anomalies. Listen for odd cries, watch for footprints, record everything you discover. In spite of what some Bigfoot researchers imply, you have no better chance of seeing a Bigfoot when you accompany a researcher into the woods than when you venture out on your own.

Above all, learn. Read books and articles, browse Bigfoot websites, glean info wherever possible, and reach your own conclusions. Remember that information pertinent to the Bigfoot mystery may appear in unlikely places, such as books about fairies. Explore a broad array of topics. Keep an open mind, and analyze every bit of data.

Too many researchers in the Bigfoot field despise new and different ideas. They cling to old ideas, like the *Gigantopithecus* theory, and cringe at the notion of considering new ones. At the same time, these researchers bemoan the way mainstream science refuses to consider that Bigfoot might exist.

Figure 10.5: To fully understand Bigfoot, we must expand our horizons to include all possibly related phenomena. For example, in December 2012 something tore out a 300-foot section of the electric tape fence surrounding my horse pasture—without leaving any tracks behind, despite the snow cover. Was this incident Bigfoot related? I doubt it, but documenting all strange occurrences means I won't overlook anything that I might later realize is indeed related to Bigfoot. Photo by Lisa A. Shiel.

Research cannot advance without new ideas. We must embrace, rather than fear, ideas that question or debunk current hypotheses. I suggest a new approach. Once each day, give a new idea a chance. Explore it, examine any evidence associated with it, let it rattle around in your brain for awhile. Don't dismiss the idea in five minutes. Give it a chance to grow in your mind. Maybe it'll become clear the idea is bunk. Maybe it holds a measure of merit. You'll never know unless you try. So the next time a new idea comes knocking, invite it in.

The old practices—ignoring evidence, chucking data, inventing statistics, invading the woods— have failed. The time has come to dump those practices, rather than the data. Once we've done that, we might find ourselves dealing with an overabundance of possibilities as a new world of evidence opens up before us. Clearly, the old ways have brought us no closer to solving the mystery. Perhaps the answers lie elsewhere.

And just maybe, they await us in the forbidden zone where Bigfoot and UFOs merge.

11
Bigfoot DNA

Over the past decade or so, one type of evidence has been hailed as the ultimate answer to the dilemma of how to prove Bigfoot's existence. This type of evidence has become so well known, and so misunderstood, that it deserves its own chapter. Of what type of evidence am I speaking?

DNA.

On blogs and in discussion forums, and particularly in press releases issued by Bigfoot researchers, genetic evidence has become the topic du jour. All of these posts and articles and press releases perpetuate the same myth—that DNA evidence will prove Bigfoot is a real, biological animal, even in the absence of a physical specimen. All we need is just

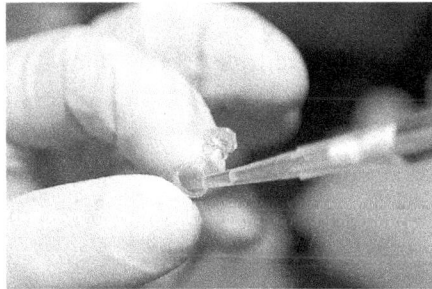

Figure 11.1: Will DNA testing provide the ultimate proof of Bigfoot's existence and identity? Photo by Maggie Bartlett, courtesy of the National Human Genome Research Institute.

one really, really, really good sample along with an open-minded scientist to perform the testing. Samples submitted for DNA testing have included hair, feces, and bits of purported Bigfoot flesh.

DNA has become the holy grail of Bigfoot research. Unfortunately, discussions about Bigfoot DNA invariably revolve around a fallacy rooted in misconceptions about the nature and reliability of DNA evidence.

Identifying the Unknown

To name and describe a new species, scientists require a physical sample known as a type specimen or holotype. A holotype is a single individual that represents an entire species. Although a single specimen may represent the entire species, multiple specimens are preferable for demonstrating that a new species has indeed been found. A DNA sample by itself proves nothing, as far as defining a new species. Comparing the new sample to existing DNA samples on file will show, at best, that the new sample does not correspond with any known species. All the sample has proven is that scientists can't identify the exact creature from which the DNA originated. This fact explains why samples purported to come from Bigfoot produce, at best, inconclusive results along the lines of "unknown primate." The genetic data gleaned from the sample may share some traits in common with known primates, but it's not an exact match.

And remember, humans are primates too. Hence, a sample labeled "unknown primate" means next to nothing. All this type of testing can demonstrate is what the sample is not. Though the sample may not match the available data on known species, this does not mean the DNA came from a new species.

Several issues plague DNA research, especially in its application to Bigfoot.

Dirty DNA

The first hurdle Bigfoot DNA must clear involves how samples are collected and preserved. Contamination is a big problem with DNA samples in general and particularly DNA samples collected in the wild. This issue becomes vital in Bigfoot research, where samples are collected by nonscientists under sketchy conditions. How much attention was paid to limiting contamination during the collection process? How long had the sample lain in the open, exposed to the elements? What other animals might've touched the sample before the researchers stumbled upon it? The answer to the first question is never offered by the researchers involved. No one knows the answers to the second and third questions.

Even scientists encounter problems with contamination. A 2008 article in *Archaeology* magazine discussed the problem of contamination in collecting DNA samples from archaeological sites. The author explained that archaeologists would need to don the equivalent of the space suits worn by astronauts in order to eliminate, or at least minimize, contamination during the collection of DNA samples from archaeological sites. DNA samples collected in the wild may have been exposed to the elements for an undetermined time. Even if they were supposedly collected straight from the source—namely, a Bigfoot—the researcher may have inadvertently contaminated the sample simply by collecting it. Do Bigfoot researchers wear space suits, or even sterile gloves?

Figure 11.2: How many Bigfoot researchers want to tromp through the woods wearing a space suit? Unless they do, however, they may be inadvertently contaminating any DNA samples they collect. Photo courtesy of NASA.

Gloves alone, however, might not provide adequate protection. Something as miniscule as a droplet of spittle or a few skin cells holds the potential to contaminate a DNA sample. Because of this problem, scientists working on a DNA sample from a 14,300-year-old coprolite (fossilized human feces) also tested the DNA of over sixty people who worked at the dig where the coprolite was found. This enabled them to rule out those individuals as the source of any genetic material recovered from the sample. But they can't rule out contamination that occurred before the dig, during the thousands of years when the coprolite lay in an Oregon cave.

A sample can become contaminated after collection too, in the laboratory where the genetic analysis was performed. Contamination is such a problem for DNA analysis that the DNA Initiative, which operates under the auspices of the U.S. Department of Justice, includes a discussion of the issue in the pamphlets it issues to law enforcement professionals.

Now consider the case of Germany's Phantom of Heilbronn. For two years, police sought not just a serial killer, but a rare female serial killer. DNA evidence collected from forty crime scenes implicated a single woman in crimes ranging from burglary to the murder of a police officer. Other people who had been convicted of some of the crimes denied any knowledge of the Phantom. The confusing menagerie of evidence finally led police to reexamine the DNA results—and conclude that the cotton swabs used to collect DNA samples had likely been contaminated at the factory that produces the swabs.

Can contamination ever be completely eliminated from DNA samples? No one knows the answer. But along with contamination, another big problem looms over DNA research.

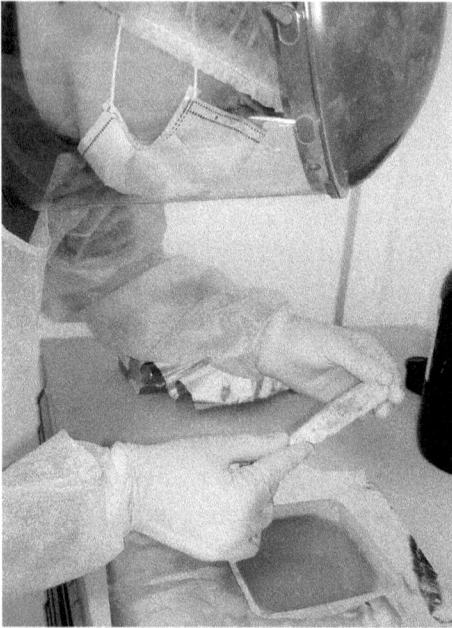

Figure 11.3: Contamination is a major concern for anyone working with DNA samples. The scientists who sequenced the Neanderthal genome, like the one shown in this photo, took precautions—but was it enough? No one knows for sure. Photo courtesy of the Max Planck Institute for Evolutionary Anthropology and the National Human Genome Research Institute.

The Genetic Jigsaw

How do scientists extract DNA from a sample? Most of us have no idea what the process involves. It seems almost magical.

DNA consists of nucleotides, molecules formed when elements such as oxygen and hydrogen bond together. Just four nucleotide bases make up all DNA on this planet, much like the three primary colors mix to create every color imaginable. These bases are called adenine, guanine,

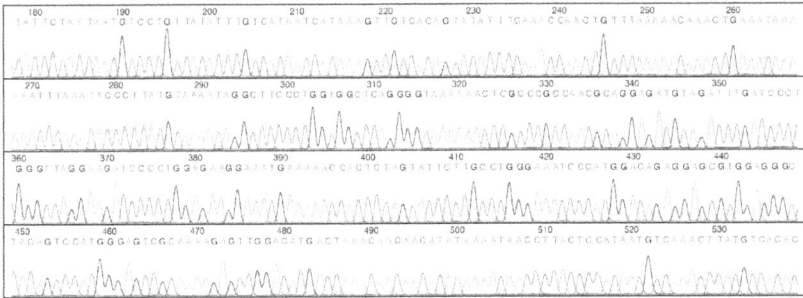

Figure 11.4: DNA analysis relies on computers to decipher the genetic data. Software is fed raw data and then spits out a DNA sequence, like the one above. Image by Darryl Leja, courtesy of the National Human Genome Research Institute.

thymine, and cytosine. The names are often shortened into the single letters A, G, T, and C. Nucleotide couples called base pairs connect the double helix, or twin spirals, that make up our DNA. The four bases combine in different sequences to spell out instructions for our cells. Like letter tiles on a Scrabble board, bases can swap positions over time—or even get replaced altogether. The order of the bases, of the letters, modifies the meaning. These changes are called mutations.

The raw data produced by DNA extraction yields a jumble of A's, G's, T's, and C's that seem like nonsense. Scientists must employ powerful computers running specialized software to find meaning in the genetic jigsaw puzzle. Herein lies the problem.

The computers used in DNA

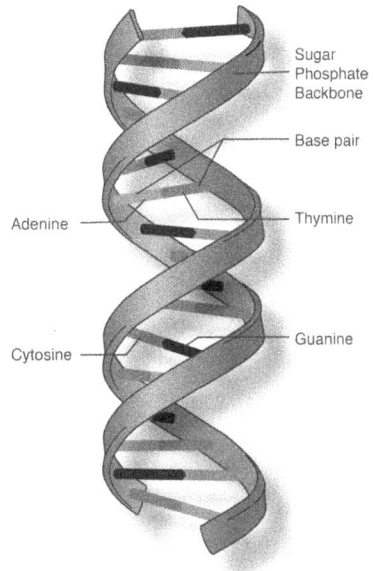

Figure 11.5: DNA takes the form of a double helix, or spiral. Base pairs connect two ribbons of sugar and phosphate. Image by Darryl Leja, courtesy of the National Human Genome Research Institute.

analysis can spit out thousands of different interpretations of the genetic jigsaw. For instance, when tracing the origins of humanity scientists have used DNA as a vital part of their evidence. Computer software dutifully swallows the raw DNA data and spits out a family tree for humanity. Yet, as geneticists themselves have pointed out, the exact same data could impart different trees depending on what software is used to process it and how many times that software analysis is run. Thousands of possible family trees might lurk inside the data collected by a single team of scientists. Which version to choose depends on what outcome is desired.

The most famous use of DNA analysis in human origins research came from scientists at the University of California at Berkeley. A scientist at another institution noted how the Berkeley team had—in two separate papers, both published in 1991—listed two different populations as the root ancestors of all humanity. In the first paper, the team listed Kung bushmen as the root; in the second, pygmies occupied that slot. Both could not be true. This case highlights the way in which software can, inadvertently or by design, influence the outcome of DNA analysis.

And the problems don't end with contamination and computers. DNA itself works against us.

Breakdown

Nothing lasts forever, not even DNA. When the cells in a living creature die, the DNA contained in those cells begins to degrade. The cells essentially self-destruct, splitting apart the DNA contained in them, slicing it into short fragments. This process may also alter the sequence of nucleotides in the DNA, much the way mutations do, which changes the meaning of the genetic information.

Cell degradation can happen for many reasons, including but not limited to the death of the organism. Cells in our bodies are constantly being destroyed and replaced. The process is natural and necessary, but it leads to problems for DNA analysis. Scientists must sort out the DNA fragments and compare them to known samples to try to determine whether the computer software has interpreted the DNA correctly. Scientists working on decoding the DNA of Neanderthals compared their samples to the DNA of humans and chimpanzees.

Such comparisons assume we know approximately what type of DNA to look for in the unknown sample. With the Neanderthal samples, for instance, scientists must begin with the assumption that Neanderthal DNA will resemble human DNA, which itself is 95-98% similar to chimpanzee DNA. But it's estimated that 90-99% of the DNA found in the Neanderthal samples stems from contamination, including bacteria. Working from the assumption that Neanderthal DNA is quite similar to human DNA, scientists will probably run their software as many times as it takes for it to spit out the expected answer. Any other answer will be deemed an error.

Dodgy DNA

We must also consider a more sinister problem—that someone might intentionally fabricate DNA evidence or falsify DNA tests. Again, science gives us evidence and parallels.

In 2009, Israeli scientists revealed the results of their study that demonstrated how easy it is to fabricate DNA evidence. The scientists fabricated (created artificially) DNA evidence by using tiny samples of real DNA or, more disturbingly, without using any real DNA at all. The team discovered they could use DNA profiles, which are basically computer files, to manufacture the desired DNA sample. According to the study, anyone with the requisite equipment and even the most basic understanding of biology, on the level of an undergraduate, could easily manufacture genetic evidence.

The ability to fabricate DNA at will casts a darker light on the practice of convicting people of crimes based on DNA evidence. Even before the Israeli study, the purported infallibility of DNA evidence had been called into question numerous times. Individual cases where scientists at crime laboratories falsified data seem disturbing enough. Now consider the case of the DNA laboratory at the Houston Police Department in Texas. The department was forced to shut down the lab after it was discovered that DNA tests conducted by nine employees had repeatedly produced false results. The misconduct affected over a thousand cases.

Falsification of data is nothing new, even among university scientists. Luk Van Parijs, an immunologist at MIT, lied in seven papers published in scientific journals, including *Nature Genetics*, a sister publication of the renowned journal *Nature*. The Office of Research Integrity, a branch of the U.S. Department of Health and Human Services, is responsible for investigating misconduct allegations. The organization found Van Parijs guilty of falsifying data. He was barred from working for or with the U.S. government, and was also fired from his job at MIT.

As discussed in Chapter 9, a recent study found that a startling percentage of scientists either admit to falsifying data themselves or know of someone else who has falsified data. The cases discussed above are, unfortunately, becoming less and less rare.

Even if we rule out the problems of evidence falsification, contamination, reliance on computers, and self-destructing cells, the road to DNA proof of Bigfoot's existence is still a bumpy one. To prove the reality of a new species requires that first we must understand what a species is. Unfortunately a solid, workable definition of the term species continues to elude scientists.

Confusion, Delusion, and Evolution

What is a species? Most of us assume that scientists know, since they announce the discovery of new species ever more frequently. Surely, no one would announce they'd discovered a new species unless they knew precisely how to define the term species. Theories about the evolution of life attempt to deal with changes on numerous levels, from generational differences all the way up to the origins of the first cell. Most of us, however, know evolution as the potter that molds new species. Yet the term species throws up an obstacle that scientists stumble over every time they encounter it.

Taxonomy

Over the course of hundreds of years, scientists have struggled to separate living things into discrete categories and to draw clear relationships between those categories. The term taxonomy refers to any such attempts to organize a tree of life. These trees are hierarchical systems, meaning that they begin with the most general category and step down through more and more specific designations. The categories are known as clades. The broadest clade is called a domain. A species is usually the bottommost clade, because it is intended to be quite specific. Sometimes a species will be divided into subspecies, but in general, a species is the most specific designation given to a living thing. To illustrate the concept of taxonomy, let's take a look at human beings.

We belong to the domain Eukaryota, which includes everything from plankton to fungi to armadillos—and of course, primates. Getting to

A Taxonomy of Human Beings

Figure 11.6. The clades highlighted in green are the ones traditionally accepted by scientists, and are modeled after Linneaus's taxonomy. Debatable clades within the family Hominidae are in gray text. For clarity's sake this list omits many unranked, tentative clades. Notice the class within a class (Mammalia within Sarcopterygii), one of the incongruities triggered by modern evolutionary theories. The chart below is a synthesis of various taxonomies of *Homo sapiens*, many of which contradict each other. Metazoa, for instance, is sometimes listed as another name for the kingdom Animalia, and other times it's given as a subkingdom.

Rank	Clade Name
Domain	Eukaryota
Kingdom	Animalia
Subkingdom	Metazoa
—unranked	Eumetazoa
—unranked	Bilateria
—unranked	Deuterostomia
Phylum	Chordata
—unranked	Craniata
Subphylum	Vertebrata
Superclass	Gnathostomata
—unranked	Euteleostomi
Class	Sarcopterygii
—unranked	Tetrapoda
—unranked	Amniota
Class	Mammalia
Subclass	Theria
Infraclass	Eutheria
Order	Primates
Suborder	Haplorhini
Infraorder	Simiiformes (aka Anthropoidea)
Parvorder	Catarrhini
Superfamily	Hominoidea
Family	Hominidae
Subfamily	Homininae
Tribe	Hominini
Genus	Homo
Species	sapiens
Subspecies	sapiens

our species, *Homo sapiens*, means drilling down through multiple clades. Traditionally, taxonomy recognized seven clades: domain, phylum, class, order, family, genus, and species. These days, however, the exact number of clades varies depending on the source consulted. Some family trees for humanity include unranked clades, categories that remain controversial and up for debate. Sometimes our species has even been divided into subspecies, with Neanderthals listed as *Homo sapiens neanderthalensis* (rather than *Homo neanderthalensis*) and modern humans as *Homo sapiens sapiens*. If this all sounds rather confusing, that's because it is!

The more specific the clade, the harder it gets to tell the difference between closely related creatures. It stands to reason, then, that the species designation, as the most specific clade, is the hardest to assign. We have no trouble telling apart animals and plants, which belong to different kingdoms (Animalia and Plantae, respectively). By the time we get down to the family Hominidae, the differences between the various creatures become harder to distinguish, especially since most of the members of this family are extinct and known exclusively from fossils. Scientists apply the term human to most members of the genus *Homo*, the clade between family and species, which further confuses matters. And now, as we finally reach the species clade, the troubles intensify.

The stumbling blocks cropped up as soon as naturalists began trying to organize the living world. Back in 1859, in his seminal book *The Origin of Species*, Charles Darwin commented that the term species was applied arbitrarily based on convenience rather than evidence. Since Darwin's day, biologists have concocted dozens of explanations, or concepts, for the term species. These days scientists prefer to say "concept" rather than "definition," because the term species is the opposite of definite. The most popular choice is known as the biological species concept (BSC).

Biological Species

In BSC, the term species refers to any population of organisms that actually does or potentially could interbreed. The inability or unwillingness to interbreed is called reproductive isolation, and it has several meanings—anatomical incompatibility, or the proverbial square peg and round hole; dissimilar mating practices; genetic incompatibility; geographic isolation, when a natural barrier such as a mountain prevents two populations from meeting; or offspring who either die off before reproducing or are sterile. Two physically identical populations of lizards separated by geographic boundaries, such as mountains or rivers, may never interbreed in the wild. Yet if brought together, say by a zoologist capturing specimens for study, the lizards might interbreed. Whether creatures like our two lizards belong to one or two species inspires debate to this day. Many versions of BSC also dictate that members of the same species must produce viable (fertile and healthy) offspring.

BSC deals exclusively with interbreeding, or sexual reproduction. Not all living things reproduce sexually, which means BSC cannot apply to all life—or even the majority of life—on this planet. Defining asexual species, like bacteria, causes just as many headaches as defining sexually reproducing species. Various criteria have been suggested for asexual species, including genetics and phenotype. A phenotype is the combination of an organism's appearance, behavior, and anatomy. Given that biologists don't monitor every population of every living thing twenty-four hours a day, no one can say for certain whether two populations can or do interbreed.

Members of the same species may produce sterile offspring for many reasons, and weaklings who die off before reproducing can be born within a single species. Scientists from the University of California, Davis, have studied three populations of salamanders thought to be two distinct species and their hybrid offspring. The hybrid offspring have a higher rate of survival than the offspring of either parent species. According to BSC, the parent species are not separate species after all. Yet biologists still call them separate species.

If differences in mating practices represent the sole barrier to interbreeding, the species could potentially interbreed. That part of the definition falls short too. The only seemingly surefire barrier to interbreeding is anatomical incompatibility.

Reproductive isolation can also refer to genetic changes that have made it impossible for two populations to interbreed and produce viable offspring. Speciation—the development of new species—requires that genetic changes accrue over time, until one species has split into two. BSC at best severely limits, and at worst completely disallows, interbreeding; therefore, it essentially disallows the exchange of genetic material. In other words, BSC allows for speciation by no means except random genetic mutation. In evolution, a mutation is a change to an organism's DNA. The change may be beneficial, detrimental, or neutral.

The problems with BSC have led some biologists to call for its death in favor of another, newer concept. But newer species concepts have problems of their own.

Genetic Species

The confusion over Bigfoot and DNA is understandable. It's easy to get confused reading news headlines that announce new species discovered using DNA. If we dig a little deeper, sometimes just by bothering to carefully read the entire article and other times by searching out the original scientific paper, the truth of the situation emerges. Most new species "discovered" through DNA analysis alone are actually cryptic species—creatures that are physiologically identical to another species, akin to identical twins in our own species. By studying the DNA of the species in question, scientists have discovered genetic differences that led them to conclude one twin is different enough from the other to be considered a new species. The new species was, in essence, hiding within another species. Scientists already had specimens of the new species, though they didn't realize it.

Here we enter the realm of another species concept that attempts to turn DNA into the magic species-detecting machine. The genetic species concept delineates species based on either genetic isolation or genetic drift. Genetic isolation means that two populations of creatures do not exchange DNA. In most cases, if interbreeding occurs then DNA has been exchanged. Genetic drift is a process that randomly selects which mutations become more or less prevalent in a population. In genetic drift, the usefulness of a mutation has little or no impact on whether it becomes prevalent, whereas natural selection (Darwin's brand of evolution) encourages beneficial changes to DNA.

The genetic species concept brings up a question: How accurate is genetic analysis in separating species?

Historically, species were differentiated based on morphology, or their anatomy and outward appearance. With the advent of genetics, scientists desperately wanted to differentiate species based on the genetic differences between them, aka their genetic distance. DNA, they hoped, would prove a far more reliable and definitive method of separating species.

The Species Problem

Figure 11.7: Cryptic species, which look identical but differ in their DNA, have been found in numerous animal populations. Most cryptic species are relatively small, like the hermit thrush (A) and the common raven (B), but studies suggest even the massive African elephant (C) may harbor a genetic secret. Some scientists think African elephants may actually be two species, based on their DNA.

Other animals, like the wolf (D) and the coyote (E), may not be separate species at all—though scientists have always listed them as such. Genetic studies indicate they may represent just one species.

U S Fish & Wildlife Service photos by Lee Karney (A), Gary M. Stolz (B and C), Gary Kramer (D), and Steve Thompson (E).

Unfortunately, studies of genetic differences often collide with morphology. Creatures that look the same get divided into separate species based on their genetics, or animals that look vastly different get lumped together as one species. Humans and chimps are a good example of the latter. Although various studies have placed the genetic similarity between humans and chimps at 95-98%, we need only look at a chimpanzee and a human to see the numerous morphological differences between us. Conversely, some species that live together and look identical nevertheless differ in their DNA. Genetics alone separates them.

Just what percentage of genetic distance is required to differentiate species? Biologists cannot agree on a standard. The authors of a study of rodents and bats suggested that any-thing less than a 2% difference *must* indicate a single species, but they went on to say that 2-11% *probably* indicates the presence of a single species. Distances of more than 11% most likely differentiate species. This standard could place humans and chimps in the same species.

Most studies of genetic distance examine one gene or a small handful of genes, rather than the entire comple-ment of DNA present in an organism (known as the genome). Geneticists can collect reams of data, but they lack the technology and knowledge to analyze all of it. Often they rely on guesswork, or assumption, in their analyses.

Figure 11.8: DNA studies tell us we share a whopping 95-98% of our genetic code with chimps, yet the differences between us and them are obvious. Image © iStockPhoto.com/Phototeam.

Scientists also cannot agree on how, or even if, genes cause speciation. Of course, in any discussion of genes we must ask the obvious question of what a gene is. Once again the answer is far from definite. In the past, scientists viewed a gene as a chunk of DNA that tells our bodies what to do with themselves—the fundamental unit of biology, akin to the atom in physics. Today, many scientists recognize the error in that analogy, because traditional genes make up about 1% of the genome. If the genome is the book, and genes are phrases in the book, then scientists are increasingly discovering that those phrases represent a fraction of the book's content. Think of declassified government documents where someone has blacked out 99% of the text. That's the state of the genome. What lies beneath the blacked-out portions? DNA that doesn't conform to the classical definition of a gene and that reacts with other molecules in ways no one understands yet, since they have just begun studying the bulk of the genome in humans, as well as other living things.

The vast majority of "new" species described based on DNA alone are animals already known to exist, the cryptic species who differ only in their DNA. The suite of problems that troubles genetic evidence explains why DNA has not been used by itself to delineate fossil species—until recently. One group of scientists has attempted to define a new type of hominid based primarily on DNA.

Denisova Man

In 2010, scientists from the Max Planck Institute announced the discovery of a new type of hominid dubbed the Denisova hominin, or Denisova Man, after the Siberian region where its fossils were discovered. A team of Russian researchers had discovered the remains of Denisova Man two years earlier, and later had samples extracted from it for DNA analysis. The remains consisted of a single bone from a pinky finger believed to date to around 40,000 years ago.

When the results of the genetic analysis were announced, news headlines exclaimed variously that scientists had discovered a new species of human, a new human relative, or a new species of hominid. The term species appeared in many of the headlines, coupled with the word new, implying that a) the scientists involved claimed to have identified a new species, and b) the results of the study were definitive and universally accepted. Neither implication is accurate.

Trouble Ahead

What is the truth about Denisova Man? First of all, the scientists who performed the genetic analysis never used the term species in the letter they submitted to the journal *Nature*, which published their report in April 2010. They refrained from assigning an official Latin name to the hominid, but simply referred to the specimen as an "unknown hominin." (The term hominin is essentially the same as hominid; both refer to prehuman species presumed to be related to modern humans. "Modern" means anatomically indistinguishable from humans alive today.)

The second problem involves the paucity of evidence concerning Denisova Man. A single finger bone comprises all the evidence for this hominid. Several months after announcing the results of the DNA analysis on the finger bone, the same scientists reported the results of their genetic analysis of a tooth found in the same cave as the finger bone. The DNA extracted from the tooth, they said, was similar but not identical to the DNA from the finger bone. Given these results, the finger bone and the tooth likely belonged to different individuals.

Little information can be gleaned from two separate, singular pieces of evidence. In science, results must be \repeatable and hypotheses must be testable. Repeatable does not mean performing genetic analysis on the same bone multiple times; it means multiple samples should be examined by multiple laboratories. Those samples should preferably come from different specimens.

Another problem with the Denisova claims also revolves around a scarcity of evidence, namely the scant amount of genetic information that is known about prehuman hominids. As we've learned, DNA degrades over time. Scientists believe that, given ideal conditions, DNA might survive for between 50,000 and 100,000 years. The majority of the prehuman hominids went extinct before 100,000 years ago. Their DNA, therefore, is past its expiration date. So far, ancient DNA has been successfully recovered from just two hominid species—modern humans and Neanderthals. This means that scientists can compare the Denisova sample with modern humans and Neanderthals, but not with any other hominids. The best the DNA analysis can accomplish is to determine that the Denisova hominid was neither a modern human nor a Neanderthal. The Denisova DNA cannot be compared to any other hominid, such as *Homo erectus* or members of the genus *Australopithecus*. This means no one knows whether Denisova DNA is similar to the DNA of those hominids.

Yet another problem is related to the one just mentioned. Scientists currently have only a handful of usable DNA samples from prehistoric humans and Neanderthals. No one knows how much genetic variation

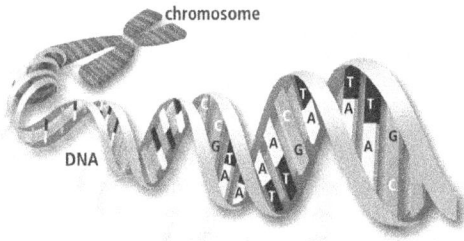

Figure 11.9: Can scientists prove a new species with DNA alone? So far, the answer is no. If scientists can't do it, then neither can Bigfoot researchers. Image courtesy of the U.S. Dept. of Energy Genome Programs/Genome Management Information System, Oak Ridge National Laboratory.

existed in populations of ancient humans or ancient Neanderthals. Scientists evaluated the Denisova DNA against the DNA of fifty-four living humans, one modern human who lived 30,000 years ago, and six Neanderthals. Over six billion humans occupy the planet today, and an unknown number of people occupied the planet in previous epochs. No one knows the size of the Neanderthal population either. So it's entirely possible that the Denisova hominid was a Neanderthal—or even a modern human, since modern human DNA from the period in question is even rarer than Neanderthal DNA.

Svante Pääbo, one of the scientists who took part in the Denisova study, told *Archaeology* magazine that declaring a new species based on DNA alone will be difficult. No one has developed a standard for what percentage of difference qualifies as a new species. Eske Willerslev, a scientist not involved in the Denisova study, told the journal *Nature* that the DNA evidence by itself couldn't prove whether the Denisova hominid hails from a unique species and that the meager information currently available for the Denisova hominid is not enough to make such a distinction.

Finally, we must consider that the Denisova finger bone turned up in association with artifacts, including bracelets, assumed to be the work of modern humans. This raises the question of how different modern human DNA from 35,000 years ago would be from modern human DNA from today. No one knows the answer. Even if we assume the Denisova DNA was not contaminated, it still could represent variation in the DNA of ancient modern humans.

Aside from genetics, another problem hinders efforts to turn a pinky bone into a brand-spanking-new species. The trouble involves the nature of fossil evidence itself.

Fragments in the Sand

While in Ethiopia hunting for vertebrate bones, graduate student Yohannes Haile-Selassie from the University of California, Berkeley, happened upon a fragment of jawbone lying exposed on the ground. Over the next four years, expeditions at several sites in the Middle Awash River Valley area would dig up more bone fragments believed to belong to eleven individuals. Later finds included bits of hand, foot, and arm bones, along with a collarbone fragment and a lone toe bone. As the discoveries earned worldwide attention in the media, the dates attached to the fossils made the newly found hominid the oldest bipedal primate found up to that time.

Do scraps of bone, none equaling an entire skeleton, furnish sufficient evidence to justify christening a new species? The medley of bones, besides falling short of a full skeleton, cropped up at multiple sites over the course of four years. Plus, the bones date to different periods; they range from 5.2 million to 5.8 million years, with the single toe bone separated from the others by at least 400,000 years and ten miles. Nevertheless, Haile-Selassie announced he'd found a new subspecies of *Ardipithecus ramidus* and designated it *Ardipithecus ramidus kadabba*. Later, he decided his specimens belonged to a separate species altogether, *Ardipithecus kadabba*.

Ardipithecus ramidus achieved species status after a specimen turned up in an area known as the Middle Awash in the 1990s. Yet *ramidus* was dated to 4.4 million years ago, about a million years younger than Haile-Selassie's specimens. How can a subspecies predate its parent species? No wonder Haile-Selassie changed his mind about classifying his fossils as a *ramidus* subspecies.

Lest it appear hominid fossils suffer from more fragmentation than other types of fossils, let's consider the remains of other species. In 1935, Ralph von Koenigswald declared a new species of extinct ape called *Gigantopithecus blacki* based on the discovery of four teeth he spotted in Chinese pharmacies. Even today, the entire body of evidence for *Gigantopithecus* consists of three jawbones, a partial fourth jawbone, and over a thousand teeth.

When paleoanthropologists do uncover more substantial evidence, they often find the bones strewn across a large section of ground. In 2004, a Spanish team announced they had dug up a significant collection of fossils—among them a tooth, part of the skull, some ribs, wrist and hand bones, and vertebrae—all representing an extinct ape they called *Pierolapithecus catalaunicus*. Salvador Moya-Sola and his team unearthed the bones during separate expeditions in 2002 and 2003, with the fossils spread over an area of approximately seventy-six square feet.

The famous fossil of an *Australopithecus* nicknamed Lucy turned up shattered and dispersed over a hillside, vulnerable to the elements, requiring an arduous search that employed multiple people to recover her bones and countless hours spent poring over the remnants to reconstruct the skeleton. With her skeleton just 40% complete, and her skull itself preserved as a handful of fragments, any reconstructions of her skeleton rely on at least 60% conjecture. Furthermore, Lucy's bones had lain in the dirt for more than 3 million years while the earth shifted and eroded around her. More than thirty years after her discovery, Lucy hangs on to her title as the most complete skeleton from the species known as *Australopithecus afarensis*. To this day, articles about Lucy and books written by paleoanthropologists refer to her skeleton as almost complete, despite the fact she has retained less than half her bones.

A newer specimen, much touted in the media, retains even less of its bones. The remains of *Australopithecus sediba*, found in 2008 by anthropologist Lee Berger and his son, include a fragmented, but

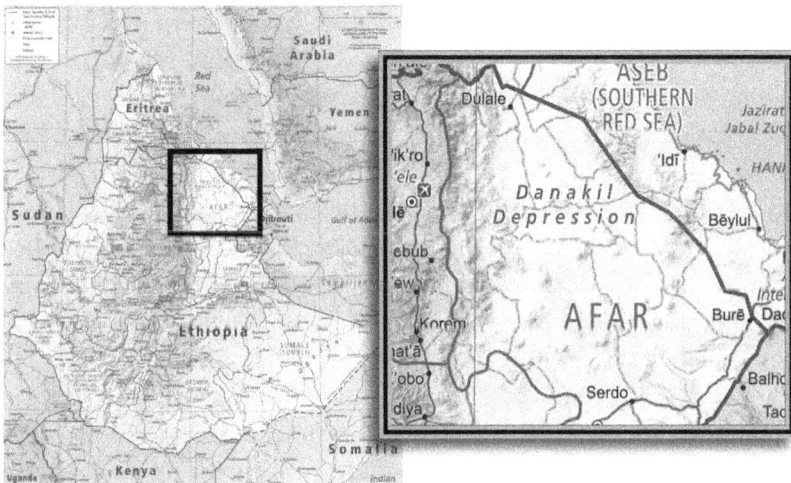

Figure 11.10: The Afar region of Ethiopia, which includes the Middle Awash, is a hotbed of hominid research, where many fossils have been found. Map courtesy of the University of Texas Libraries.

mostly complete, skull accompanied by scattered bits of the skeleton. A second skeleton of *Australopithecus sediba* included a nearly complete arm but only a few fragments of the skull and widely scattered pieces from the remainder of the skeleton. The fossils have been dated to just under 2 million years old.

Although Berger assigned the fossils to the genus *Australopithecus* and christened them a new species, *Australopithecus sediba*, other experts have disagreed with the designation. They suggest the *sediba* fossils actually belong to an already described species known as *Australopithecus africanus*, or perhaps even to a very archaic species in the genus *Homo*. When dealing with evidence in the form of bits of bone, no one can say anything for certain. But this doesn't stop researchers from declaring that every new find represents a new species. What's going on here?

This question thrusts us into the overlapping realms of paleontology and paleoanthropology. Paleontologists scrutinize the fossilized traces of any life-forms, whether animal or plant. Paleoanthropologists study the fossils and other evidence, such as stone tools, left behind by hominids. Though the two disciplines often intersect, such as when paleoanthropologists study the fossils of prehuman primates, paleoanthropology focuses primarily on understanding the origins of humanity. Both disciplines rely on the evidence gleaned from fragmented fossils.

So why do paleoanthropologists want to christen every new fossil as a new species? The answer is as complicated as the fossils. First, egos play a starring role in the drama surrounding human origins research. Scientists like to promote themselves as unbiased and objective, unaffected by any emotion or personal prejudice. The hard sciences focus on repeatable experiments, falsifiable data, and mathematically precise calculations. We often describe disciplines such as paleoanthropology as "soft" sciences because they lack repeatable experiments, little of the data is falsifiable (meaning it can be proven false or true), and a lot of fudging goes into the calculations. Then we must add into the mix the fact that careers are made on one big find—and lost over failure to produce anything new. The pressure to make a stunning discovery, coupled with the egotistical desire to coin a new species and go down in history as its discoverer, propels the creation of new genera (plural of genus) and species.

In his 2003 article in the journal *Science*, Tim White brings up an example from paleontology that demonstrates how the imaginations of scientists can exaggerate the diversity of extinct animals. In the early twentieth century, paleontologists working in the western United States uncovered fossils of ancient animals known as oreodonts, relatives of pigs and sheep. The number of fossils recovered stirred paleontologists to invent an equally great number of oreodont species, with no real evidence to support their assertions. Paleontologists essentially manufactured oreodont diversity—which in turn served as evidence for a type of evolution called adaptive radiation, wherein one species turns into many as individuals seek to occupy different niches in the environment. In the last century, recognizing the fallacy of oreodont diversity, paleontologists have trimmed the ranks of oreodont species to a more manageable level.

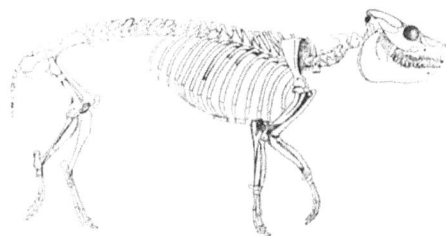

Figure 11.11: Oreodont fossils like this one drove paleontologists to imagine more diversity than likely existed. Drawing from the *South Dakota School of Mines Bulletin 13*, November 1920.

Paleoanthropologists have overstuffed the fossil record for hominids in a similar manner to puff up the case for ordered diversity, in lieu of the chaos engendered by the fragmentary evidence. When a paleoanthropologist unearths a new fossil, he may assign it to a new species without ever bothering to compare the new fossil to those already known and described. New specimens also may linger in top-secret limbo, viewed only by members of the team that discovered the fossil, making it impossible for anyone to compare their latest fossil to the newest finds made by other paleoanthropologists.

In 1994, Tim White's team announced the discovery of fossils they assigned to a new species, *Ardipithecus ramidus*, yet details on the discoveries stayed top secret for a further fifteen years, when they were finally revealed in the journal *Science*. Louis Leakey's team dug up the first *Homo habilis* fossils in 1960-1963; the specimens tarried in the shadows, unpublished, for some thirty years. The record holder for longest unpublished fossil, however, goes to a Neanderthal specimen. Although Neanderthals got their name from a skullcap unearthed in the Neander Valley of Germany in 1856, two discoveries predate the Neander

Valley skullcap—a skull found in Belgium in 1828 and another dug up on Gibraltar in 1848. More than 160 years after its discovery, no one has published a detailed report on the Gibraltar skull.

Paleoanthropologists safeguard their finds as jealously as a dog protects his favorite bone, refusing to let anyone outside the discovery team have a look at it until the discoverers "publish" their fossil. Since new fossils often attract lots of media attention, most people assume the hullabaloo means that a passel of paleoanthropologists from multiple institutions have examined the fossil and approved its status as a new species.

Nope. What about after the discoverers publish a short piece about the new fossil in one of the scientific journals? Nope again. Paleoanthropologists consider their finds top secret until the fossils are "published." Discontent with simply bickering over names for their fossils, these folks also quarrel about the meaning of the word publication. An initial, brief piece in a scientific journal equates to an "announcement," not publication. A fossil is deemed unpublished until its discoverers pen an exhaustive description of the fossils, known as a monograph. The publication of a monograph, as we've seen, may not happen until many years later.

Announcements of new discoveries in scientific journals, without the publication of an ensuing monograph, lead to the discovery team's unproved and unquestioned interpretations becoming accepted fact. The new fossils, assigned to newly minted species, sneak into textbooks without any real discussion. No debate can occur, since a select few are permitted to view the fossils. Other researchers know the discovery team may even limit access to casts of the bones, which are themselves inferior surrogates of the real thing.

Under these circumstances, it should come as no surprise that the initial claims about a new species often get overturned. In 1995, a team led by anthropologist Russell Ciochon announced that in China they had discovered a piece of a hominid jaw dated to 1.9 million years ago. The jawbone, they said, belonged to a relative of *Homo habilis*. The discovery pushed back the date for the arrival of hominids in Asia by nearly a million years. Then, in 2009, Ciochon reversed his opinion on the Chinese fossil in an essay published in the journal *Nature*. He now believes the fossil represents a previously unknown type of ape. After fifteen years in the hominid family tree, the Chinese jawbone must now find a new home on a completely different tree. But what about all the scientific papers and books that cited the Chinese discovery as proof of a far earlier presence of hominids in Asia? Will the authors of those works change their opinions, or reject Ciochon's reappraisal? The answers are unclear.

Top-secret fossils, exaggerated diversity, reversals of opinion, untrustworthy DNA results—what should we take away from all of this? Whenever a new fossil "species" is announced in the media, beware of jumping on the bandwagon. It may not have any wheels yet.

Broken Promises

When we consider all the weaknesses inherent in DNA studies, one fact becomes inescapable and crystal clear. DNA alone will never prove a thing about Bigfoot.

On the surface, DNA seems to offer the promise of ultimate proof and a final solution to the Bigfoot mystery. But digging a little deeper reveals that DNA alone can't prove what Bigfoot are or even that they exist as real animals. If we want scientists to accept Bigfoot's existence, we must present them with complete physical specimens, not bits of hair or feces or flesh purported to come from a Bigfoot. It's time we accept this fact and move on from it.

Let's examine a hypothetical scenario. A Bigfoot researcher presents a geneticist with a sample of the type mentioned above (hair, feces, flesh, or even blood). Let's assume the sample was collected in a perfectly sterile manner, with zero chance of contamination. The DNA test comes back as an unknown animal or, at best, an unknown primate. This has not proven Bigfoot exists. It has not even proven the researcher discovered a new species of animal. The test has proven only that the specific DNA sample in question can't be identified with any DNA currently documented. DNA databases do not yet include samples for every known organism on the planet. They also do not include samples from every individual within every species, or even from a wide variety of individuals.

No reputable scientist will proclaim, based on this DNA evidence alone, that Bigfoot is a real animal. They can't even say the sample definitely came from a Bigfoot. The most the DNA can reveal is that the sample of unverified origin most likely came from a nonhuman primate. For all the scientist knows, however, the sample in question was taken from someone's pet chimpanzee and by the time it reached the laboratory the DNA had degraded to the point where it was no longer clearly identifiable as chimp DNA. The sample might also have come from a human being but, by the time the Bigfoot researcher found it lying around in the woods, the DNA had degraded until it was unidentifiable. The point is that no one can know for certain from what type of animal the sample originated. If the Bigfoot researcher swears he obtained the sample directly from a living or deceased Bigfoot but refuses to provide the complete specimen, the outcome is the same. No reputable scientist will take the word of a Bigfoot researcher in lieu of a type specimen.

Result: the skeptical scientific establishment will roll their eyes at the "proof."

Consider recent goings-on in the Bigfoot research community. For quite some time, a group of researchers has claimed to have Bigfoot DNA that was undergoing analysis by Melba Ketchum, a veterinarian who runs a DNA testing company called DNA Diagnostics Inc. Ketchum has, through social media and press releases, hyped this study as proof of Bigfoot's existence and identity. Despite Ketchum's claims that her paper on the subject was undergoing peer review at a scientific journal, in 2013 she published the paper herself in a journal she bought and renamed *DeNovo Journal of Science*. Though information about where precisely the DNA samples came from is sketchy, Ketchum stated that some of them came from food samples placed in plastic containers and left out for Bigfoot to munch on and, therefore, leave behind DNA. The study of 111 DNA samples also included bits of hair and feces.

The genetic analysis found two varieties of DNA—nuclear DNA (nuDNA), which comes from the nucleus of a cell; and mitochondrial DNA (mtDNA), which comes from structures outside the nucleus known as mitochondria. We all inherit our mtDNA from our mothers, and nuDNA from both parents. Ketchum's study revealed that the mtDNA was entirely human, while the nuDNA was also human but with anomalies. Ketchum says that the anomalies prove this DNA came from a new species, a cross between humans and an as-yet-un-identified hominid ; presumably, this would mean a human mother and a father of a different species. Mainstream scientists who have read Ketchum's paper say that the anomalies suggest contamination of the

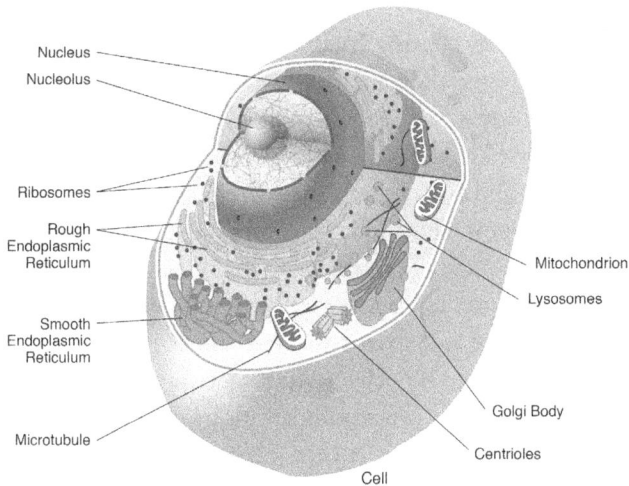

Figure 11.12: The anatomy of a cell is complex, but DNA is found in just two parts—the nucleus and the mitochondria (plural of mitochondrion). Image by Darryl Leja, courtesy of the National Human Genome Research Institute.

samples , not cross-species breeding. According to the science website Phys.org, Ketchum's paper also makes no mention of her team comparing the anomalous DNA with the DNA of known, nonhuman species. Without absolute proof of where the DNA samples came from, and considering the problematic issue of contamination, the scientific establishment will not accept such bold claims about Bigfoot based on one study and without a body to examine.

On July 1, 2013, a science blogger for the *Houston Chronicle*, Eric Berger, announced the results of a study he had helped coordinate. The study, conducted by a lab that Berger did not name, retested some of Ketchum's DNA samples. Internet rumors have identified the lab as being associated with the University of Texas, but so far no official reports have been published on the study. The results of the retesting, according to Berger, showed the DNA belonged to an opossum and other known species. Ketchum immediately denounced the findings on her Facebook page, even going so far as to suggest a possible conspiracy to cover up her findings. This kind of statement does little to enhance Ketchum's credibility, particularly with the mainstream scientists she claims to want to convince. Without their approval, her results will remain fringe science.

Another DNA study is being conducted jointly by geneticists at Oxford University in the UK and the Lausanne Museum of Zoology in Switzerland. The results of the study were supposed to be published in the fall of 2012, but as with Ketchum's study, the release has been delayed—apparently to allow Bigfoot researchers and other parties to submit additional samples. However, in February 2013, the Oxford-Lausanne group released the results of their study of purported Russian Bigfoot hairs. The three hairs came from a bear, horse, and raccoon—not an unknown primate. Does this foreshadow their final results? Only time will answer that question.

Bryan Sykes, the lead geneticist in the project, stated in a 2012 interview that DNA testing provides foolproof identification of species. At least one aspect of Sykes's own study calls that statement into question, however. The hair that was identified as bear belongs to a North American black bear, but the sample supposedly came from Russia. This raises once again the question of contamination, for how else might an American bear drop its hair in Russia? Sykes suggested a bear escaped from a circus, but this seems farfetched to say the least. The sample Sykes received may have been a hoax too, which seems more likely than a circus runaway. In another similarity with Ketchum's study, so far the Oxford-Lausanne team has been vague about where the samples were collected, by whom, and in what manner. Whatever the case, this enigma highlights the fact that DNA testing is only as good as the sample tested.

As we've learned in this chapter, despite what scientists claim, genetic evidence is far from foolproof. When it comes to Bigfoot, the problems are compounded by the elusive nature of the animal being studied and the far-from-ideal circumstances in which samples are collected. Does this mean DNA analysis is useless in Bigfoot research? Of course not. The problems with DNA analysis do mean, however, that we should not expect genetics to offer the ultimate proof of Bigfoot's existence—especially not without a body. And it may take more than one body.

We lack the evidence to prove to the scientific community that Bigfoot is real and is a previously unrecognized species. We can, however, speculate as much as we like about what Bigfoot might be.

Evidence from the fossil record provides interesting clues.

12
Bigfoot Fossils

Scientists estimate that upwards of 98% of all the species
that have arisen in earth's history have gone extinct. This means that to
understand the history of life on earth—to understand what types of
living things once inhabited the planet, what they looked like, how they
lived, and how they interacted with each other and their environment—we
must rely on the evidence from fossils.

The Fossil Record

A fossil is any remnant of a long dead living thing, from bones to feces
to impressions of body parts, that scientists unearth from the ground or
find lying around on the surface. The youngest fossils date back about
10,000 years. The process of fossilization alters the chemistry of the
carcass by adding, taking out, or substituting minerals. Other kinds
of remains, such as mummies, are not technically fossils. To figure out
how species evolved, paleontologists search for fossils and attempt to
interpret the fossil record, the apparently linear progression of fossil
life-forms through time as viewed in the geologic record (the layers of
rocks and dirt).

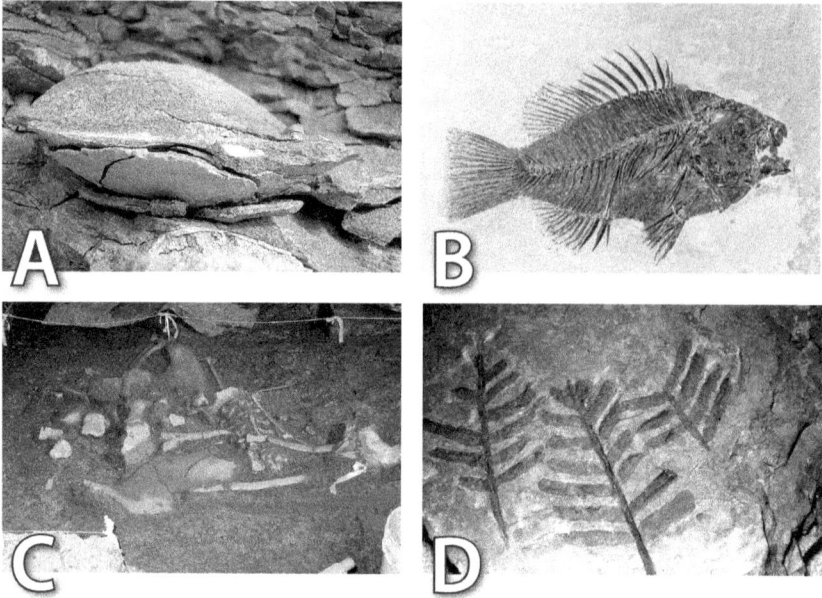

Figure 12.1: The fossil record preserves evidence of many life-forms, both extinct and currently living—including marine fossils (A/B), large mammals like the mammoth (C), and even plant species (D). Photo A courtesy of the National Park Service; U.S. Geological survey photos by W.R. Hansen (B), Paul Carrara (C), and E.D. McKee (D).

How many species does the fossil record preserve? No one knows for certain. Of the species we know existed, those named in our catalog of the natural world, over 80% coexist with us today. The rest exist only in fossil form, and most fossils preserve only hard parts, not soft parts like skin or internal organs. Some scientists estimate the fossil record preserves at most 10% of all species that have ever lived, but that estimate may be far too high. Other scientists think the number is closer to .1%, if not less. This means that at least 99.9% of the species that once existed have disappeared, not just from the face of the planet, but from geologic history itself. We have no way of knowing what those creatures looked like and how, or indeed if, they fit into the evolutionary story of life.

Scattered Clues

The fossil record is necessarily fragmented, as numerous geological and chemical processes act on the remains of living things. When a creature dies, its body begins to decay and disintegrate. A fortuitous combination of circumstances leads any single carcass or group of carcasses to undergo the fossilization process. A creature must die in the right place at the right time, and even then the remains must survive thousands or millions of years' worth of exposure to geological processes.

Water, such as from rivers or floods, may rip the skeleton apart and scatter the bones across a wide area. The remains might also be destroyed or torn asunder by earthquakes, landslides, water seeping through the soil, the natural shifting of sediments, volcanic eruptions, or numerous other natural phenomena. The longer the fossil lies buried, the greater the chance geologic processes will deform, crush, scatter, or outright destroy the specimen.

Missing Pieces

The fossil record exists within the geologic record, like chocolate chips in a cookie. Like the fossil record, the geologic record provides a less-than-complete picture of our planet's history. The layers of rock and soil that make up the geologic record contain vast gaps. These holes, known as unconformities, represent time periods during which either no rock was laid down or the rock was later destroyed. Erosion might've worn away the layers, or the rock might've been recycled through other geologic processes.

One of the largest unconformities appears in the rock strata of the Grand Canyon in Arizona. Here the gap, known as the Great Unconformity, gobbles up as much as a billion years of the geologic past. Around the world, in countless locations, gaps measuring hundreds of millions of years or more interrupt the sequence of layers in the geologic record. Who knows what creatures might have lived during those eons? Since the earth failed to preserve a record of those vast spans of time, we will never know the answer.

From unconformities to the vagaries of fossilization, flaws in the record of our planet's past make it impossible for anyone to know for certain what types of life may have existed in the distant, or even not-so-distant, past. The fossil record contains a mere fraction of the life-forms that once populated this planet.

Still, fossils do provide us with some interesting clues. So what might the fossil record tell us about Bigfoot?

Unconformities

Figure 12.2: The great angular unconformity (above) lies within the Grand Canyon, on the banks of the Colorado River. In 1875, famed explorer John Wesley Powell viewed a similar unconformity and drew this illustration (below) of it. The unconformity occurs between level B and the levels above and below it. Images courtesy of the U.S. Geological Survey; top photo by E.D. McKee.

The Bigfoot Record

No one has ever found the remains of a Bigfoot. Right? Well, maybe we shouldn't be so quick to dismiss the notion. We can say only two things for certain—that no mainstream scientist has identified any remains as belonging to Bigfoot, and that no specimens in museums have been labeled Bigfoot remains.

The scientific establishment rejects the idea that a humanoid-but-not-human primate walks the earth today. This means that no mainstream paleontologists or paleoanthropologists are looking for Bigfoot fossils and, if they found some, they wouldn't identify the bones as relating to Bigfoot. They might label the fossils as an unknown primate or unknown hominid—or, more likely, they would declare that each specimen represents a brand-new genus or species.

Considering these facts, the possibility remains that we do have Bigfoot bones, or at the very least bones of their ancestors. Museums and universities around the world house the bones of bipedal humanoid creatures, which mainstream scientists call ancient hominids and fossil primates. Perhaps the debunkers who bemoan the lack of physical evidence for Bigfoot's existence have ignored the evidence right in front of their noses. Maybe Bigfoot researchers have too.

Any discussion of Bigfoot and the fossil record must inevitably begin with the hypothesis favored by many Bigfoot researchers. It's an idea that sounds reasonable, especially when the facts are glossed over or outright omitted. This hypothesis is often called the *Gigantopithecus* theory, sometimes shortened to the Giganto theory. The idea gets its name from the fossils of an extinct ape. *Gigantopithecus* forms the foundation of the Bigfoot-is-just-an-ape theory, but does the fossil record really bear out this theory?

Gigantopithecus

For about 700,000 years, beginning one million years ago, a giant ape lumbered around Asia. This extinct creature, known to science as *Gigantopithecus*, today acts as a scapegoat for a mystery that stymies those who examine it. Bigfoot researchers finger *Gigantopithecus* as the ancestor of modern-day Bigfoot. Many organizations dedicated to

Bigfoot research, especially on the American West Coast, subscribe to the Giganto theory.

And why not? The idea sounds reasonable, like a perfect fit. After all, *Gigantopithecus* was a giant, bipedal primate standing six to ten feet tall and sporting a massive jaw that dwarfs the mandible of a modern gorilla. Anyone who has watched a television documentary about Bigfoot has likely seen a reconstruction of *Gigantopithecus* in the form of a statue of a colossal ape, usually displayed with a man alongside it to highlight the enormity of the beast. Such reconstructions give a twofold impression—that scientists have unearthed the complete remains of at least one member of the genus *Gigantopithecus*, and that we know exactly how the creature looked in life so we can say with certainty it looked much like Bigfoot.

But how much can we really know about *Gigantopithecus*?

Giganto History

The first hints that a giant ape once roamed Asia cropped up just before World War II. The German paleoanthropologist Ralph von Koenigswald had begun searching Chinese pharmacies for fossils, which the locals called "dragon teeth" or "dragon bones" and which they used in homeopathic remedies. The Chinese pharmacies had earlier aided von Koenigswald in his quest to dig up remains of *Homo erectus*. In 1935, von Koenigswald stumbled across a tooth he surmised belonged to a colossal ape. Further hunting netted him three more teeth. On the basis of these four teeth, von Koenigswald declared a new genus of extinct ape that he christened *Gigantopithecus*, or "gigantic ape."

Another scientist, Franz Weidenreich, studied casts of the fossil teeth and reached a differing conclusion. Noting the curious bulk of some *Homo erectus* fossils found on the Indonesian island of Java, Weidenreich theorized that the teeth von Koenigswald had discovered belonged to a giant version of *Homo erectus*, and that modern people had evolved from this species through a process of gradual shrinking. As paleoanthropological theories go, Weidenreich's was no more fanciful than most. In fact, for years afterward, his theory supplanted von Koenigswald's vision of a giant ape.

During the 1950s, Chinese paleoanthropologists initiated a new search for the giant ape. Tracking down the source of the fossils in the pharmacies, the Chinese researchers located a cave high in a natural rock tower, a site that yielded teeth identical to the ones von Koenigswald had found twenty years earlier. At a site further to the north, another member of the team learned of a farmer who'd found a giant jawbone. Excavations yielded another jawbone at the same cave where the farmer happened upon his treasure. The new jaw retained most of its teeth, with just three missing. Now paleoanthropologists could compare the teeth already found to the ones still affixed to the jawbone. Analysis proved to them that the original specimens did indeed belong to a giant ape.

In the ensuing decades, excavations have brought in a handful of additional mandibles and even more teeth. No other remnants of *Gigantopithecus* have turned up so far.

How Many Gigantos?

The genus *Gigantopithecus* encompasses three species—*Gigantopithecus blacki, Gigantopithecus giganteus,* and *Gigantopithecus bilaspurensis.* Fossils of the first two have turned up in China and Vietnam; fossils of the third have been found in India. The remains of *Gigantopithecus bilaspurensis* date to an earlier period than the other two species, somewhere between 6 and 9 million years ago. The evidence for all the species of *Gigantopithecus* is limited to teeth and mandibles (lower jawbones).

Figure 12.3: Was *Gigantopithecus* really a giant version of a modern apes like this gorilla? Many Bigfoot researchers hope so, because they want to paint Bigfoot as a giant ape too. Photo by Lisa A. Shiel.

The reasons for separating the various *Gigantopithecus* fossils into distinct species are the same reasons discussed in the previous chapter, in reference to hominid fossils. Everyone wants to discover a brand-new species, and this desire leads paleontologists and paleoanthropologists to see the slightest difference as evidence of a distinct species. Also, with *Gigantopithecus bilaspurensis*, the fossils were found in different locations and dated to different time periods than the fossils for the other species.

Gigantopithecus bilaspurensis was apparently smaller too. Whether the difference in size indicates different species or simply a difference between the sexes, no one really knows. Pinning down size disparities between the sexes within a single species requires more evidence than some jawbones and teeth can provide.

Gigantopithecus fossils present other dilemmas as well. Paleoanthropologists have run into trouble when trying to differentiate the fossil teeth of hominids from those of *Gigantopithecus*, and the teeth of *Gigantopithecus* from those of other apes. Orangutan teeth that fall on the larger end of the scale can be misidentified as belonging to a species of *Gigantopithecus*. Similarly, smaller orangutan teeth may be erroneously identified as belonging to a hominid, such as *Homo erectus*.

Another difficulty arises when attempting to sort out from how many individuals the teeth came. If the fossil assemblage includes a pile of teeth and a few mandibles, does this necessarily mean the teeth came from just two individuals? Or could the teeth have come from more than two individuals, and the other mandibles were destroyed at some point before scientists discovered the assemblage? The answers to these questions are unclear.

How Big Was Giganto?

Though reconstructions of the beast imply we have a complete skeleton of *Gigantopithecus* to work with, in reality artists build their conceptions of the giant ape from a collection of mostly fragmented jawbones, a pile of teeth, and a hefty measure of imagination. Even Russell Ciochon, one of the top experts on *Gigantopithecus*, admits in his book *Other Origins* that any reconstruction of a fossil animal involves at least as much art as science and produces only one of many plausible visions of the creature.

All reconstructions of *Gigantopithecus* rely on conjecture, since the entire catalog of *Gigantopithecus* fossils consists of jawbones and teeth. Scientists must estimate the skull size by comparing the jawbones to those of living apes, as well as other fossil apes. Then they must guess at the head-to-body ratio in a similar manner. Estimates generally range from six to ten feet for height, and 600 to 1200 pounds for weight.

Ciochon and his colleagues commissioned one of several reconstructions in existence. Rather than contracting a scientist or forensic sculptor, they

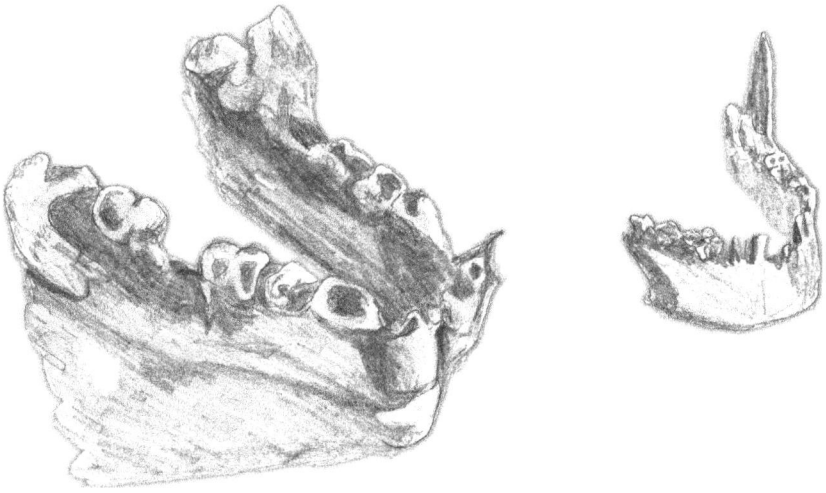

Figure 12.4: The jawbone of *Gigantopithecus* (left) dwarfs that of a modern human (right). But teeth and a few jawbones are all the evidence we have for Giganto. Drawings by Kerrie Shiel.

joined forces with a Hollywood special effects guru named Bill Munns, who has also constructed models of living primates. The model Munns created for *Gigantopithecus* stands ten feet tall. Critics of the model have observed the reconstruction resembles an orangutan, though other models take their cues from the gorilla. Critics also point out that the Munns reconstruction uses the largest possible dimensions for the creature, rather than a median size. Most estimates gauge the height of *Gigantopithecus* based on the average standing height of gorillas, with the assumption that the long bones of *Gigantopithecus* would measure 20-25% longer than those of a gorilla. The average standing height of the male gorilla is about six feet. This would make *Gigantopithecus* just over seven feet tall.

The available fossils reveal another puzzle too. During the earlier period of the accepted timeframe for the genus, *Gigantopithecus* seemed to increase in size. Yet the *Gigantopithecus* fossils dating to the later end of the accepted timeframe are smaller in size. The evidence suggests these creatures first grew larger, and then shrank. If this is indeed the case, then we could logically expect any surviving populations of *Gigantopithecus* in existence today to be smaller in stature than the example depicted in the Munns reconstruction.

But these aren't the only problems for the Giganto theory.

Did Giganto Walk Upright?

The majority of experts who have studied the jawbones, including Russell Ciochon, believe *Gigantopithecus* preferred a quadrupedal gait known as knuckle-walking over bipedal locomotion. The question of stance is pivotal in any discussion of what fossils Bigfoot most resembles.

Only one primate alive today walks upright exclusively—humans. Other primates may walk upright on occasion, but spend the vast majority of their time either swinging from branch to branch or knuckle-walking. The gibbons and siamangs of Asia, for instance, adopt bipedal locomotion on occasion but swing amongst the trees 90% of the time. Orangutans have been observed walking in a bipedal stance on tree branches, when they can hold onto other branches for support. But human beings hold onto our status as the sole primate currently in existence that walks on two feet as its standard mode of locomotion. All other primates lack the appropriate anatomy for bipedalism.

Most Bigfoot researchers, a troop that includes a handful of biologists and anthropologists, seek reasons to believe *Gigantopithecus* walked upright. They mention how the jaws of *Gigantopithecus* spread out toward the back in a manner consistent with the shape seen the jawbones of bipeds. Yet comparing the *Gigantopithecus* jaw to those of living apes and humans points up the similarities to ape jaws, and the disparity with the mandibles of humans and the ancient hominids.

Human teeth sit in a parabolic curve; ape teeth align in two parallel rows. Ape jawbones exhibit a V shape; human jawbones have a more rounded appearance. The jaws of *Gigantopithecus* exhibit a V shape, in line with living apes. Relative to the other teeth, *Gigantopithecus* canines are much larger, another trait seen in modern apes. The Giganto jaws are also much deeper than human jaws.

These features, along with the other evidence concerning *Gigantopithecus*, suggest an affinity with nonhuman, quadrupedal primates rather than with humans. Yet to stand as the ancestor of modern Bigfoot, Giganto needs to have walked upright. To name *Gigantopithecus* as the ancestor of Bigfoot requires us to accept that, while no other primate before or since has adopted a bipedal gait its modus operandi, for some reason Giganto did—despite its apelike anatomy, as evidenced by and inferred from its teeth and mandibles.

Figure 12.5: Fossils of *Gigantopithecus* have turned up in China, Vietnam, and India. Map courtesy of the University of Texas Libraries.

So here's the story the Giganto theory writes for us. Apes enjoyed their knuckle-walking status for millions of years then—boing!—*Gigantopithecus* pops out of the evolutionary box as a biped. In spite of its bipedalism, Giganto retains its apelike jawbones and teeth. Despite growing smaller during the latter part of its fossil record, for unknown reasons Giganto became a giant once more. Oh, and it became distinctly more humanlike in appearance too.

And they say the UFO connection is outlandish!

Not one of the reconstructions of *Gigantopithecus* resembles Bigfoot, save for the large stature. Each reconstruction takes its cues from the ape world, a prudent approach considering the similarities between the jawbones of Giganto and other primates. In contrast, witnesses who've seen hairy hominids mention the humanness of the creatures' faces. Their testimony provides many clues that simply don't mesh with the Giganto theory. Now consider the opinion of an expert on primates and anatomy, primatologist Esteban Sarmiento. In an interview with a Texas newspaper, he said that the Bigfoot seen in the Patterson film does not look like an ape but, if it's a real animal, must represent a whole new species closer to man than to ape.

Since we have so few other bones of *Gigantopithecus* from which to deduce its appearance, we can do no more than imagine how it looked. Imagination provides fertile soil for growing theories. Unfortunately, none of the ideas that sprout up have enough strength to mature.

The fossil record, however, holds other possibilities that offer far more evidence—clues that are both greater in number and superior in quality.

Fossil Hominids

Long, long ago in a time before humans walked the earth lived a pair of species called *Homo erectus* and *Homo heidelbergensis*.

Oops! I almost forgot that "human" means any creature that paleoanthropologists want to cram into the genus *Homo*, whether it looks like an ape-man or a human man. *Homo heidelbergensis* and *Homo erectus* are two such species. They're so similar that paleoanthropologists often have trouble distinguishing the two, which suggests perhaps they aren't separate species after all. What sets these species apart from us? The list of differences includes

- ↬ smaller brains,
- ↬ more robust and often larger bones and teeth,
- ↬ pronounced brow ridges,
- ↬ receding foreheads, and
- ↬ no chins.

These hominids sound a lot more like *Homo erectus* and the Neanderthals than like us. Unlike with previous hominids, such as *Australopithecus*, evidence suggests members of *Homo heidelbergensis* and *Homo erectus* could reach or exceed six feet in height. Far more muscular and robust than modern people, these species do resemble a creature we know—Bigfoot.

The larger breeds of Bigfoot, especially in the Pacific Northwest, share many traits in common with *heidelbergensis* and *erectus*. Bigfoot come in all shapes and sizes, just like the ancient hominids, but as with the ancient hominids no one has proven that shape and size distinguish a species. All the varieties of Bigfoot might easily represent one species. The same goes for the ancient hominids.

Fossils of *erectus* and *heidelbergensis* have turned up in Africa, Europe, and Asia—unlike *Gigantopithecus*, the favorite fossil of some Bigfoot researchers, which has been found in Asia only. According to scientists, fossils of neither ancient hominids nor *Gigantopithecus* have turned up in North America. What should we conclude from the available evidence? Well, the fossil record has left us far more evidence about what ancient hominids looked like and how they lived than about what *Gigantopithecus* looked like or how it lived. After all, *Gigantopithecus* bequeathed to us nothing more than teeth and a handful of (mainly fragmented) jawbones. Conversely, the fossil record provides near-complete specimens of *Homo erectus* along with various skulls and bones of *Homo heidelbergensis*.

Let's sum it up. Two species of bipedal, robust, apelike-yet-not-ape creatures lived around the world. These species have been, most likely in error, labeled as members of the genus *Homo*. We have their fossils, which provide us with a great deal of information about their anatomy and appearance. Maybe what we have represents not archaic human fossils, but instead Bigfoot fossils.

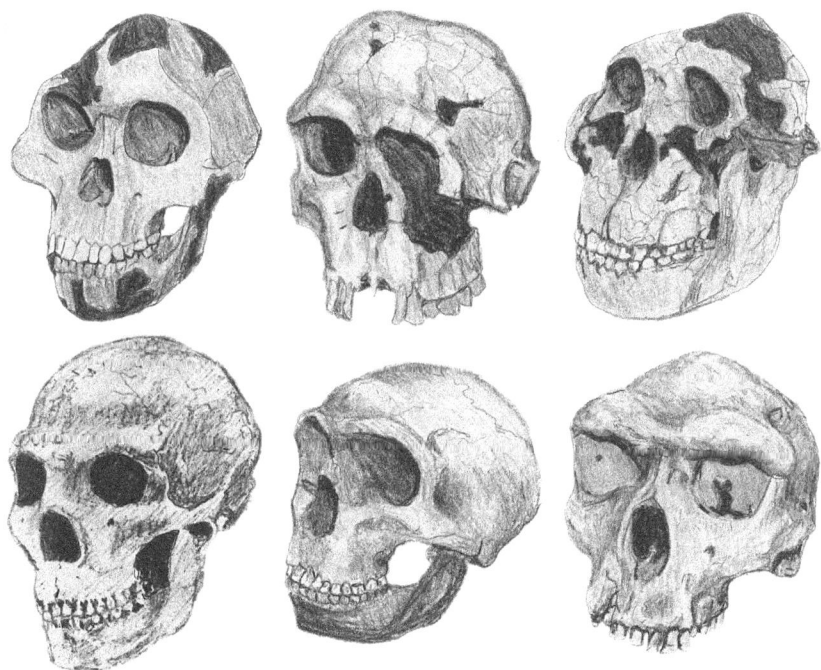

Figure 12.6: The skulls of (clockwise from top left) *Australopithecus afarensis, Homo habilis, Australopithecus boisei, Homo erectus, Homo neanderthalensis,* and *Homo heidelbergensis.* Black portions indicate missing parts of the skull. Drawings by Kerrie Shiel.

But *heidelbergensis* and *erectus* are not the only candidates for fossil Bigfoot. The fossil record offers up other examples of nonhuman hominids that also share traits in common with our favorite cryptid. Which of these species looks most like Bigfoot? Do any of them look like Bigfoot? Consider these additional candidates:

- ⊘ *Australopithecus afarensis*. This small hominid lived about 2-3 million years ago. The famous fossil known as Lucy hails from this species. Specimens have been found in Africa.
- ⊘ *Homo habilis*. This species was also small, though somewhat larger than *Australopithecus*, and lived about 1-2 million years ago. Specimens have been found in Africa and possibly also in the Republic of Georgia.
- ⊘ *Australopithecus boisei*. A heftier version of Lucy's kin, this species lived at about the same time as *Homo habilis*. Sometimes this species is called *Paranthropus boisei*.
- ⊘ *Homo erectus*. Paleoanthropologists mark this species as the first to emigrate out of Africa into Europe and Asia. Its fossils date from about 2 million to 300,000 years ago.
- ⊘ *Homo neanderthalensis*. Commonly called Neanderthals, this species is sometimes labeled as a subspecies of *Homo sapiens*. Neanderthals lived in Europe between about 200,000 years ago and 30,000 years ago. Neanderthal is alternately spelled Neandertal.
- ⊘ *Homo heidelbergensis*. This species was initially known only from specimens in Europe, but later on examples turned up in Africa. These sophisticated hominids existed from about 800,000 years ago to 150,000 years ago.

The questions of when these hominids first appeared and when, or indeed if, they went extinct are open to debate. It's entirely possible that all these hominids represent variation within one species. The dating of hominid fossils generally relies on dating the layer of earth in which the fossil was found. Often, though, the fossils turn up on the surface or lying exposed in a ravine. This makes it difficult to accurately date the fossils.

Can we ever prove that the bones in museums belong to, or are closely related to, Bigfoot? Probably not, at least until we have a dead body or live specimen of a modern Bigfoot. Does it really matter if we ever prove what Bigfoot is (or isn't)? That's a question we each have to answer for ourselves.

13
The UFO Connection

Witnesses have reported Bigfoot sightings that involve mysterious lights. This is a fact. Anyone who disputes that such reports do exist either outright lies or suffers from an ignorance of the data. Sometimes ignorance stems from laziness or lack of access to data; in other cases, however, ignorance is a choice. Avoid looking at the data and, voilà, for you the data does not exist.

Damned Data

Scientists often take this stance where the paranormal is concerned. Charles Fort, a chronicler of the strange and scientifically rejected, referred to this kind of ignored evidence as "damned data"—information condemned to the fringes of knowledge because it calls into question accepted dogma. Fort wrote about this problem in his best-known work, *The Book of the Damned*, published in 1919. It's amazing that almost a century later the mentality of "damned data" continues to hinder science. Folks who aspire to expose the ignored evidence sometimes call themselves forteans, after Charles Fort.

An awful lot of Bigfoot researchers apparently aspire to become the anti-Forteans. They seem to specialize in the art of damning any and all data that questions the just-an-ape assumption. Take UFO-related Bigfoot sightings.

They happen. Period.

To counter this fact, many researchers from the just-an-ape camp fall back on one of two tactics. For sighting reports submitted to them directly, they toss the report in the trashcan. For all other Bigfoot-UFO sightings, either they dismiss them as hoaxes or delusions or they claim any hairy bipeds seen in conjunction with UFOs are not Bigfoot at all, but some other type of creature. UFO-related creatures are often referred to as hairy humanoids or even Wookies (after the Bigfoot-like creatures from the *Star Wars* movies).

Must a Bigfoot-type creature seen with a UFO be called something other than Bigfoot? Many researchers would say yes. They often propose quasi-logical explanations to justify the claim that creatures spotted with UFOs aren't Bigfoot, even though the beasties look like Bigfoot. The real explanation, however, hides in the underbelly of Bigfoot research—in the psyches of the researchers themselves. Too often emotion becomes entangled with the investigation, as the researchers struggle to justify throwing out sightings that simultaneously disturb them and cast doubt on their preconceived ideas. High strangeness associated with Bigfoot

Figure 13.1: If a Bigfoot-type creature steps out of a UFO, must we label it a hairy humanoid instead of a Bigfoot? Photo by Lisa A. Shiel, of a sculpture at Lakenenland Sculpture Park, Harvey, Michigan.

clearly disturbs a lot of people, and it certainly casts doubt on the just-an-ape idea. Consequently, researchers from the just-an-ape camp must distinguish the so-called flesh-and-blood Bigfoot from the so-called paranormal Bigfoot. Any reasoning will do, no matter how flimsy.

In reality, the distinction between "flesh and blood" and "paranormal" exists solely in the minds of the researchers. Bigfoot are by their very existence both paranormal and flesh and blood. "Paranormal" means simply that 1) science cannot as yet explain it because the phenomenon is so rare that it cannot be replicated for scientific verification and 2) the phenomenon exhibits characteristics that *appear* to defy natural laws. For instance, Bigfoot seem to survive without a large population, an obvious food source, or a place to lay their heads down to rest.

We've already explored some of the Bigfoot-UFO sightings in previous chapters. But what might this connection signify? To answer that question, let's begin by examining a particularly controversial aspect of the Bigfoot-UFO connection.

Synchronicities

A synchronicity is when two phenomena seem connected but share no direct causal relationship. The two phenomena will occur in the same small geographic area at different times. Often, the same witnesses will see both phenomena. A connection exists, but one that traditional science cannot explain. Synchronicities do not adhere to traditional notions about cause and effect. If I drop an egg and it breaks on the floor, I know I caused the egg to break. One might argue that gravity, or the force of the impact, caused the egg to break, but my clumsiness is still the root cause for the effect of the egg shattering.

Now imagine I've just set an egg on the counter. Suddenly, a glowing orb flies through the kitchen. I watch the orb flit out the window, out of sight, then I look down to discover the egg has broken. Nothing touched the egg, it hasn't moved, and nothing fell on it. But the egg broke precisely when the orb flew through the kitchen. The events seem related; however, I cannot prove the orb caused the egg to break. I might formulate a dozen other explanations for what happened to the egg, all of which deny the orb affected the egg. Although the explanations sound reasonable, I'm left with one big problem. No egg before or since has ever broken when lying undisturbed on the counter.

In situations like this, rational explanations begin to strain the boundaries of the definition for rational. Similar problems crop up with the synchronicity of Bigfoot and UFOs (a category that includes glowing orbs). In cases where the witness saw a Bigfoot inside or in front of a UFO, the connection is obvious. What about cases where the two phenomena seem related but have no direct cause-and-effect relationship?

What hidden connections might lurk in the forbidden territory of synchronicities?

Hidden Connections

Imagine that I have just spotted a UFO hovering over the woods. When I go into the woods to investigate, I see a Bigfoot. I never observed the Bigfoot coming out of the UFO. I can prove no direct connection between the two. If this happened once, or even twice, I might dismiss it as coincidence. If I encounter such coincidences ten, twenty, thirty times...what then? At what point does coincidence become absurdity?

Several years ago, I received a report about two brothers who had a Bigfoot encounter near Paulding, Michigan, in the western Upper Peninsula. In November 1988, Aaron and his brother observed three hairy humanoid creatures, brown in color, walking through a clearing alongside Robbins Pond Road. One creature appeared to be taller than the others, leading the witnesses to wonder if the smaller ones were juveniles. The creatures walked upright and had long arms.

Paulding also hosts a mystery light, an orb-type occurrence that happens every night in the vicinity of the utility right-of-way along Robbins Pond Road. The witness who reported the Bigfoot sighting did not mention seeing the mystery light, though he did mention that his sighting happened in the same area where the Paulding Light appears. This is another type of synchronicity, in which Bigfoot and UFO sightings are reported in the same area at different times and by different witnesses. If the two phenomena share a connection, then we should expect to find sightings of both in the same areas. But must we always find sightings of both in the same areas?

And what does it mean when we don't—or when we do?

Cursed Coincidences

A closer examination of a portion of the available data about Bigfoot sightings and UFO sightings reveals something unexpected. It shows correlations that many researchers on both sides, Bigfoot and UFO, prefer to ignore. It reveals synchronicities—or, to coin a phrase inspired by Charles Fort, the sightings data expose a series of cursed coincidences.

The available sightings data shows locations where Bigfoot sightings occur but no UFO sightings have been reported, and vice versa. Hawaii, for instance has no recorded Bigfoot sightings (native Hawaiians do have legends about hairy dwarves, known as *menehune* or *mu*). Researchers who balk at the idea of a connection sometimes point to locations like Hawaii as proof that no connection exists between Bigfoot and UFOs. If they're connected, the logic goes, then they must always both occur in the same areas. If we apply this tenet in other areas, however, the falseness of the logic becomes apparent. In many locations around the world, we see human beings but no cars. Does this mean there is no connection between cars and people?

Beware of false logic. It's a favorite tactic of debunkers, and of Bigfoot researchers intent on snuffing out the idea of a Bigfoot-UFO connection. Keeping the opposition on the defensive frees the attackers from the discomfort of having to defend their own claims.

The fact remains that witnesses continue to report encounters with both Bigfoot and UFOs, though often the encounters occur separately. The witnesses don't connect the two. They report whatever strange things happened to them, wanting someone to listen, someone who won't ridicule them. If a Bigfoot witness starts talking about the UFO she saw on another occasion in the same area, too many Bigfoot researchers will laugh, walk away, or simply tune out the information.

Here's an interesting correlation between Bigfoot and UFO sightings. One of the biggest databases of Bigfoot sightings available online is maintained by the Bigfoot Field Researchers Organization (BFRO); one of the biggest databases of UFO sightings available online is maintained by the National UFO Reporting Center (NUFORC). The states with the most UFO sightings, according to NUFORC, are California and Washington—which just happen to be the states with the highest number of Bigfoot sightings in the BFRO database. The order is reversed for the two types of sightings, with Washington #1 for Bigfoot and California #1 for UFOs, but the correlation is striking.

Bigfoot/UFO Sightings

Figure 13.2: The first table shows the top ten states with the most UFO sightings and Bigfoot sightings, respectively. States common to both lists are in **bold**. The second table shows the population of each state in the top ten list, along with its rank (by population) among all states. Information based on data from the Bigfoot Field Researchers Organization, the National UFO Reporting Center, and the U.S. Census Bureau.

UFOs	Bigfoot
1. **California**	1. **Washington**
2. **Washington**	2. **California**
3. **Texas**	3. Oregon
4. **Florida**	4. **Ohio**
5. **New York**	5. **Florida**
6. **Illinois**	6. **Texas**
7. Arizona	7. **Illinois**
8. Pennsylvania	8. **Michigan**
9. **Ohio**	9. Colorado
10. **Michigan**	10. **New York**

State	Population	Rank
California	37,253,956	1
Texas	25,145,561	2
New York	19,378,102	3
Florida	18,801,310	4
Illinois	12,830,632	5
Ohio	11,536,504	7
Michigan	9,883,640	8
Washington	6,724,540	13

Of the top ten states for Bigfoot and UFO sightings, eight are common to both lists. An anti-Fortean might say this is to be expected because these states host the largest populations. The more people living in a state, the more potential witnesses there are in that state. Although California does rank as the most populous state in the nation, Washington ranks thirteenth—yet it's number one for Bigfoot sightings and number two for UFO sightings. If population alone explained away the synchronicity, then we should expect the #2 state for both Bigfoot and UFO sightings to be Texas. It's not. Texas ranks third for UFOs but sixth for Bigfoot.

According to estimates published by the U.S. Census Bureau, as of 2010 Michigan's population outnumbered Washington's, yet Washington has amassed far more reported sightings of both Bigfoot and UFOs. Clearly, population alone cannot account for the synchronicity concerning which states have accumulated the most reported sightings.

The synchronicities just keep piling up at our feet. If we ignore synchronicities, we may miss a vital piece of the puzzle. Ignoring evidence because it disturbs us, or because it doesn't fit our preconceptions, or because we don't understand what it's telling us, invalidates the research. No one can trust the research of individuals who accept only the data that pleases them.

One particular type of UFO seems to trigger the most knee-jerk reactions.

The Mystery of Glowing Orbs

Sightings involving glowing orbs and Bigfoot, though apparently rare, do occur. Glowing orbs also associate themselves with fairies and with other types of UFOs. The synchronicity of Bigfoot and glowing orbs seems even more prevalent than sightings of the two together. Let's begin the discussion there.

Little UFOs

Whether we think of glowing orbs as spirits or electrical phenomena, they are UFOs. No one knows what glowing orbs are, so they belong in the UFO category. While some witnesses have seen glowing orbs with Bigfoot, the two phenomena also share a synchronicity. Both phenomena will occur in the same small area—say, on one person's property—at different times. But what are orbs, and why do they occur with or in the same area as Bigfoot?

With photos of glowing orbs, the favored "explanation" is dust particles or raindrops. With eyewitness sightings, the top scapegoat is ball lightning. The idea sounds reasonable, superficially. But there's one serious problem with the ball lightning hypothesis.

Has anyone bothered to ask whether we know what ball lightning is?

The answer is no. Although most UFO researchers discount ball lightning as irrelevant to their research, they ought not. An aerial phenomenon, whether ball lightning or flying saucer, that remains unexplained and utterly incomprehensible is, in fact, a UFO. Whether we define UFO as Unidentified Flying Object or Unconventional Flying Object, ball lightning qualifies.

The Scientific Viewpoint

A 2008 news story from Australia outlines the views of a scientist who says ball lightning continues to circumvent all efforts to understand it. Two main theories attempt to account for the phenomenon—one explains ball lightning as a type of plasma that travels from its parent lightning bolt through conductive paths in the ground; the other theory describes a chemical reaction between lightning and silica and carbon in the ground. The latter theory requires the creation of silicon nanoparticles that pop out into the air as glowing balls. French scientists only recently demonstrated that invisible silicon nanoparticles can be created by electricity.

In 2006, National Geographic News also noted the ongoing mystery of ball lightning. In the National Geographic story, physicist Graham K. Hubler of the U.S. Naval Research Laboratory explained that scientists still don't know what ball lightning is. Hubler suggested ball lightning may involve a new kind of physics, science beyond what we know today. No one knows what it is—or what causes it. Debunkers often dismiss eyewitness sightings of glowing orbs as ball lightning, as if this solves the mystery. To call glowing orbs ball lightning, however, serves only to lock one mystery inside another. For, as scientists readily admit, nobody knows the cause or composition of ball lightning.

Competing theories explain the phenomenon as plasma or oxidized silicon nanoparticles, and a stranger hypothesis links them to miniature black holes. None of the theories can either satisfy all the apparent qualities of ball lightning or produce definitive evidence to support it. Scientists have managed to create tiny orbs in the laboratory, similar to ball lightning, but the orbs last for a matter of seconds. They also have not been shown to exhibit the stranger traits of ball lightning, such as passing through windowpanes, repeatedly bouncing into a person's head, and moving against the wind and gravity.

Ball lightning is often associated with thunderstorms. Glowing orbs can occur anytime, anywhere. Of course, a scientist confronted with reports of glowing orbs spotted nowhere near a thunderstorm will likely dismiss the reports as hoaxes or the delusions of nutballs. Not long ago, the majority of scientists refused to admit ball lightning existed; today, they admit it exists but have no clue what it is.

Burning Questions

Ball lightning can move against the wind and against gravity, just as glowing orbs do. Ball lightning can hover, bounce around, go through walls, and appear from and disappear into thin air. Glowing orbs exhibit the same behavior. Debunkers brush off glowing orbs as ball lightning. I agree that the two phenomena may be the same thing—which does not make them natural. Another possibility is that orbs are a natural phenomenon, but they've been enhanced artificially or controlled to perform a certain function.

My game camera has captured numerous photos of orbs, or under various conditions where the standard debunking explanations—dust,

Figure 13.3: Ball lightning has proven harder to capture on film than cloud-to-ground lightning. Time-lapse image courtesy of the NOAA Photo Library, NOAA Central Library, and OAR/ERL/National Severe Storms Laboratory (NSSL).

raindrops, snowflakes—don't apply. On one night in June 2004, my game camera captured multiple glowing orbs *when the camera's flash was not activated*. This suggests the orbs were self-illuminated.

Witnesses have seen orbs with the naked eye. In 2005, during the most intense thunderstorm I've ever experienced, I saw two orbs that joined together in a dumbbell shape. After a few moments the orbs winked out, vanishing in an instant, leaving behind a tiny shower of sparks that sizzled out after a few seconds. I talked to a witness who saw a glowing orb as wide as a two-lane highway. The witness and her sister were driving home from Minneapolis when, near the town of Paulding, a strange light began to trail them. The orb followed the witness all the way back to her home in the Keweenaw Peninsula, approximately eighty miles from Paulding. Remember Paulding? It's home to a mystery light, and it was the site of at least one Bigfoot encounter.

Let's dump the old "dust particle" nonsense right here. Glowing orbs exhibit behavior that goes beyond the scope of debunking explanations. These balls of light seem controlled by an intelligence. I view orbs as a combination of the natural and the technological, possibly the result of manipulating a natural phenomenon to create tiny probes, which are then sent out to keep an eye on people or animals or whatever the controllers of the orbs wish to study. We send probes to other planets. We leave game cameras in the woods to spy on animals. An advanced race, whether alien or otherwise, might very well do the same.

Now that we've examined the evidence, it's time to bring it all together.

A Hypothesis

Whenever I give interviews or speak at a gathering, I talk about the Bigfoot-UFO connection and how a lot of researchers want to censor sightings in order to avoid any connection. My discussion of this link invariably brings up the same question: What exactly is the connection between Bigfoot and UFOs?

Of course, nobody knows with any degree of certainty. Nothing about Bigfoot or UFOs is known for certain. After examining the evidence, however, I have reached a few conclusions about what may connect Bigfoot and UFOs. This is my Bigfoot-UFO hypothesis.

Somebody pilots all those UFOs. From small drones to mile-wide mother ships, UFOs must have an intelligence behind them in order to exhibit the behavior they do. Some people think UFOs are earthquake lights or manifestations of group consciousness or some such thing, but neither of those theories fits the evidence or even makes sense when we examine it in depth. Earthquake lights, sometimes also called earth lights, emanate from the ground during earthquakes or immediately before or after them; therefore, this type of light could not explain all UFO sightings. None of these ideas can explain instances where witnesses see clearly technological craft that exhibit capabilities beyond any technology known to exist on Earth.

Everything I am about to say stems from one hypothesis—UFOs represent technology created by an advanced race. Whether that race originated on Earth or hails from elsewhere, whether they are aliens or earthlings, the evidence from UFO sightings indicates the beings behind these craft harness types of technology our "modern" society can't come close to replicating. Historical evidence suggests UFOs have been visiting, or inhabiting, this planet for thousands of years or longer. Cave paintings seem to depict stereotypical flying saucers. Other ancient artwork depicts strange-looking beings and mysterious craft.

Bigfoot have probably lived on this planet longer than humans. They resemble the ancient hominids far more than we do; legends of hairy man-beasts date back centuries, perhaps millennia. Tales of UFOs extend back equally as far. In fact, it would seem that as long as UFOs have existed, Bigfoot have existed too.

The Truth about Bigfoot

Everything we've examined so far, all the damned data and cursed coincidences, reveal a pattern. The uncensored data shows us the true nature of Bigfoot. When we look at the annals of Bigfoot sightings, several characteristics emerge that don't fit within either the just-an-ape framework or the not-paranormal framework:

- Bigfoot that disappear into thin air.
- Strange lights associated with the appearance and/or disappearance of Bigfoot.
- Footprints that end abruptly, as if the creature vanished.

- Similarities between Bigfoot, UFOs, fairies, and other paranormal phenomena.
- A distinct lack of evidence supporting the idea that Bigfoot is nothing but an ape.
- Another distinct lack of evidence concerning how Bigfoot survive in large enough populations to reproduce and thrive.
- A correlation between the geographic areas where the most Bigfoot sightings and the most UFO sightings are reported.
- Sightings of Bigfoot and UFOs together, and of the two separately but in the same area.
- The strangely elusive nature of Bigfoot.
- Waves of sightings that dissipate as if the creatures responsible had left the area.

The direct correlations and the synchronicities between Bigfoot and UFO sightings virtually scream at us, if we bother to look at the data and listen to what it says. How can a creature that's seen as often as Bigfoot apparently is remain scientifically undocumented? Why are they so elusive? The last item in the above list also makes little sense for dealing with a normal animal that has no connection to paranormal phenomena.

Sighting reports illustrate that Bigfoot sightings often come in waves, similar to UFO flaps. In 1971, residents of the Arkansas town of Fouke experienced a string of Bigfoot sightings. Only sporadic sightings have been reported since. A wave of sightings occurred in 1951 in the vicinity of Charlotte, Michigan, in a place nicknamed "gorilla swamp." In 1964, also in Michigan, previously sporadic sightings of the Sister Lakes Monster exploded into a wave that garnered tremendous media attention. Why should a wave of sightings crop up in a certain area, then fade away as if the creatures have left?

Perhaps the Bigfoot did leave the area. Perhaps they caught a ride on a UFO.

Exploration, With Caution

Think about this: We send probes to other planets to check them out. Our probes collect soil samples and analyze them on the spot. We even sent a probe to crash into an asteroid—and our Voyager 1 probe has traveled over eleven billion miles from Earth and counting. Now, imagine we have time-traveled into the future, to a time when humans have developed the technology to send manned missions to other worlds. What would we do if we journeyed to a planet, only to discover sentient beings living there? These beings possess technology far inferior to ours; in fact, they seem downright primitive in comparison. What would we do?

Humans would have three options: 1) leave to find another planet or go home; 2) introduce ourselves to the natives; or 3) observe without being detected.

I doubt we would choose option one. We go to other planets in search of life. Yet option two could cause conflict. We might frighten the natives, or they might see us as invaders. We could introduce diseases to them, or they could infect us with their diseases. Nobody would want to risk that, especially since it has already happened in our past when people from one part of the world traveled to a new part of the world they had never visited before. In fact, we still risk this today anytime we travel to a foreign country.

Figure 13.4: Why wouldn't aliens send probes to planets like Earth? After all, we send probes to other worlds—probes like Voyager 1 and Voyager 2, which sent back photos like this one of Jupiter's "red spot," a giant storm. Photo courtesy of NASA/JPL-Caltech.

Option three would give us the freedom to observe an alien race without interfering in their development or risking contamination on either side. Sound familiar? This idea has become familiar to many of us from the television series *Star Trek* and its spinoff movies. In *Star Trek*, they called this concept the Prime Directive. If we traveled to other planets, it seems logical that we'd follow a similar rule. We have learned from past mistakes in exploration. Scientists today worry about the contamination unmanned probes could cause to other worlds, such as the probe they'd like to send to Jupiter's moon Europa to dive down below its icy surface into the depths of its hidden oceans.

Back in 1967, before the first man landed on the moon, the U.S. and other nations signed a U.N. treaty dealing with the possibility of contaminating extraterrestrial worlds during exploration. The treaty requires nations to examine the risks of contamination and adopt protocols to prevent or minimize it. Considering that at least a hundred microbes can survive on a single square millimeter of human skin, the task is daunting. Radiation does not necessarily kill microorganisms. Some animals can even survive the vacuum and radiation found in space—like the tiny invertebrates (creatures without internal skeletons) known as tardigrades. Nicknamed water bears, these little guys have demonstrated in experiments their amazingly hardy nature. Neither the vacuum of space nor space radiation could destroy them.

Life is hard to stop, even in outer space.

Now consider UFOs. An alien race with advanced technology frequents our world, avoiding direct contact for the most part but enjoying the chance to toy with us. To them, we are nothing more than animals. Earth serves as their wildlife park. They come to observe, to keep us in line, to monitor the animal life. They take samples of that life back to their ships for study. They engage in experiments to see how the humans will react if they drop off a shipload of Bigfoot in one spot.

For us, a wave of sightings ensues. For the aliens, the experiment grows tiresome and they collect their Bigfoot specimens to return them to their home in the remote woods. For us, the wave of sightings ends abruptly. We are left to wonder where the Bigfoot went and why we can't find them again.

As discussed in Chapter 8, a definite trickster element runs through UFO and Bigfoot sightings. From the beings who pilot UFOs to the beings who appear to us as Bigfoot, whatever lies behind these phenomena clearly enjoys toying with us. Perhaps the trickster element is less of a "fringe" topic in ufology, but in Bigfoot research the notion lingers at the outskirts of acceptable topics. Discussing such things invites ridiculed, and invariably leads to the question of why anyone would want to taint Bigfoot research with ideas drawn from the "lunatic fringe."

The Evolution Connection

If we dare to examine the trickster element, doors open up for us. Why do these phenomena toy with us? Is it possible that the beings who operate

UFOs have undertaken research similar to our own? Perhaps to these beings our home planet as a laboratory, a zoo, or just a fun destination for summer vacation. If we consider the research angle, then Bigfoot might play a central role in their experiments.

Consider the Cambrian Explosion, a time 500 million years ago when life erupted into countless bizarre varieties of life-forms. The Cambrian Explosion remains a mystery. How did it happen? Why did it happen? A mass extinction later wiped out most of the Cambrian creatures. Throughout our planet's history, life has gone through cycles where life blossoms then is struck down by mass extinction.

Could a connection exist between the cycle of extinctions, the Cambrian Explosion, and evolution? Imagine an alien race first visited our world eons ago. They found primitive life-forms, bacteria and the like. These aliens possess advanced technology. They see a primeval world in need of molding. A great experiment ensues.

The aliens tinker with the life-forms already present on Earth. They create a mind-boggling array of creatures, just to see if they can. Maybe the creatures they made eventually got too wild, or perhaps the aliens got bored with them. Either way, they decided to make a fresh start. They lob an asteroid at Earth, or perhaps use a weapon that leaves a meteor-like crater. Bam! Extinction.

The aliens could've repeated this cycle many times. Cook up some life-forms, study them, kill them off, and start again with a new batch. Human researchers will use animals in their experiments, then kill the animals once they've completed their study. Human researchers also try to create new life-forms. A truly disturbing trend in science is the creation of transgenic animals. In transgenics, the genome of an animal is altered via the introduction of foreign DNA. From glow-in-the-dark mice to goats that make spider webs, scientists are creating these animals today for use in laboratory experiments.

What does any of this have to do with Bigfoot? The evidence we've examined so far suggests three things:

- UFOs have visited our planet for hundreds of thousands, perhaps millions, of years.
- UFOs and Bigfoot-like creatures share a connection.
- The ancient hominids (Homo erectus, etc.) share more in common with Bigfoot than with human beings.

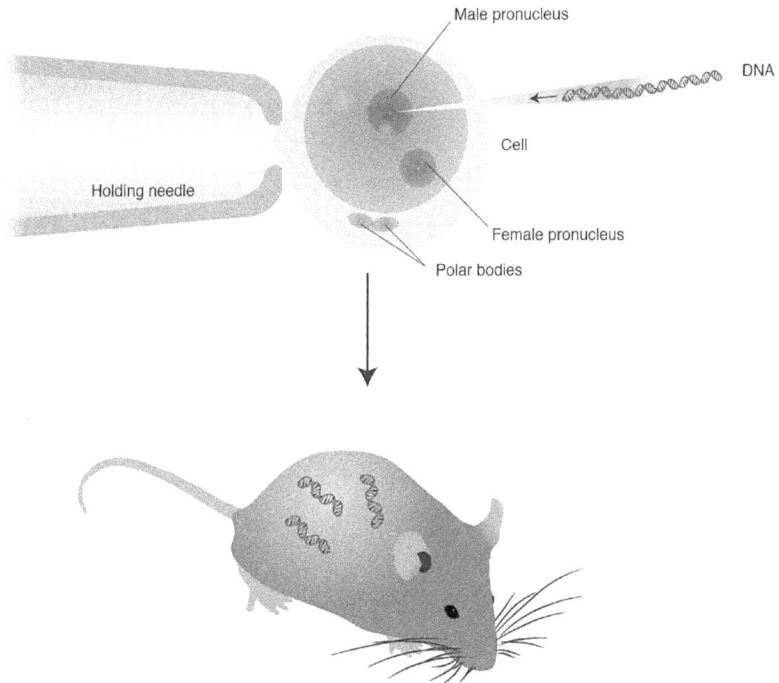

Figure 13.5: This illustration shows how foreign DNA is inserted into a fertilized egg or embryo, thus creating a transgenic creature. Image by Darryl Leja, National Human Genome Research Institute.

Hominid species seem to pop up from nowhere, then gradually fade away. The evolutionary family tree contains so many branches that anthropologists can't agree on how to link the branches, or even where exactly to split the branches. Now consider transgenics.

What if, millions of years ago, the UFO entities decided to experiment with transgenics? They took an embryo from an apelike creature and inserted their own DNA into the embryo's genome. Maybe the offspring didn't turn out quite like they had planned. So they try again. And again. Eventually, they get what they wanted—a bipedal, intelligent creature well adapted to life in the wild, a creature that could serve as a workhorse. What creature has the requisite strength?

Bigfoot.

Transgenics is not science fiction. Today we have genetically modified food, as well as genetically modified living things. If we can do it, so can "they." And if the unknown entities behind the scenes of these paranormal phenomena have developed technology far in advance of ours, as the evidence suggests, then their transgenics probably makes ours look like the tinkering of children.

This is one hypothesis. Is it accurate? Is it total nonsense? Nobody knows for certain either way, just as nobody knows much of anything about Bigfoot for certain. If one day someone proves Bigfoot and UFOs have no connection to one another, then at least we'll know *one* thing for sure. If one day someone proves scientifically and irrefutably that the Bigfoot species is nothing but an unusual type of ape, then at least *one* mystery will be solved. But before any researchers can attempt to answer any of the questions surrounding Bigfoot, they must be willing to talk about all aspects of the phenomenon—even the disturbing and baffling ones.

If we ever hope to understand the Bigfoot mystery, we must approach it with open minds, not domgatism and ridicule.

Ancient Bigfoot

How long has Bigfoot existed? The media and debunkers might say Bigfoot has been around since the 1950s, when one or maybe two guys hoaxed some footprints in the Pacific Northwest. Yet an ever-growing pile of intriguing circumstantial evidence suggests that Bigfoot has existed for much, much longer.

Historical Evidence

Beginning in 2010 and ending in June 2012, an exhibit at the Washington State History Museum in Tacoma explored the long history of Bigfoot legends and sightings. Focusing on the Pacific Northwest, the exhibit included ancient Indian artifacts that depict apelike-yet-humanoid creatures. Peoples around the world have left us similar artifacts that suggest humans have encountered Bigfoot-type creatures throughout history.

Bigfoot Art

The earliest artwork dates to a period called the Paleolithic (literally, "old stone"), commonly called the Stone Age, which began about 4 million years ago. Figurines dated to this period depict beings with features reminiscent of Bigfoot. For instance, an artifact unearthed in Dolní Vestonice (Czech Republic) shows the head of a humanoid with a pronounced brow ridge and facial features reminiscent of the creature seen in the Patterson-Gimlin film of 1967. Lines on the carving also suggest a hairy neck and, by extension, body. In my book *Backyard Bigfoot*, I discussed at length ancient artwork that may represent Bigfoot-type creatures.

I believe ancient artwork from around the world illustrates the presence of hairy hominids far back in human history. Archaeologists, on the other hand, look at the artwork and see "earth-mother goddesses" or fertility symbols. When I look at ancient artwork, such as cave paintings or petroglyphs, I strive to view them in a straightforward manner. I don't look for arcane religious symbolism, for which there is no solid evidence, since ancient peoples left no written records. If the figure in a cave painting or ancient statuette looks like a Bigfoot, why shouldn't it be one?

We have a tendency to view history through the lens of modernity. We think of ourselves as representing the pinnacle of social and technological evolution. Ancient people were superstitious simpletons. They worshiped big stones—or so we presume. How smart could they be?

Yet monuments like Stonehenge and the Great Pyramid at Giza tell a different story. If we accept that ancient peoples had the smarts to build sophisticated monuments, then we should look at their artwork as equally sophisticated and realistic. The cave paintings of Europe evidence a level of sophistication and realism not seen again until the Renaissance. If ancient artists painted something that looks like a Bigfoot or a UFO, we should take it at face value.

Ancient people may well have succumbed to superstition on occasion, just as modern people do. Some of the ancient artwork may represent superstitious symbols. However, we also know that ancient peoples represented real animals in their art. Take, for instance, the cave art of Europe. The artists painted realistic bison and other animals. Ancient artists of the American Southwest also painted real animals. If we see a large, bipedal, humanlike-yet-not-human figure alongside a realistic representation of a bison, why should we assume the bison is real yet the figure is symbolic?

Consider the context, as archaeologists love to say. A realistic, known animal alongside an unknown biped provides a realistic context for the bipedal figure.

Ancient Artwork

Figure 14.1: Might ancient artwork depict Bigfoot-type creatures? These three examples bear intriguing similarities to descriptions and photographic evidence of Bigfoot's appearance. A mammoth-ivory carving from Dolní Vestonice (A), Czech Republic, dates to about 24,000 BC. Another ivory figurine (B), this time from the ancient Dorset culture of Greenland and eastern Canada, dates to between 600 and 900 AD. A wooden figurine (C) attributed to the Thule culture—an ancient people who spread from Alaska eastward into Greenland and are thought to be the ancestors of modern Inuits—dates to about 1000 AD. Drawings by Kerrie Shiel.

Wild Men

Although in many people's minds the Pacific Northwest is *the* hot spot for Bigfoot, the phenomenon spreads around the world and throughout history. In the nineteenth century, traveling sideshows frequently showcased a "wild man of Borneo," often a hoax but inspired by real sightings of wild men (hairy, bipedal creatures). In researching my book *Forgotten Tales of Michigan's Upper Peninsula*, I dug up dozens of newspaper stories from the nineteenth and early twentieth centuries about mysterious wild men roaming the woods of the Upper Peninsula. Even back then, debunkers found silly excuses to dismiss the sightings. A common scapegoat was escaped mental patients. John Doe broke out of the mental hospital, therefore he must be the wild man seen 200 miles away.

These "wild men" generally matched a description similar to that of the creatures we call Bigfoot today. Hair covered their bodies and they wore no clothes. They made strange cries and screams, threw objects at surprised witnesses, and stuck to the woods. One such being terrorized the western U.P. back in 1901.

The incidence unfolded in the woods near the town of Crystal Falls, which sits a stone's throw from the Wisconsin border. First, a group of hunters happened upon the "wild man" along the banks of the Deer River. They observed the creature consuming a skunk, then the beast noticed his observers and snarled at them before bolting into the deeper woods. Several more sightings occurred, including one

Figure 14.2: A dancer from the Kwakiutl tribe of British Columbia, dressed in garb representing a "wild man of the woods." Photo courtesy of the Library of Congress, Prints & Photographs Division, Edward S. Curtis Collection, LC-USZ62-52220.

instance when the wild man gave a tough lumberjack quite a start by unleashing a series of cries the witness described as "unearthly yells." Despite a three-day search, authorities never found the wild man.

Whenever we talk about Bigfoot we must remember the deep history of legends and sightings. Though sightings from before modern times are easy to dismiss, and ancient artwork hardly offers concrete evidence, both types of historical evidence presents us with intriguing clues. These lines of evidence also demonstrate that the idea of Bigfoot creatures, unlike the term Bigfoot, are not a modern invention.

The antiquity of Bigfoot leads to a question. In what ways might ancient humans have interacted with Bigfoot?

Mystery of the Big Stones

Around the world, mysterious ancient races built enormous monuments out of equally enormous stone blocks often referred to as megaliths (literally, "big stones"). Megalithic sites include Stonehenge in Britain, the Giza pyramids in Egypt, the temple of Baalbek in Lebanon, and Sacsayhuaman in Peru. Archaeologists insist the ancients used rudimentary methods to construct these megalithic monuments—sledges rolled across logs or hauled up long ramps, megaliths tilted down into pits to raise them vertically, ramps to drag the stones up to great heights, tools made of soft metals like copper, and other similar methods. Why would ancient people go to so much trouble?

Figure 14.3: Like the monuments at Giza, Stonehenge in England's Wiltshire region was built from massive stone blocks up to 24 feet high. Some of the stones were transported a great distance from the Preseli Mountains in Wales. Stonehenge is at least 5,000 years old. Photo courtesy of the Central Intelligence Agency.

Archaeologists also explain away the dilemma of why. They proclaim that the ancients made these monuments for religious purposes. Because they were so pious, they toiled for decades to construct monuments out of huge, unwieldy stones when much smaller stones would've gotten the job done equally as well. But what if the ancient builders didn't toil at all? What if they built megalithic structures because it was easy for them to do so?

The ruins at Tiahuanaco in Bolivia include a massive stone structure known as the Gateway of the Sun (a modern name, since no one knows what its builders called it). The structure weighs an estimated ten tons and was hewn from a single slab, making it a true megalith. Sacsayhuaman in Peru includes walls made out of even larger megaliths, each carved into an irregular polygon shaped, all of them fitted together so tightly a sheet of paper can't fit between them. Many of the megaliths at Sacsayhuaman weigh one hundred tons or more, and some of these enormous stones were lifted up to form lintels for gateways. Other megalithic sites include stones of similar or greater size, and involved similar feats of construction.

Why bother?

Thanks to the TV show *Ancient Aliens*, the idea that aliens may have influenced human development and culture has become well known,

Figure 14.4: On Egypt's Giza Plateau sit the Great Pyramid, the Sphinx, associated temples, and two more large pyramids, along with several smaller ones. These structures were built mostly from huge blocks of stone, some of which originated hundreds of miles away. The Giza monuments are over 4,000 years old at a minimum. Photo courtesy of the Central Intelligence Agency.

even to people who have never read a book by Erich von Daniken. The idea is often labeled the "ancient astronaut" theory. Mainly, the theory contends that evidence found in myths and artwork from ancient civilizations points to an alien presence on Earth throughout human history. The theory is often extended to encompass the mind-boggling engineering feats of ancient cultures, explaining those accomplishments as the result of alien technology.

Ancient Apocalypse

Pictorial and textual evidence does offer tantalizing evidence that UFOs may have visited our planet since the dawn of time. I firmly believe that aliens have visited our planet in the past and continue to visit us today. However, I am not convinced that aliens ever gave us technology. I believe human beings are responsible for those mind-boggling feats of engineering. Advanced human civilizations could've arisen in the distant past, only to be wiped out by natural disasters. As recently as about 74,000 years ago, the Toba volcano on the Indonesian island of Sumatra erupted. The Toba eruption stands as the largest known volcanic eruption in the last two million years, leading scientists to label it a supervolcanic eruption.

A volcanic event of this scale certainly triggered global devastation. It's even been suggested that the Toba eruption caused a population bottleneck, a catastrophe in which so many humans died that it caused a constriction in the genetic diversity of our entire species. Geneticists do claim to have found evidence of an ancient bottleneck, buried in the DNA of modern humans. This has led some scientists to blame the Toba eruption for the bottleneck. Yet

Figure 14.5: The Toba caldera, remnants of a supervolcano, as it looks today. Image courtesy of NASA/GSFC/MITI/ERSDAC/JAROS, and the U.S./Japan ASTER Science Team.

no one can agree on when the genetic bottleneck occurred, and a study of mammal fossils from the time period of the Toba eruption revealed no obvious die-off of animals.

Nevertheless, and eruption on the scale of Toba must've caused devastation. Any human civilization existing at the time, however advanced, would have suffered both from the initial impact of the eruption and from its aftermath. The study of ice cores, long shafts of ice drilled out of frozen places like Antarctica, suggests that the Toba eruption triggered a "volcanic winter" that lasted for centuries. A cataclysm on the scale of Toba could easily wipe out the sophisticated civilization. And Toba was not the only cataclysm in the relatively recent history of our planet. The advances and retreats of glaciers, which covered vast swaths of the globe at various times in the past, scoured the earth's surface. Smaller, yet still devastating, volcanic eruptions erased whole regions. The 79 AD eruption of Mount Vesuvius in Italy destroyed the Roman cities of Pompeii and Herculaneum. Only by an accident of fate did remnants of those towns survive for archaeologists to unearth them nearly 2,000 years later.

A number of researchers have suggested that the flood myths we find all around the world, including the biblical tale of Noah, represent cultural memories of a global cataclysm. In his book *Underworld*, Graham Hancock presents intriguing scientific evidence that sea levels rose catastrophically at the end of the last Ice Age, about 17,000 years ago. Before the hypothesized flood, sea levels measured nearly 400 feet lower than today. The English Channel had not yet formed, meaning that dry land connected southern England to France. Entire islands that once protruded from the Mediterranean Sea now lie sunken. Coastlines around the world included significantly more land than they do today. Australia, Tasmania, and New Guinea constituted a single landmass known as Sahul. In fact, according to Hancock, geologists estimate that we've lost 5% of our planet's surface area due to the melting of the glaciers at the end of the last Ice Age. Though 5% may not sound like much, it equates to about the same amount of land found in the United States and South America combined.

Who knows what may lie under the waters of our modern oceans. Who knows what evidence of ancient advanced civilizations may have been washed away by the cataclysmic surging of sea levels when the last ice age ended. As with volcanic disasters, the cataclysmic flood holds the power to destroy entire civilizations. In December 2004, an undersea earthquake off the coast of Sumatra generated a massive tsunami that killed nearly 230,000 people. Now imagine this kind of horrifying destruction expanded to a worldwide event. This scenario may have played out thousands of years ago.

Volcanic eruptions and massive floods represent just two of the possibilities for worldwide catastrophes. Both possess the power to decimate human populations and certainly to annihilate cities, possibly even whole civilizations.

What types of materials would survive for thousands of years? Stone, for sure. Metal might, given the right conditions, but even metal cannot last forever. Human civilizations of the distant past may have preferred stone over metal or other materials, for reasons we can't fathom. We should not assume ancient cultures, even advanced ones, would've used the same materials and technologies that we use. Stone structures like Sacsayhuaman, Tiahuanaco, and Stonehenge present difficulties in terms of dating their construction. No one can say for certain when these structures were built.

Figure 14.6: The 2004 tsunami, triggered by an earthquake off the coast of Sumatra, caused significant damage even thousands of miles away in American Samoa. Photo by Dr. Bruce Jaffe, U.S. Geological Survey.

Lost Civilizations

How did the ancients build their monuments with such precision? How did any of the astonishingly precise monuments found around the world, and attributed to various ancient cultures, come to be? Stone tools won't hack it. Copper hammers won't either. And when we consider that many of these monuments contain astoundingly large, heavy slabs of stone, the mystery deepens.

The answer may be both simple and complex. Those ancient cultures must've possessed technology far more advanced than archaeologists like to believe, but that technology was likely also quite different from anything we use today. Therefore, we may run into great difficulty when trying to puzzle out how the ancients did what they did. Does this mean we need to turn to aliens for the answers? Just because we can't figure out how it was accomplished doesn't mean humans aren't responsible.

Evidence for lost, technologically advanced civilizations has been uncovered. Such evidence forks down two different but related paths: 1) the existence of modern humans in anomalously ancient times, and 2) the possibility of anomalously advanced civilizations in prehistoric times. In their book *Forbidden Archeology*, Michael Cremo and Richard Thompson provide nearly a thousand pages worth of evidence for the first possibility. For example, in 1899 a human femur was discovered near Trenton, New Jersey, in geological deposits dating to approximately 107,000 years ago. Modern humans were supposed to have not left Africa yet at that time, much less emigrated to North America. In the 1850s, a skeleton turned up at Savona, Italy, in deposits dated to the Pliocene epoch, which spans the time period from 5.3 million to 1.8 million years ago. Even in Europe, relatively close to the so-called Cradle of Humankind in Africa, no modern humans should've been alive during that epoch.

Also in the nineteenth century, different kinds of evidence leading to similar conclusions were discovered around the world. A shell found in England in deposits 2 to 2.5 million years old had a human face carved onto its surface. A copper object resembling a coin turned up in Illinois, dug out of deposits approximately 200,000 to 400,000 years old. The object had symbols and humanoid figures etched onto it. In 1928, miners working in an Oklahoma coal mine reportedly found a concrete block wall and a barrel-shaped block of silver two miles into the mine. The most stunning example of anomalous evidence, however, comes in the form of a metallic sphere with grooves etched around its middle. The grooves appear so carefully etched that they seem to have been machined, or at least carved by human hands. The sphere was discovered during the twentieth century in a South African mine—within 2.8 billion-year-old deposits. Yes, that's 2.8 *billion*!

Figure 14.7: The two faces of the coin-like copper object found in Illinois, which has been dated to at least 200,000 years ago. Drawing from *Sparks from a Geologist's Hammer* by Alexander Winchell, published 1881.

Although none of this evidence qualifies as conclusive, at least according to mainstream scientists of today, the existence of such evidence points to a shocking conclusion. Human beings may have existed for far longer than the few hundred thousand years scientists allot to our species.

A Little Help

Perhaps the ancient builders marshaled more than technology to help them build the megalithic monuments. Perhaps they had help from beings much stronger than themselves—beings capable of hacking gigantic stones out of the earth, transporting those stones with ease, and hefting them up as high as needed. The ancient builders may have used a combination of technology and muscle power. But those muscles didn't belong to humans.

They belonged to Bigfoot.

Why not? The idea makes as much sense as the fanciful theories proposed by archaeologists. Evidence suggests Bigfoot have existed as a species for a long, long time. Eyewitness testimony indicates that these creatures are very, very strong. With advanced technology and powerful, if nonhuman, workers on their side, the ancient builders would've had little trouble erecting megalithic structures.

Perhaps ancient peoples built megalithic monuments for practical, rather than superstitious, reasons. Building with megaliths might've proven more efficient for them, given their technology and resources. Why waste time piecing together many small pieces when they could slam together giant rocks in a jiffy? With the help of their powerful, hairy neighbors, they might've needed far less than twenty years to construct a monument like the Great Pyramid.

Well, why not?

Bigfoot Wars

Ancient artwork from around the world appears to depict hairy hominids. In many of the same locales, humans retreated into barely accessible areas, clearly hiding from something. But what?

In the Americas, many mysterious tribes inhabited the land thousands of years ago—the Hohokam, Anasazi, and Fremont of the Four Corners region; the Mississippians of the central U.S.; the Olmec of Mesoamerica; and the enigmatic architects of the monumental structures in South America, such as Macchu Picchu and Sacsayhuaman. In Europe, during the Paleolithic, humans crawled deep inside caves to remote, hard-to-reach spots where they stayed long enough to paint masterpieces on the walls. In Turkey, at various points in ancient history, residents of the Cappadocia region carved out underground cities and fortresses. Why did ancient people go to such lengths to hide themselves?

Consider the Anasazi. They first emerged, according to mainstream archaeology, around 200 BC and by 1300 AD they'd vanished. In late thirteenth century AD, the Anasazi did something strange—they began to build fortresses high up in steep cliffs that modern people find next to impossible to access. Some of the cliff dwellings lie near springs, but many do not. In fact, the majority of them lie in or on the boundaries of winding networks of canyons. Kiet Seel, a cliff dwelling in Arizona, houses 155 rooms. The largest of the cliff-top fortresses, Cliff Palace at Mesa Verde in Colorado, features 200 rooms. Cliff Palace perches high up on a cliff face, under a rock overhang. Archaeological evidence shows the people lived in these fortresses for long periods. Why would the Anasazi create virtually inaccessible homes, after years of constructing ground-based structures?

Evidence points to warfare. Archaeologists have discovered headless skeletons, skeletons with smash skulls, and evidence that fires devastated Anasazi strongholds. These ancient people died violent deaths at a time when, as a culture, they abruptly decided to desert their comfortable

Ancient Fortresses

Figure 14.8: The Anasazi, a mysterious people who lived in ancient America, built enigmatic and imposing structures that are hard to reach and would be even harder to attack. Cliff Palace (top) at Mesa Verde in Colorado clings to the side of a steep cliff. At Hovenweep (bottom), on the Utah/Colorado border, lie the remnants of one of many watchtower-like structures built by the Anasazi. Photos courtesy of the National Park Service.

accommodations atop mesas and in valleys. They moved into fortified villages and, oddest of all, dwellings tucked into cliff faces high above the valley floors. Cliff dwellings incorporated multiple rooms and multiple stories, evidencing their use as homes rather than simply military outposts. The Anasazi also built imposing stone towers at strategic locations throughout their territory. Then a few hundred years later, just as mysteriously and suddenly as they had switched their living habits, the Anasazi abandoned their homeland.

The cliff dwellings protected them from two kinds of threats—those from the ground and those from the sky. What fierce enemy could reside on the ground and have a connection to the sky? What enemy possessed enough strength to overwhelm the Anasazi, to the point where retreating into inaccessible cliff fortresses in inaccessible canyons seemed the only option?

Next, consider ancient Europeans. Paleolithic peoples of Europe lived in their own version of a hard-to-access homestead. They retreated into deep, narrow caves—many so difficult to reach that people must've crawled backward into them. In these caves, the ancient Europeans painted some of the most beautiful and sophisticated artwork in human history. Some of the artwork created by Paleolithic Europeans seems to depict hairy hominids. The caves, however, served as more than art galleries. Ice-age humans lived in them, or at least hid in them for extended periods. Evidence of hearths and the existence of fossilized footprints, sometimes found hundreds of feet inside the caves, points to more than a ritual significance for these cave art sites. In the bowels of the cave at Niaux, France, hundreds of fossilized footprints demonstrate that both children and adults frequented the cave.

Paleolithic cave art emerged around 30,000 years ago, according to mainstream estimates. Some cave art sites, like France's Lascaux, contain large chambers. Nearly all the cave art sites lie deep underground. The Paleolithic people also lived in rock shelters—ledges shielded by overhangs, situated on the sides of cliffs. Like the Anasazi, they seemed intent on shielding themselves from the skies. We might dismiss rock shelters as simply places to hide from rain and other inclement weather, but no one needed to crawl hundreds of feet into barely accessible caves to escape the weather.

With the Paleolithic caves, archaeologists tell us the people used them for religious ceremonies, despite the evidence that adults and children occupied the caves and the lack of evidence for religious activities. No one knows what religious ceremonies, if any, the Paleolithic people performed since they left no written record. Why would ancient Europeans, like ancient Americans, hide? They needed protection from the ground, from a threat too powerful to fend off in the open. They needed fortresses they could block off more easily, fortresses to protect them from the sky and the ground.

The ancient inhabitants of Turkey also went to a lot of trouble both to hide and to fend off an unknown enemy. These ancient people carved out whole underground cities in the region of Turkey today known as Cappadocia. Some archaeologists attribute the earlier underground structures to the Hittites, an ancient superpower on a par with Egypt, who reached their heyday during the thirteenth century BC. No one knows for certain, however, what culture created the subterranean cities because some of them seem to date to an earlier time than even the Hittites.

What we do know is that the underground structures of Cappadocia are vast, sophisticated, and heavily fortified. In fact, we might more accurately call them underground fortresses. These underground complexes contain multiple levels with air shafts, wells, chimneys, rooms for food storage, and

Figure 14.9: This is just one of the massive stone disks used to block the doorways of ancient underground structures in the Cappadocia region of Turkey. Photo © iStockPhoto.com/Claudio Beduschi.

accommodations for waste disposal. From inside the fortress, residents could seal themselves off by rolling huge stone disks three to five feet in diameter across the doorways. Tunnels miles long connected these subterranean fortresses that lay scattered across the area. Soot coating the walls and ceilings testifies to the frequent use of torches, which suggests people hid in these fortresses for extended periods.

Why take such extreme measures to elude a human enemy? Perhaps the ancient people of Cappadocia needed extreme measures to fend off an extraordinarily powerful enemy. Perhaps they faced a similar enemy as the Paleolithic Europeans before them and the Anasazi of the Americas after them. Archaeologists say the Hittites built their underground fortresses to fight off the Sea Peoples. Yet the ancient Egyptians fought the Sea Peoples too—without underground fortifications. Maybe the Sea Peoples weren't the enemy the Hittites feared most. Maybe the enemy wasn't even human.

The fortifications employed by the Hittites suggest several characteristics of their enemy:

1. Great strength.
2. Dominance over the land and sky.
3. An ongoing presence throughout history and around the globe.

In other words, the enemy was hard to kill and harder to hide from because they weren't tied to the ground like the ordinary folks of the ancient world. What kind of enemy would have those characteristics?

Maybe, just maybe, their enemy wasn't human. Maybe they hid from hairy, bipedal creatures who worked together with sky-based entities. Maybe their enemy was Bigfoot and their UFO kin.

Of course, this is all conjecture. But so is virtually everything we "know" about Bigfoot and much of what we think we know about ancient history. Did ancient people battle Bigfoot and their UFO buddies? Did they build hidden fortresses to fend off this powerful enemy?

We may never know for certain.

15
A Universe of Theories

Anyone who seriously studies the topic of Bigfoot must come to accept one simple, if undesirable, fact. We know next to nothing about Bigfoot. We can't even prove irrefutably, much less scientifically, that these creatures exist. Virtually everything we say about Bigfoot is conjecture—albeit, hopefully, based on an examination of the available evidence.

Some researchers may engage in various unethical practices, such as

- throwing out data that displeases them,
- exaggerating the quality of the evidence,
- ridiculing anyone who disagrees with them,
- ignoring certain facets of the phenomenon that disturb them,
- and worst of all, fabricating evidence.

Why do some people resort to unethical behavior? Some do it deliberately, but others slide into this behavior unconsciously because they simply cannot handle what the evidence suggests. Researchers who deliberately engage in unethical behavior do it for money, for fame and glory, due to mental unbalance, or some combination of the above.

One of the main issues hindering Bigfoot research is the double-edged sword of theories. On one side, we find researchers who eschew theorizing because they claim not having any opinions or ideas about Bigfoot makes them more scientific. On the other side, we encounter the people who find a theory and cling onto it with all their might no matter how flimsy the evidence for the theory might be and no matter how much evidence piles up against it. Outsiders gazing in the community of Bigfoot researchers might conclude that only two options exist—not theorizing at all, or selecting one theory to cherish forever.

Yet theorizing need not to turn into an either/or situation. Analyzing the evidence should lead to conclusions, which in layman's terms we call theories. A theory may be proposed, then later discarded. Given how little we know (versus believe) about Bigfoot, we ought to feel free to propose theories about any aspect of the phenomenon. These ideas, necessarily based on inconclusive evidence, should not be limited by what we think mainstream science might accept or buy what fits within our personal comfort zones. The truth is that mainstream scientists will scoff at anything to do with Bigfoot, and cowering within our comfort zones serves only to hinder our research.

If we step outside the bright light within our personal zones, into the twilight beyond, who knows what we might discover?

In this book, I've presented a number of theories—some rooted in scientific evidence, some relying on more abstract reasoning, and still others based chiefly on my opinions. I've spent years poring over books and articles about topics as varied as theoretical physics, psychic phenomena, ancient history, Bigfoot and other legendary creatures, and anything else that struck my fancy. Thus, even my wackiest theories about Bigfoot rest on a foundation of concrete knowledge. Maybe no one else would bother keeping an eye out for possible connections between Bigfoot, ancient megalithic structures, and Anasazi cliff dwellings. Maybe that's the problem with Bigfoot research.

Most Bigfoot researchers seem unwilling to draw connections.

Are any of my theories correct? The better question might be, are anyone's theories correct. For now, no one can answer these questions. Perhaps one day we will find the elusive "ultimate proof" that Bigfoot exists, coupled with irrefutable proof of what they are. This is the holy grail of Bigfoot research. It may also prove to be the cryptozoological version of fool's gold.

Does this mean we should stop searching? No. But anyone venturing into the field of Bigfoot research ought to start by understanding and accepting the limitations of such research. Only then do we free ourselves to explore all avenues, where ever the evidence may lead.

Let's recap the theories I've presented in this book:

1. **All paranormal phenomena are connected.** From Bigfoot to UFOs to fairies to psychic phenomena, and everywhere in between, paranormal phenomena exhibit similarities and connections. They cross the boundaries we draw out for them. They taunt us. If we listen to the evidence, what might we discover?

2. **Synchronicities are meaningful.** Bigfoot and UFOs seem to share some kind of connection, and direct sightings of the two together represent the tip of the metaphorical iceberg. Some locations host both the Bigfoot and UFO sightings, though separately. Another synchronicity lies in which states host the most reported sightings of the two phenomena. What mysteries might resolve by diving into the ocean of synchronicities?

Figure 15.1: Might Bigfoot have a connection to ancient megalithic monuments? Newgrange (shown above) is one such megalithic site in Ireland. The so-called tomb may not really be a burial place, but perhaps it's another fortress to defend against a powerful, unknown enemy. Newgrange also illustrates another interesting fact—that certain symbols are universal, found at prehistoric sites around the world. In this case, the symbol is the spiral. What does it mean? No one knows. Image © iStockPhoto.com/UnaPhoto.

3. **Bigfoot is unusually elusive.** No zoo in the world houses a Bigfoot. No museums display stuffed Bigfoot. The overwhelming majority of Bigfoot witnesses experience brief, fleeting encounters. Video and photographic evidence has proven inconclusive, and usually so blurry no one can tell what the image shows. DNA purported to come from Bigfoot leads to inconclusive results. Why has Bigfoot turned out to be the most elusive species on earth?

4. **Bigfoot resembles fossil hominids far more than apes.** The famous, or perhaps infamous, *Gigantopithecus* theory lacks anything resembling solid evidence. The fossil record does, however, contain evidence relevant to Bigfoot research. If we compare the fossil hominids to Bigfoot, we find that these two types of creatures resemble each other far more than either of them resembles human beings. Might Bigfoot be a descendent of those ancient hominids?

5. **Historical evidence points to the deep history of Bigfoot.** Ancient artwork seems to depict Bigfoot-type creatures at least as far back as the Paleolithic. Sightings of "wild men," whose descriptions mirror those of Bigfoot, date back hundreds of years. How long might Bigfoot have coexisted with us?

6. **Bigfoot could've helped build megalithic monuments.** They certainly possess the strength required to hew gigantic stones out of the earth, as well as to transport those stones and use them to build megalithic structures. Why wouldn't an ancient human society have taken advantage of this natural resource for labor?

7. **Bigfoot could've fought with ancient humans.** All over the world, at specific points in time, ancient human populations sought refuge deep in caves and high on cliff faces. They hid from a powerful, unknown enemy. Might Bigfoot have played a role in terrorizing ancient peoples?

Some of these theories are uniquely mine, and others have been proposed before by different researchers. When it comes to Bigfoot, evidence is abundant—if not conclusive or concrete. If we ever hope to dig any answers out of the mounds of evidence heaps at our feet, we must be willing to examine all the clues. We must take a chance on forming opinions and developing theories, and we must risk publicly exposing those opinions and theories. Debunkers, and even other Bigfoot researchers, may ridicule our ideas. But so what?

The gathering of evidence requires research.

Research demands an open mind.

Analyzing the evidence raises questions and suggests conclusions.

Answering those questions demands an open mind.

Accepting and revealing those conclusions...

Well, that may require the greatest effort of all. But daring to theorize, and letting the world know what we've concluded, may offer the best chance we have of figuring out the Bigfoot mystery.

Part Three

Backyard Phenomena

Truth is born into this world only with pangs and tribulations, and every fresh truth is received unwillingly.

Alfred Russel Wallace

16
A Mystery Is Born

Every story has a beginning and an end. But do mysterious phenomena have start lines that we can distinguish? Sometimes they do, most often they don't. When did humans first spot strange lights in the sky and recognize them as something out of the ordinary? When did the first Bigfoot sighting occur? We might pinpoint the first documented sighting of a hairy, bipedal creature or the first written account of bizarre lights in the skies, but we have no way of knowing precisely when these phenomena first emerged. For all anyone knows, they have always existed.

Each individual, however, remembers that first encounter with something unsettling and seemingly inexplicable. I was fourteen when I experienced my first UFO sighting. I was twenty-nine when I first encountered another phenomenon, one for which I would become known within the community of Bigfoot aficionados.

Stick signs.

In 2006, I published my first nonfiction book. *Backyard Bigfoot* dealt with several controversial aspects of the Bigfoot mystery and included what is, as far as I know, the first documented research on the stick sign phenomenon. I had found my first stick sign three years earlier while living in north-central Texas. As I continued to find more and more signs, even after moving to Michigan in 2004, I scoured books, magazines, and websites for any mention of discoveries similar to mine. I found none. Some Bigfoot researchers talked about finding bent saplings, trees snapped off high above the ground, or teepee-like formations made from long sticks. I found not even a passing mention of the kind of signs I was running across on regular a basis.

I joined e-mail lists devoted to Bigfoot. My tentative questions about the stick signs and other strange things I was finding triggered nasty responses from list members. If anyone else found similar signs and mentioned them to Bigfoot researchers, they might've encountered the same ridicule dressed as skepticism. No wonder I found no public discussions of anything similar to what I'd discovered. Yet I became convinced that someone *should* discuss it. As with the Bigfoot-UFO connection, stick signs seemed to engender an inexplicable knee-jerk reaction from the very people who claimed to want to find answers to the Bigfoot mystery. How on earth can we really learn about a phenomenon, however, if we refuse to look at all aspects of it? Even before I stumbled onto the stick sign phenomenon, that question spurred me to embark on a career in Bigfoot research.

Of course, career isn't exactly the right word for it. Yes, some people might get into Bigfoot research in hopes of attaining fame and fortune. Most of us realize this isn't likely to happen. We work day jobs to earn a living, and investigate Bigfoot on the side—as a hobby, or sometimes as an obsession. We do it out of fascination and a genuine interest in learning the truth.

Well, *most* of us want the truth. One class of researchers seems intent on molding the Bigfoot phenomenon to fit their preconceived notions, dismissing or outright denigrating any evidence to the contrary. These researchers deem certain topics, from

Figure 16.1: Who makes stick signs? In my previous book *Backyard Bigfoot*, I presented the theory that—guess who—Bigfoot might be the sign-maker. Artwork by Kerrie Shiel, from the *Backyard Bigfoot* book cover.

the UFO connection to Bigfoot-is-not-an-ape theories, to be thoroughly unacceptable and therefore verboten.

Take stick signs, for example.

The Start Line

I go for walks every day in the woods surrounding my home. I know what was there the day before and what has changed. A downed tree or a new pile of scat (animal feces) will pop out at me as I set out on my daily hikes. Back in Texas in 2003, during one of these walks, I spotted an arrangement of sticks alongside the trail. Two short sticks, perhaps a foot in length apiece and half an inch in diameter, lay one crossed over the other like a plus sign. The formation had not been there the day before and lay away from the edge of the woods, sitting in the open like some sort of marker—though what it marked, I couldn't say. The formation looked so out of place, and so unnatural, that I snapped a photograph of it. Then I forgot about the incident.

Figure 16.2: This was the very first stick sign I ever found, in Texas. November 3, 2003—photo by Lisa A. Shiel.

Until I found another sign. And then another. And another.

Over the years, the evidence mounted—and grew stranger and stranger. Simple plus signs and parallel sticks gave way to more-complicated formations. I started calling these formations stick signs, since they nearly always involved sticks of approximately the same length and diameter. Yet the phenomenon has also grown to involve other media, from reeds to dog bones to scraps of green mesh and even feathers. Other strangeness has cropped up to accompany the stick sign phenomenon as well. Stones that look very much like ancient stone tools

A Typical Stick Sign

Figure 16.3: Sticks signs, like the one above, are often made from two sticks that started out as one. In the photo below, it's clear that the two sticks fit together; the inset shows the broken end of the left-hand stick. May 26, 2005—photos by Lisa A. Shiel.

have turned up far from any possible source of such rocks. Strange balls of light, often called glowing orbs, haunt the very same woods where the stick sign phenomenon occurs. And finally, braids more intricate and precise than any simple tangle have shown up in my horses' manes. This final phenomenon, mane braiding, has been reported around the world and is frequently associated with Bigfoot.

The Culprit

What leads me to conclude Bigfoot is responsible for stick signs? Clearly something or someone creates these purposeful formations. The stick signs stand out from everything around them, as out of place as a whale in the desert. The signs share a number of traits in common with each other that seem to indicate a common source.

Physical Characteristics
- The sticks have been snapped or cut off a branch or larger stick; sometimes the ends can be fit back together to re-form the larger stick. See Figure 16.3 for an example of this.
- They each measure about a foot long.
- Each stick is approximately half an inch in diameter.

Figure 16.4: This photo (left) shows a stick sign and its surroundings, as well as where it lay in relation to my house. The inset provides a close-up of the stick sign itself. May 16, 2007—photos by Lisa A. Shiel.

Other Characteristics

- ↔ Stick signs look distinctly unnatural.
- ↔ The signs appear overnight.
- ↔ No footprints are visible in the vicinity of the signs.
- ↔ They show up along trails, especially pathways forged by horses or wildlife such as deer.
- ↔ The formations often occur in areas where it's unlikely they simply fell onto the ground in a distinctive shape (e.g., in open areas or away from concentrations of fallen sticks). See Figure 16.4 for an example of this.
- ↔ When stick signs include other items, such as reeds or stones, the source of the items is unknown or located too far away for the items to have blown or fallen there.

In the lists above, I mentioned that no footprints show up in the vicinity of stick signs. I have, however, found unusually large humanoid tracks in the same areas where stick signs and other phenomena occur—but the tracks appeared on different days than the stick signs.

Big Evidence

In Texas on August 10, 2004, I discovered just such a track. It appeared in the sandy loam of one of my main walking trails, which was originally blazed by my horses. The footprint measured about twice as long as my shoe and much wider, it lacked the arch visible in human footprints, and the stubby toes lined up almost straight across the front of the print. These are all traits common to tracks attributed to Bigfoot.

A couple years later, two fellow Bigfoot researchers presented me with a gift. It was a plaster cast of a Bigfoot track, a copy of a cast made at the site of perhaps the most famous Bigfoot encounter in history—Bluff Creek, California. The cast given to me is a replica of a footprint left by the creature seen in the Patterson-Gimlin film, the one piece of Bigfoot footage nearly everyone has seen. After receiving the cast, I compared it to photos of the track I found in Texas. The similarities struck me immediately.

The footprint I found looked strikingly similar to the track left by the Bluff Creek Bigfoot.

On the same day that I found the full footprint, I also photographed a second partial footprint. Later, in Michigan, I found a possible footprint

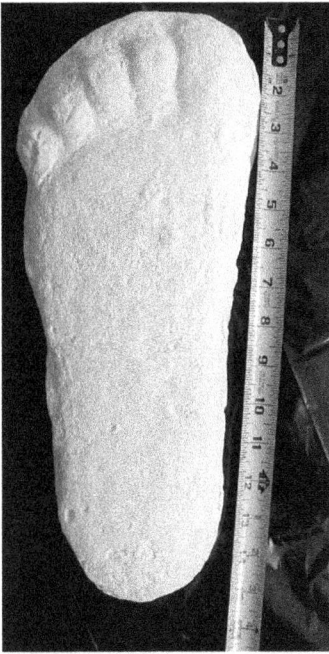

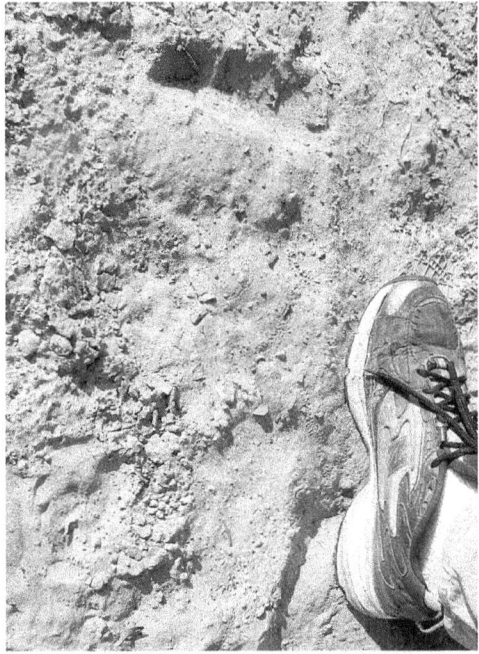

Figure 16.5: On the left is a cast of a track left by the creature in the 1967 Patterson-Gimlin film, taken at Bluff Creek, California; on the right, a track I found near my house in Texas on August 10, 2004. Photos by Walt Shiel (left) and Lisa A. Shiel (right).

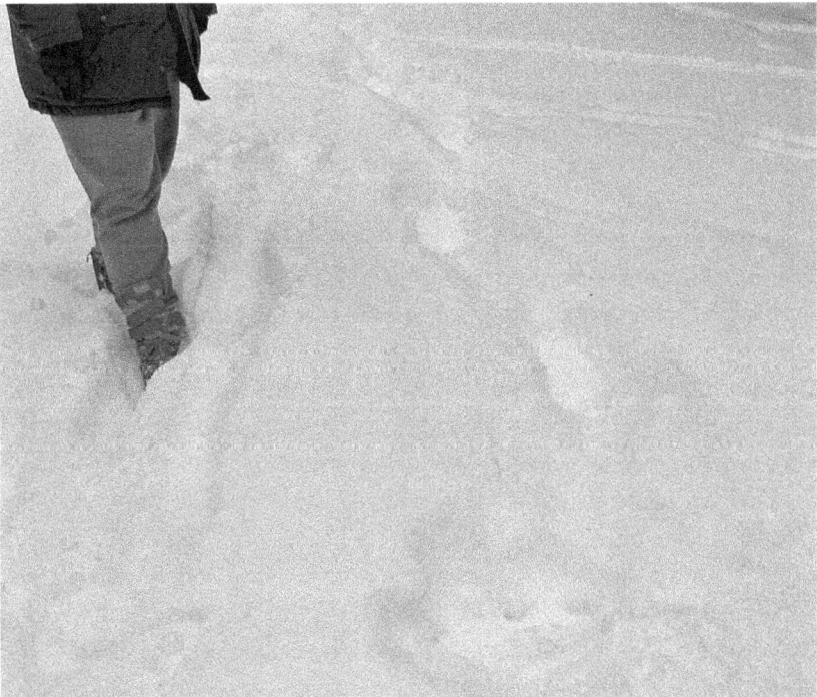

Figure 16.6: These tracks in the snow were not left by horses or deer. February 21, 2007—photo by Lisa A. Shiel.

in a swampy area near my house. Though smaller than the footprint from Texas, it shared many traits in common with that track. Unfortunately, the new track did not photograph well due to the color and texture of the soggy soil. On February 21, 2007, I came across less-distinct tracks in the deep snow. The tracks were not from the horses, or from deer. They had the general shape of humanoid footprints, very large in size. No tread, such as from snow boots, was visible in the tracks.

I've also heard strange whooping sounds and screams like nothing else I've heard in the woods. On April 23, 2005, at 12:45 AM, I awoke because my bedroom had gotten stuffy. I climbed onto my knees to unlatch and open the window above the head of my bed. Just as I slid the window open, the brightest shooting star I've ever seen in my life streaked across the sky above the treetops. I knelt by the window for awhile hoping to see another shooting star. In the distance, a pack of coyotes yipped. After seeing no more meteors for several minutes, I lay back down on the bed. The window I left open.

At that moment, off to the northwest, a creature whooped. The sound was loud, clear, and unmistakable. The vocalization sounded like "eee-YOOP"—a short call, high-pitched with deep undertones, as if it resonated from within a large chest. The call echoed off the trees, which meant it must've originated within the five-acre clearing behind the house. A second later, overlapping voices answered from the distance. A moment after that, a series of thumps issued from behind the house. I jumped up, certain someone was breaking down the basement door. When I looked out the west windows, however, I saw no one. I lay awake for over an hour listening for more calls. None came.

Owls, foxes, and bears can make some weird noises. Yet the whoops, screams, and thumps I've heard remain unidentified and unexplained—although they closely resemble sounds recorded by other Bigfoot researchers, who believe their recordings capture the vocalizations of the creatures we call Bigfoot.

Once I did get a glimpse of something in the woods. While walking along the edge of the woods south of my house, I noticed ravens squawking as they circled above the trees. They seemed especially interested in a small clearing perhaps thirty feet from where I stood. The clearing was well lit, with sunlight streaming down into it. The woods between me and the clearing were darker, though not impenetrable. I gazed through the trees attempting to see what had caught the ravens' attention. Suddenly, a shape caught my eye. Something dark-colored and very tall stood next to a tree. Before I could approach it for a better look, the figure stepped behind the tree and I lost sight of it. Whatever the figure was, I'm certain it was no deer or bear. I've seen black bears at relatively close range. Even if a bear stood up on its hind feet, it would not look like what I saw that day. Bears have sloped shoulders and snouts. The figure I saw possessed neither.

Bigfoot is no stranger to the Keweenaw Peninsula, my home territory. During the years that I ran a Bigfoot research group, I collected reports of sightings that took place less than twenty miles from my home. Even after I shut down my research group, I spoke to people who told me about sightings their friends and relatives had in locations within as little as ten miles from where I live. Though most of the witnesses don't want to come forward, for fear of ridicule, their experiences suggest that I'm not the only one who may be encountering Bigfoot in the woods of the Keweenaw.

I'm not the only one discovering stick signs either. Often people tell me they have never looked for stick signs, since they hadn't heard of the phenomenon until they read *Backyard Bigfoot* or heard me on the radio talking about stick signs. Now they keep an eye out for such signs. A fellow Bigfoot researcher, Thom Powell, told me this was the case for him as well. When I interviewed him for *Forbidden Bigfoot*, he mentioned that after reading *Backyard Bigfoot* he and his son began to

Figure 16.7: The Keweenaw Peninsula, where I live, is covered in dense forests where large animals can easily hide. Photo by Lisa A. Shiel.

keep an eye out for stick signs during their hikes. They found quite a few. The Powells even tried my technique of creating stick signs in hopes of receiving responses from the sign-maker.

Is Bigfoot responsible for the stick signs and other phenomena? No one can say for certain—not even the skeptics. I believe Bigfoot is responsible.

What you believe…well, that's entirely up to you.

17

Stick Signs Update

l have never stopped looking for stick signs. Every day as I walk through the woods, the same woods I walk through daily and the woods in which I live, I keep an eye out for anything strange. *Backyard Bigfoot* documented all my experiences through early 2006. Since then, I've continued to find distinctly unnatural formations of sticks, along with other unexplained phenomena. Here I present a chronological overview of the best and most interesting stick signs that have turned up since the publication of *Backyard Bigfoot*. This chapter also includes a number of photos that did not appear in the original e-book of *Backyard Phenomena*.

At the end of the this chapter, I'll offer my advice for anyone interested in becoming a stick-sign hunter.

First up, though…the sticks.

2006

Backyard Bigfoot, published in March 2006, included the best stick signs from the early part of that year. The remainder of 2006 offered up several stick signs worth mentioning.

April 18: A large Y-shaped stick with two parallel sticks. Other signs have also made use of Y-shaped sticks, sometimes by themselves and sometimes paired with other elements.

March 26: This X or T sign was made from a stick and a strip of bark.

Figure 17.1
The Best of 2006
photos by Lisa A. Shiel

May 5: A cross or X with smaller sticks placed nearby.

May 14: An X fashioned from strips of bark.

May 14-27: A cluster of signs made with stout sticks. Though most of the signs employ sticks about a half inch in diameter, these were twice as thick. I've also found other signs made with thicker sticks. Probably the sign-maker uses whatever sticks are at hand, or perhaps whichever ones look the nicest.

June 14: This complex sign combines several rocks with thin sticks; it showed up in right my driveway.

June 24: Two stout Y-shaped sticks paired with two equally thick straight sticks.

October 27: These two signs showed up on the same day; the larger one (above) uses a strip of bark.

November 9/12: This pair of signs appeared three days apart—first the smaller one, and then the larger one. Both signs were created using the same strips of carved wood, which look like they came from furniture or interior decorations such as molding or baseboard—but they did not come from anywhere in the vicinity of the stick sign. I had kicked apart the first sign.

September 7, 2006: A cross made with thin sticks—though one is much longer than the usual type seen in stick signs.

December 27, 2006: A delicate sign pairing a short, fat stick with a daintier one. The thin stick was balanced on the fat one.

2007

The year 2007 proved to be a good one for stick signs. A few winter signs turned up, but as in most years, summer was the most prolific for stick signs. I guess stick signs have a season, just like baseball or football.

Standing Up to Scrutiny

Can the stick sign phenomenon stand up to scientific examination? Well, that's a matter for debate. Mainstream scientists and even a number of Bigfoot researchers would say no. Some stick signs, however, refuse to lie down in the face of skeptical scrutiny. Take this little guy that turned up on January 4, 2007, during a midwinter thaw. One stick is propped up on another so that it pokes upward toward the sky. Several other signs showed up on the same day. Apparently, Bigfoot enjoy a break from the snowy, cold weather as much as humans do.

The Boughs of Bigfoot

The first week of April 2007 brought a late blizzard to the U.P. of Michigan, with over a foot of snow at my house and two feet in some other places on the Keweenaw Peninsula. I've often found signs of Bigfoot—braided manes, stick signs, possible footprints—just after a snowfall. Bigfoot, like other animals, can probably sense a change in the weather coming. They take advantage of the oncoming snow to conceal any tracks they might leave during their forays into human territory. Yet in April 2007, a stick sign appeared *before* the onset of the blizzard.

On April 2, my dogs had shown an intense interest in a path that leads away from the gate north of the pole barn, straight into the woods. The

Figure 17.2: I found this trio of signs on the same day. The top photo is the sign that included one stick pointing skyward, propped up by another stick. The middle photo shows a sign that makes use of a bark strip. The bottom right photo is a classic cross. January 4, 2007. Photos by Lisa A. Shiel.

path is a game trail, not one of my usual walking trails. I didn't go down the trail at that point, as the dogs were too excited by whatever scent they'd picked up. The next day, I returned to spot and discovered two large branches, each about six feet long, had been carefully braced across the trail in an X formation. Unlike the usual stick signs, which lie on the ground, these branches stood upright, propped between brush and trees. A light snow had fallen that morning, which made the branches show up well in photos.

Later that day, a blizzard dropped over two feet of snow, impeding further investigation until the following week. Then, I conducted a field investigation of the area, to answer four questions:

1. **From what kind of tree did the branches originate?** The branches appear to have come from a type of pin cherry.
2. **Did the branches fall off a nearby tree?** The trees in the vicinity are maples, aspens, and pines. No cherry trees of any sort grow in that section of the property; therefore, the branches could not have fallen off a pin cherry and landed in the position in which they were found.
3. **Had the branches broken off or been cut?** One end of each branch was undamaged, while the other had been broken off the tree. Examination of the branches showed the broken ends were sharp rather than frayed. When I attempted to snap off the opposite end of one branch, the flesh would not snap off cleanly but instead stripped off a section of bark.
4. **Were the branches jammed into the ground or balanced on the ground?** The branches had been carefully propped up between trees. The ends rested on the ground, rather than being jammed into it.

The sticks used to construct ground-based stick signs have similarly cut ends on them. The stick signs also employ twigs about half an inch thick; the branches used in this sign also measure approximately half an inch in diameter. I had determined at the time of discovery that no tracks, animal or human, could be found in the vicinity. The hardness of the ground prevented the impression of tracks.

What was the purpose of the cross-trail sign? As with all stick signs, I can't say anything for certain, but can only postulate about the purpose and meaning of each formation. Ground-based stick signs seem to mark trails. The upright X sign seemed to block the trail. Another sign composed of two parallel sticks lay on the ground near the upright crossed sticks. The upright X sign might well have served as a warning to other Bigfoot to steer clear of that area for some reason, or perhaps it was a message for me. If it was meant as a warning, the nearby ground sign might've been meant to offer more information. Whatever the case, the mystery remains unsolved.

One fact is clear to me, however—the upright X did not appear naturally.

Figure 17.3: The photo above shows the large, crossed sticks that blocked a game trail; the inset provides a closer view. Another sign (bottom) also turned up on the same day, near the upright X. April 3, 2007. Photos by Lisa A. Shiel.

Figure 17.4: A large L-shaped sign next to my house. April 14, 2007. Photo by Lisa A. Shiel.

Summer Signs

Some interesting formations cropped up in the late spring and summer. Along with the common parallel arrangements, I also discovered geometric and X shapes, plus a T-shaped sign that appeared right next to my house. One sign that looked vaguely like an arrow consisted of two sticks, one of which had been bent into a V shape.

Fanning the Flames

On September 3, 2007, I found a stick sign on my property that looked different from the arrangements I'd found previously. Mostly I find crosses, T shapes, and parallel sticks. Once I found a bunch of sticks arrayed in a circle, and I've also seen arrows, geometric shapes, and box-like formations that imitated signs I'd made.

The sign I discovered on September 3, 2007, displayed a different style (see Fig. 17.6 for a photo). The formation included a straight stick below (or beside, depending on your viewpoint) a fan-like shape unlike anything I've seen prior to that day or, indeed, since that day. The sign, like the others, appeared overnight in the horse pasture behind my house. Ten days later, another formation with similarities to the fan-shaped sign turned up in the same area. This time, the sticks were fanned out in a wider array with a clump of hay inside the stick formation. The two signs were similar in their fan-like quality but strikingly different in overall appearance. The original fan-shaped sign stands a unique entry in the catalog of stick signs.

Later in the fall, on November 10, I found a sign that bore a striking resemblance to one I'd found more than three years earlier in Texas. A sign from June 28, 2004, incorporated a feather into a T-shaped formation. The feather was tucked under the longer of the two sticks. The sign that appeared on November 10, 2007, also integrated a feather

Figure 17.5

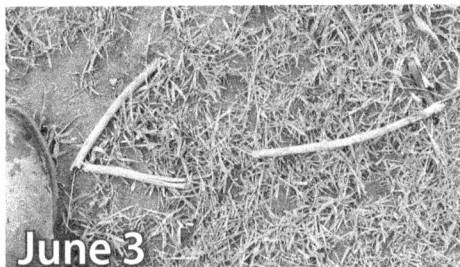

Summer Signs of 2007
photos by Lisa A. Shiel

into the arrangement, though this time the feather lay a few feet from a small stick (see Fig. 17.7 for photos). The similarity is still intriguing.

2008

Stick sign activity was lighter in 2008 than in previous years. Conversely, or perhaps in response, the traditional wildlife returned in full force. A pack of wolves made their den on my property, deer abounded, rabbits frolicked everywhere, and bears came to eat the wild cherries and blackberries. The sign-maker, however, left fewer stick signs than usual—if stick sign activity can be considered usual!

Debunking the Debunkers

Some people like to claim that stick signs are made by bears or raccoons. If that were the case, then the increased presence of wildlife in 2008 should've increased the number of stick signs. The exact opposite proved true. More wildlife equaled fewer signs. The evidence suggests that perhaps the sign-maker's presence chased away the wildlife in previous years. The resurgence of wildlife accompanied by a decline in stick sign activity also debunks the bear/raccoon theory.

Of course, debunkers have another explanation too. Wind, they say, must blow the sticks down from the trees and onto the ground, where they fall in random patterns that wackos like me interpret as purposeful arrangements. But does the evidence support this idea?

Let's take a look at the weather in 2008, the year of few stick signs. The wind theory implies that more wind means more stick signs. Hence, a very windy year ought to produce a plethora of signs scattered through-out the woods and pastures on my property. After all, trees predominate out here. The summer of 2008 brought an abundance of windy weather coupled with a drought that left the vegetation parched—and the tree branches primed for getting ripped down by the wind. Yet, as I've already said, I found less stick signs in 2008, not more. The dearth of signs worsened in the summer months, in direct opposition to the increase in wind.

Sorry, debunkers. The wind theory fails too.

Don't feel sorry for the poor debunkers, though. I'm sure they'll come up with another harebrained explanation very soon.

Figure 17.6: This unusual design looks like nothing else I've found. September 3, 2007. Photo by Lisa A. Shiel.

Figure 17.7: These eerily similar designs showed up more than three years apart and half a country distant from each other. In Michigan on November 10, 2007 (top); in Texas on June 28, 2004 (bottom). Photos by Lisa A. Shiel.

The Best of 2008

The year may have been lackluster in terms of quantity, but several of the signs I found in 2008 displayed new and interesting designs or appeared in surprising locations.

Figure 17.8
The Best of 2008
photos by Lisa A. Shiel

Two parallel sticks with a third one perpendicular to the first two (left). This formation appeared right outside my house. I kicked the sign apart, spreading the sticks far from each other and their original location. The next morning, the sign had been reconstituted in a spot within inches of its original position. May 21, 2008.

A vertical stick planted in the dirt (bottom left). The stick was positioned out in the open, away from trees. On the same day, a small cross sign (bottom right) turned up not far from the upright stick. May 29, 2008.

A large, fat stick balanced on a small log, with a third chunk of wood nearby. June 26, 2008.

A tiny cross-shaped sign. This one turned up inside my pole barn, the front of which serves as a garage while the back contained a horse stall that has since been removed. The tiny stick sign was placed directly in front of my car, just inside the doorway. I wondered if this sign might be a response to the carved-wood cross that sits in my kitchen window, clearly visible from outside too. June 29, 2008.

This small stick beside a clear marble was also in the pole barn, further from the door, between my car and the horse stall. The marble did not come from nearby. Before this sign showed up, I'd found other marbles in the pole barn, with no clue where the objects originated. (I can hear the obvious joke about marbles that debunkers will undoubtedly pounce on with glee. Well, I did take away their two favorite theories, so I should give them something to make up for it!) June 29, 2008.

Another stick sign right beside the house, next to a chair. July 3, 2008.

A small cross or plus sign fashioned from bark strips. June 4, 2008.

A T-shaped sign made from slender pieces of hay. August 26, 2008.

Thicker sticks form a curving sign. October 29, 2008.

2009

The next year turned out to be even slower. Most of the stick signs I saw didn't look good enough to photograph because a) they were too vague for me to definitively identify them as stick signs, or b) the surrounding vegetation obscured the sign in photographs (though in person they looked okay). If the sign is made from small, brown sticks and the surrounding area is covered in brown grass, then a photograph will not reproduce the sign very well.

In March 2009, I found two signs laid out on the snow, and then on October 26 I found one good sign that is clearly visible in the photograph. It also looks virtually identical to similar parallel formations I've discovered both before and since.

Figure 17.9

The Best of 2009
photos by Lisa A. Shiel

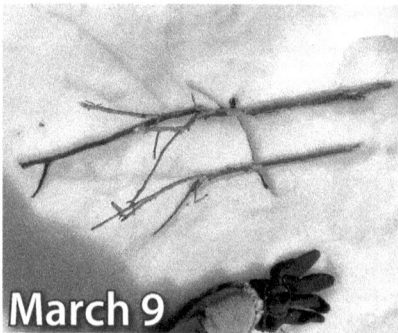

2010

The lull in stick sign activity continued into 2010. Possible signs were vague and not worth photographing for the most part. See Fig. 17.10 for the best of 2010.

2011

Once again, stick sign activity was low. But noteworthy signs did emerge Fig. 17.11 shows the highlights of 2011.

2012

Stick sign activity picked up in 2012, with a number of intriguing signs throughout the year. Signs in the snow, signs in the horses' favorite orchard pasture, signs in the driveway—the year 2012 had everything. See Fig. 17.12 for the year's best.

Some of the 2012 signs turned up surprisingly close to my front door—my literal front door. Now someone might ask how anyone could creep around in my yard, and even on my deck, without being noticed. I live in a two-story farmhouse that was built back in the days when they used thick boards made from solid wood. Trust me, a sound has be quite loud to penetrate this house. Someone skulking through the yard would make no more, and probably less, noise than the horses make walking around in their pasture, which comes right to the house. If their nocturnal activities don't wake me, even with my bedroom window open, then the sign-maker could certainly enter the yard without disturbing me or my pets.

Stick Signs Statistics

When I started work on the full version of this book, I decided to undertake a detailed analysis of the stick sign phenomenon as I've experienced it. I wondered if any patterns might emerge. Although

Figure 17.10

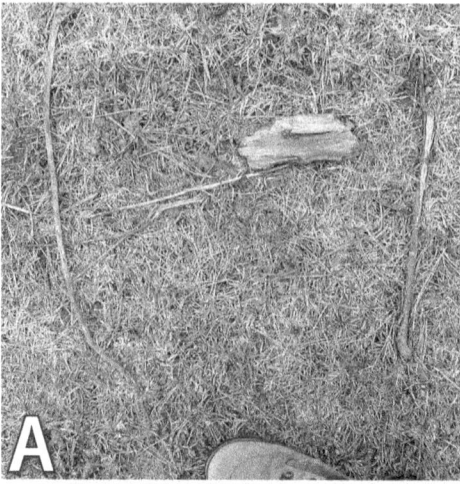

The Best of 2010
photos by Lisa A. Shiel

April 3: Two thin sticks book-ended a broken chunk of wood (A), and a long line of parallel sticks ending with a V-shaped stick (F).

April 11: Parallel sticks sat along a trail (C), and two wood strips are set in a T shape (D).

May 4: Parallel sticks lay right outside the door to the pole barn and directly in front of the attached horse shed (B).

June 9: A triangle-shaped sign was made from three separate thin sticks (E).

Figure 17.11

The Best of 2011
photos by Lisa A. Shiel

June 16: Widely spaced parallel sticks lay smack on a trail, as if trying to block the way or mark a particular section (A). Near the parallel sticks sat a delicate little cross formation (inset). Nearby, a large stick lay directly over the trail (B), atop a skid mark where a horse slid in the mud.

June 17: A lovely T formation (C).

June 25: Another cross, this time made of wood strips (E).

August 11: A complex sign composed of three sticks (F).

October 30: An apple between parallel sticks (D). No apple trees grow in the immediate vicinity, though some do grow elsewhere on the property.

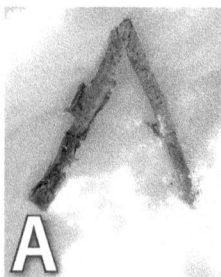

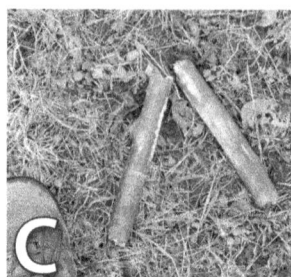

Figure 17.12

The Best of 2012
photos by Lisa A. Shiel

February 5: A V-shaped sign (A) in the snow—no tracks nearby.

March 31: A large cross (B).

April 1: Another V-shaped sign (C), this time made with fat sticks. This sign showed up the very next day after the cross sign. (Yes, it was April Fool's Day. I give another gift to the debunkers!)

April 7: Two chubby sticks (E), with one of them sticking straight up (F) out of the ground. These turned up in my front yard.

June 2: A delicate little T (D).

June 3: A large, spread-out T (H). This one appeared on my birthday, inside a section of the horse pasture where apple trees grow. The orchard pasture is right across the road from my house. (It's a dead-end gravel road way out in the country.)

August 1: A large cross (G) beside an old hand trowel (inset). This sign was left inside the orchard pasture, mere feet from the fence and the road. I don't know where the hand trowel originated.

August 1: A little parallel formation in my driveway (I).

August 1: The parts of this T sign (J) started out as one stick, which was broken in half (inset).

August 2: I found this T sign (K) in the same spot where the T and hand trowel had been the day before. I'd destroyed that sign by scattering the sticks—but the next day the sign had been remade using different sticks and minus the hand trowel.

August 6: This cross (L) with one stick balanced on the other appeared on the deck right outside my door! The sign was laid out right next to a turtle-shaped lawn sprinkler. The sprinkler, which was already on the deck before the stick sign appeared, had not been moved.

August 16: This L formation (M) used the same sticks from the previous sign and was also left on the deck. I'd piled the sticks near the deck steps, but ten days later the sign-maker moved them to create this arrangement.

August 21: Another T (N), made from slender sticks.

I found no obvious patterns, the statistics derived from my analysis do offer some interesting insights into a controversial phenomenon. I offer here a selection of my data, in the form of charts. Take in the data, consider it, and decide for yourself what it all might mean.

What are the most intriguing bits of data? Here's a sampling of points that caught my eye. All data is from the period starting November 2003 and ending November 2012.

The Peak

Stick sign activity peaked in 2004. My first book on the subject, *Backyard Bigfoot*, was published in March 2006. Is there a correlation to the publication schedule for my books? Not really. Activity dropped precipitously in the two years before *Backyard Bigfoot* came out, rose slightly immediately after its release, and then plummeted again. Since 2009, activity has climbed gradually. My second nonfiction Bigfoot book, the e-book *Creature of Controversy*, came out in December 2011—stick sign activity did not increase measurably until the following spring. See Fig. 17.13 for the yearly distribution.

The Busy Month

Combining the data for all years, the month with the most stick sign activity is August; February has the least activity. I've found stick signs in every month of the year, though when the snow pack is deepest (typically late January into February), I find the least signs. A number of signs have turned up during midwinter thaws, when the snow pack might melt away completely. As might be expected, however, activity peaks in the summer months. See. Fig. 17.14 for the monthly distribution.

Most of the signs found in August occurred in 2004. The year of 2008 saw the most signs in October, while 2007 was the only year to have January signs (thanks to a midwinter thaw). See Fig. 17.15 for the monthly distribution divided up by years.

The Shapes

Stick signs come in all shapes and sizes, just like Bigfoot them-selves. The top shape is not really a shape at all—I call this type of formations complex signs because, well, they're just too complex to call them a particular shape (like a square or a triangle). Complex

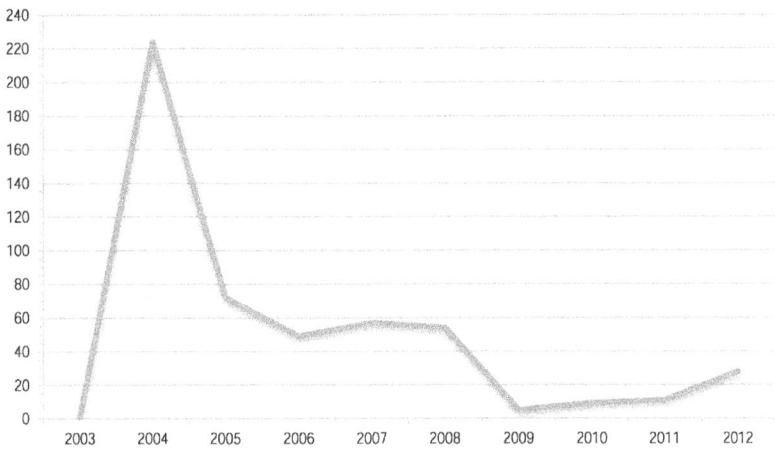

Figure 17.13: Stick sign distribution by year. Chart by Lisa A. Shiel.

Figure 17.14: Stick sign distribution by month. Chart by Lisa A. Shiel.

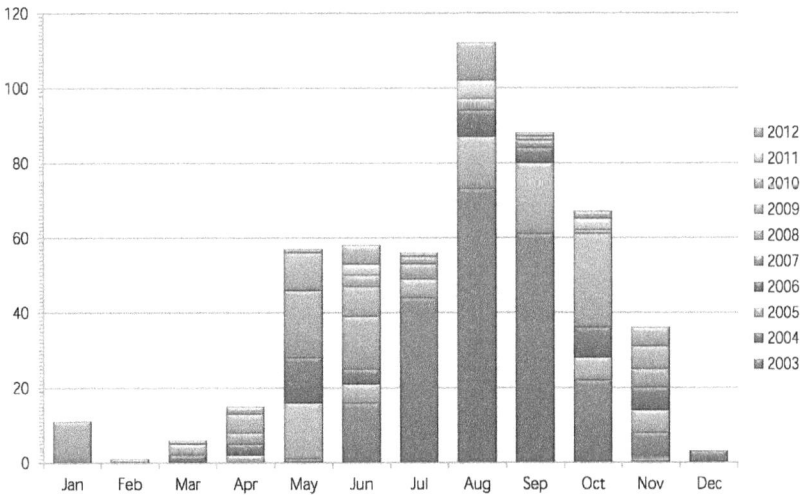

Figure 17.15: Stick sign distribution by month and year. Chart by Lisa A. Shiel.

signs are often larger than other signs. They involve multiple sticks arranged in distinctly unnatural, but hard to classify, arrangements that might include multiple geometric shapes or different types of non-stick elements. For instance, I've found signs that incorporated wires, rocks, and bits of mesh.

The second most frequent arrangement is the parallel formation. This usually involves two sticks laid out parallel to each other, but it can also include more than two sticks. Cross and T shapes are also relatively common, though far less so than complex or parallel signs. See Fig. 17.16 for more the frequency of shapes.

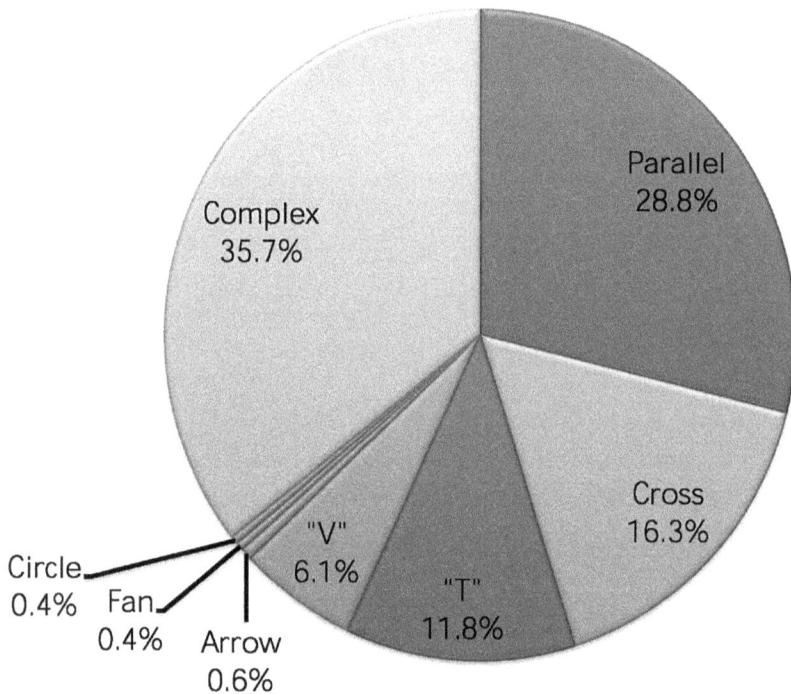

Figure 17.16: Frequency of stick sign shapes. Chart by Lisa A. Shiel.

How to Hunt for Stick Signs

To conclude this chapter, I'd like to offer my advice to anyone interested in hunting for stick signs. Here are the top 5 things a prospective stick sign hunter should do.

1. **Buy property in a remote area, preferably one with a history of Bigfoot sightings.**
    Alternatively, find a site owned by a friend or relative willing to accommodate your stick sign investigations. If you choose the friend/relative route, make sure the landowners don't host ATV clubs or similar group activities on a regular basis. You want an area with restricted public access. For this reason, public lands (such as state and federal parks) do not work well for stick sign research because you never know who may have traipsed through the area and how often they did so. Maybe children decided to play games with sticks. Unless you control the property, you just can't be sure.

2. **Walk the property every day, paying attention to the trails and what lies on or near them.**
    Visiting your research area once in awhile might be okay if your goal is to hunt deer. But searching for stick signs demands an intimate knowledge of the area. Walking the trails every day isn't enough by itself either. You must note what was there on each day, so that you'll recognize when something new has appeared overnight. Also pay attention to the weather. Was there a powerful windstorm the night before you found the stick sign? Tracking everything that might affect your research is key.

    It's important to get to know the existing trails too. When I says "trails," I don't just mean walking trails cleared by humans. I also mean game trails, like those carved out by deer.

3. **Remove any twigs that already lie along the trails and in open areas.**
    Clearing the area when you haven't visited it before is key. Also, if you've visited the area but have never paid close attention to the ground before, you should also make a point of clearing the trails. This leaves a clean slate that you can use as a baseline when hunting for stick signs. After the trails are cleared, if stick signs show up in the area, you'll know they weren't there before.

4. **Watch and listen for other signs of Bigfoot—such as footprints or unexplained whoops/screams.**
   Once again, paying attention is key. Get to know the normal sounds of nature in the area. Buy a book on animal tracking to help you differentiate normal tracks from unexplained ones. You don't need to become the world's expert on these things, but developing a working knowledge will only help your research.

   Most importantly, don't let naysayers embarrass you into giving up on your research. If you can't identify a call you heard in the woods, contact someone who might know. If that person tries to make you feel stupid for not knowing that was the mating call of the Sneezing Whatsahoozit, say thank you and move on. We learn by seeking knowledge—which means ignoring obnoxious people who try to stand in the way. And in the future, you'll recognize that weird sound as the Sneezing Whatsahoozit.

5. **Document anything unusual you find—photograph it and note where and when you found it.**
   Evidence must be documented, else why bother conducting research? Digital cameras are pretty cheap and you don't have to print every photo you take. You don't have to be a professional writer to write things down for future reference. Keep track of dates, places, and events. Maybe that scream you heard happened the night before you found a passel of stick signs. Unless you write that down, you might easily forget the possible connection.

Of course, I could give much more advice than this. But these tips will help any aspiring researcher get started on a quest to discover evidence of a unique form of communication. You might even try creating your own stick signs to see if you get a response. If you do create your own signs, photograph those as well; if your sign gets altered, you can use the photo to compare your original sign to the alteration.

Happy hunting!

18
Mane Braiding

Stick signs engender much controversy among Bigfoot researchers, yet they are not the only phenomenon related to Bigfoot that riles up the just-an-ape camp. Proponents of the idea that Bigfoot is an ape, and nothing more, revile any evidence that suggests otherwise. They might accept that Bigfoot bend over saplings or use simple tools made out of sticks like chimpanzees do, but in their minds anything more sophisticated is impossible.

The just-an-ape theory represents Door A. The evidence from stick signs offers us Door B. And behind Door B, we find even more strange and confusing phenomena related to Bigfoot.

Take, for instance, mane braiding.

I first encountered the mane braiding phenomenon while living in Texas. In the beginning, I allowed myself to dismiss them as natural tangles or perhaps the handiwork of the neighbors' grandchildren. As time went on, however, I found it more and more difficult to stick to my original hypotheses. I continued to find mysterious braids in my horses' manes after I moved back to Michigan in 2004. The best mane braids to date showed up in the spring of 2005.

Yet where I currently live there are no children nearby—no easy scapegoats. The idea of a natural origin no longer makes sense either. It really only made sense as long as I didn't think about the problem too much. As often happens with unexplained phenomena, my mind simply couldn't accept that anything as bizarre as mane braiding could happen. My experiences with stick signs opened me up to other possibilities. If Bigfoot make stick signs, why not mane braids as well?

The Mane Evidence

What makes a mane braid different from a tangle? The braids consist of locks of mane interwoven and twisted together in a complicated pattern similar to a French braid, though vastly more intricate, with a tight knot at the end that's woven back into the braid. Braids display some unique characteristics not seen in natural tangles:

1. Individual locks within the braid are twisted.
2. These twists are woven into a larger braid composed of coiled, interlocking twists.
3. The whole braid is finished off by tucking the end up inside the braid and tying a tight knot around it.
4. These braids are difficult to untangle.

Concerning the last point, I've never had any luck untying the strands. They can only be removed by cutting them out of the mane. As someone who grew up having long hair, I know what normal braids look and feel like, from a simple three-strand braid to a French plait. The braids in my horses' manes differ from any braiding style I've encountered. The technique used to create them is extremely complex and must take a great deal of concentration, practice, and time to achieve the effect.

Why is mane braiding attributed to Bigfoot? To answer this question, we must begin by examining related evidence from mythology and fairy lore.

A Twisted History

In Part One, I talked about the long history of Bigfoot sightings. Mane braiding also appears to have a deep history—evidence from

Figure 18.1: The best mane braid to date, which illustrates all the traits mentioned. May 11, 2005. Photo by Lisa A. Shiel.

eyewitness accounts meshes with legends attributing mane braids to mythical creatures from giants to fairies. The same lore that speaks of mane braiding also speaks of hairy, manlike creatures.

Hairy Legends

William Shakespeare immortalized mane braiding in his play *Romeo and Juliet*, in which he blamed the phenomenon on the fairy queen Mab. Shakespeare did not, however, invent the notion of fairies braiding manes. The phenomenon already enjoyed a long kinship with the various types of fairy beings, as evidence by numerous legends. In his 1911 book *The Fairy-Faith in Celtic Countries*, W.Y. Evans-Wentz recounted a wealth of fairy lore that involved both hairy beings and more humanlike entities. Mane braiding, coupled with a general affinity for horses, weaves through all of fairy lore. A legend from the island of Islay involves a giant whose daughter wore necklaces fashioned from twisted hair.

Pixies are a type of fairy known in various locations throughout the British Isles. (They've also been known as piskies, particularly in Cornwall, but I'll use the name familiar to readers in my part of world.) The frisky pixies apparently like to ride horses at night and plait their manes, leaving the horses in a state of agitation or exhaustion. The human owners of the horses found they could not undo the braids, which seemed too complex to be manmade. Evans-Wentz related the eyewitness account of a woman who told him that, twenty years earlier, she'd watched tiny pixies dance across a horse's back and climb up its mane. Another eyewitness described pixies chasing a horse, perhaps trying to catch it. Fairies of many varieties are said to ride horses.

Figure 18.2: William Shakespeare, who wrote about fairies and mane braiding. Image courtesy of the University of Texas Libraries, the University of Texas at Austin.

Another type of fairy being, known from French folklore, also braids the manes of horses. The *lutins* are ubiquitous spirits, akin to household gods. People believed the good health of their horses came from the blessing of the *lutins*; conversely, if the *lutins* were angered, they might braid the horses' manes as a trick to punish the owners for neglecting the *lutins*. As with the pixies, *lutins* often left the horses agitated or exhausted. Farmers would hang brass rings in the horses' manes to ward off the *lutins*.

More legends about mane braiding and Bigfoot turn up all over Europe. Jacob Grimm—a mythologist and one of the Brothers Grimm, authors of *Grimm's Fairy Tales*—mentions several legends about mane braiding in his book *Teutonic Mythology*. When pixies braid the manes of horses, he explains, the braid is called a pixy-seat. Another being, called a *schrächel*, was believed to braid horses' manes too. European mythology also abounds with tales of wild men, humanoid creatures with hair-covered bodies.

In the Americas, folk tales speak of hairy dwarves that live in remote canyons and valleys in the Andes. Locals say these mini-Bigfoot love to ride horses, but their small stature makes it impossible for them to ride on the horses' backs. The creatures braid locks of mane into stirrups so that they may enjoy horseback riding.

But the evidence for mane braiding is not limited to mythology and local legends.

Sightings and Suspicions

In December 1896, a newspaper in Michigan's Upper Peninsula reported on an unusual situation. A local man named John Pomroy was baffled by the happenings in his barn. Every evening, Pomroy said, he would comb out his horse's mane—and every morning he would find the mane braided in a distinctly unnatural way. What could cause this, he wondered. The mystery deepened when, one morning in December, he walked out to his barn to find the door locked from the inside. Pomroy had to knock down the door to his own barn to gain entry.

Other folks he shared the story with had suggested pranksters might be to blame. But how could pranksters lock themselves in the barn and then escape from it without breaking down the door? Pomroy decided the culprit must've been a ghost.

In the nearby town of Lake Linden, the French-Canadian population still preserved legends of the mane-braiding *lutins*. Apparently, Pomroy never heard those tales. The U.P. also has its fair share of Bigfoot sightings, both in modern times and back in Pomroy's day. Back then, of course, no one connected mane braiding with Bigfoot. In fact, the creatures were known simply as wild men and often dismissed as being escaped mental patients.

In the book *In the Footsteps of the Russian Snowman*, researcher Dmitri Bayanov presents the story of a young Russian researcher who witnessed mane braiding firsthand back in the early 1990s. The region encompassing Russia and the Caucasus has a history of sightings of a Bigfoot-type creature known as the *almasty*. Gregory Panchenko staked out a barn where a farm caretaker reported finding braids in his horses' manes. Panchenko hid inside the barn one night, in a spot where he could see one of the horses, and waited for the *almasty* to appear. He fell asleep but, awhile later, was awakened by snorting noises from the horse. When he looked, Panchenko saw an *almasty* standing beside the horse, apparently braiding the mane.

Yet mane braiding is not limited to remote regions. In 2009, British newspapers began reporting on a spate of bizarre incidents in rural parts

Figure 18.3: According to most archaeologists, ancient people built mysterious megalithic monuments as places of religious worship. So maybe pagans celebrated the summer solstice by braiding horses' manes inside the Standing Stones of Callanish on Scotland's Isle of Lewis...hmm, I don't think so. Photo courtesy of the Central Intelligence Agency.

of the nation. Reports of mysterious braids turning up in horses' manes appeared in online forums devoted to all things horsey. Owners were dumbfounded by the incidents. One theory postulated that thieves used the braids to mark horses they wished to steal, but this idea crumbled in the face of facts. No horses have been stolen.

Police consulted an unnamed warlock, who supposedly identified the braids as "knot magick" used in white magic rituals. Horse owners remained largely unconvinced, however, since warlocks would need to cross electric fences and other barricades in the middle of the night and wrangle the horses, who wouldn't like being messed with by strangers. At least one horse owner also had three dobermans who were not awakened by whatever or whoever braided the horses' manes. In July 2012, *The Nottingham Post* quoted a practicing pagan, Dave Dominic, as saying that he knows of no rituals involving braiding horses' manes.

The mane braiding incidents have continued sporadically. In late 2009, horse owners in southwest England reported twenty incidents in three months. Still, none of the offered explanations fit the evidence.

Great Britain does have a history of Bigfoot sightings. As recently as November 2012, the newspaper *The Independent* reported on the latest in an ongoing wave of sightings in the town of Tunbridge Wells, forty miles outside London. Witnesses described the creature as eight feet tall and covered in hair, with frightening red eyes. Here in the U.S., witnesses have also described Bigfoot with red eyes. Great Britain has such a complex history of Bigfoot sightings that Nick Redfern, an author and investigator of all things strange, announced on the blog Cryptomundo that his forthcoming book about Britain's Bigfoot will be the longest book he's ever written.

The data leads to an inescapable conclusion. Wherever mane braiding occurs, we find Bigfoot—and vice versa. Does this mean that Bigfoot are definitely the culprits? Well, we don't know much about Bigfoot definitively. The best we can say is that the evidence, when viewed without prejudice, points strongly to a connection between Bigfoot and mane braiding.

Figure 18.4

Mane Braids
photos by Lisa A. Shiel

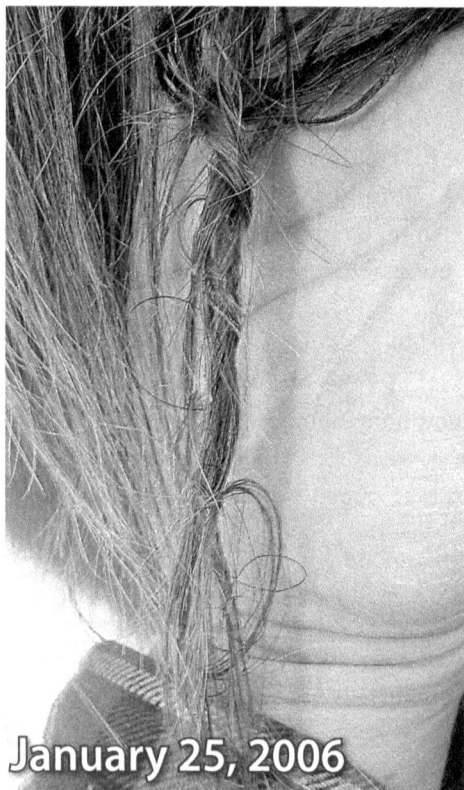

September 20, 2005

September 23, 2005

January 25, 2006

May 18, 2006

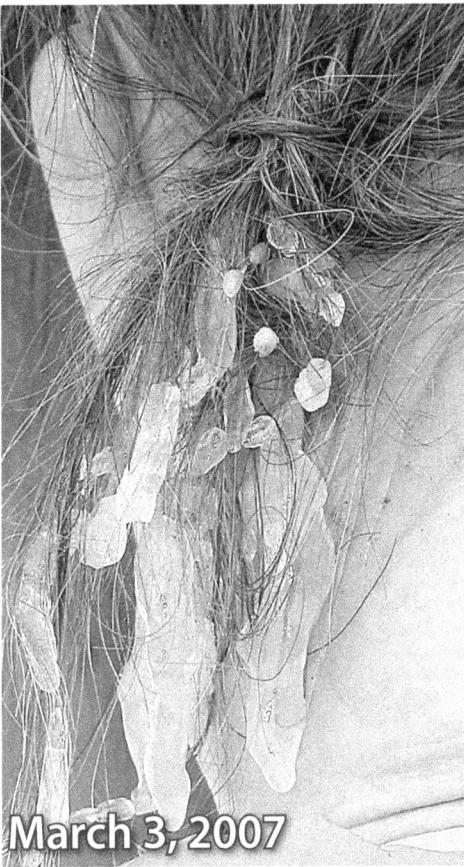

March 3, 2007

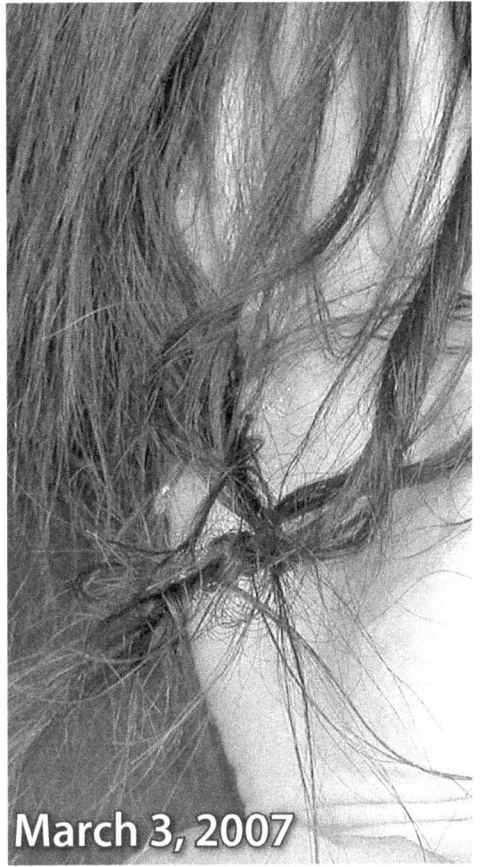

March 3, 2007

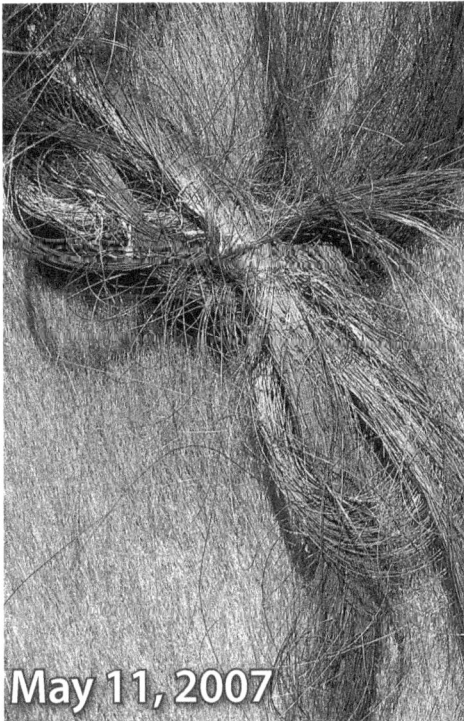

May 11, 2007

April 15, 2007

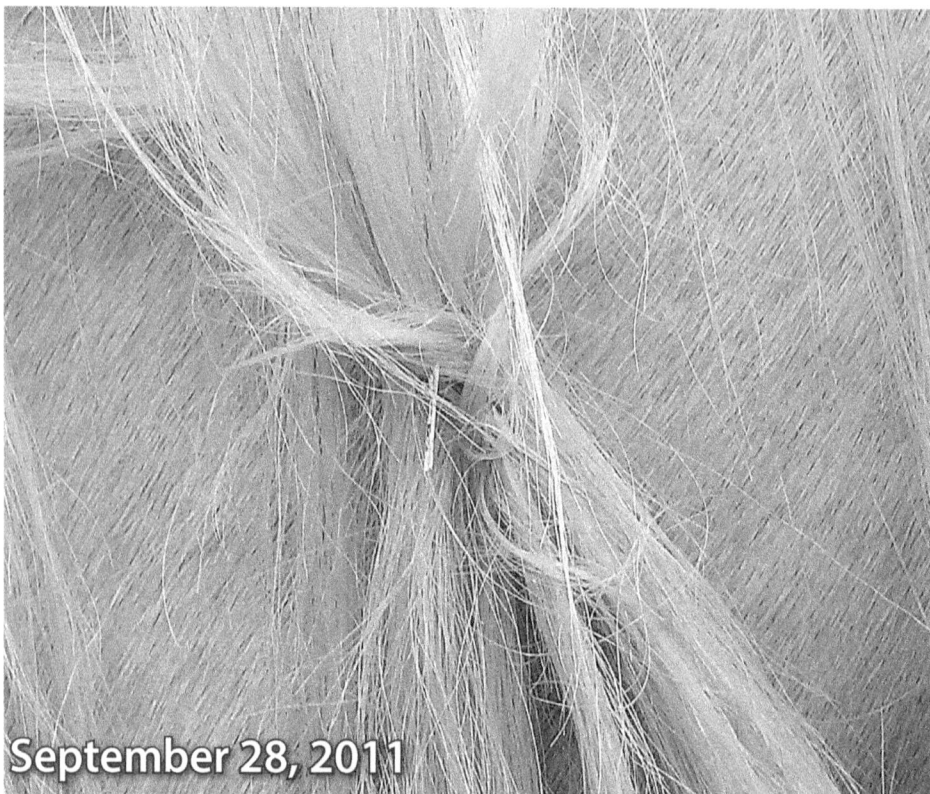

September 28, 2011

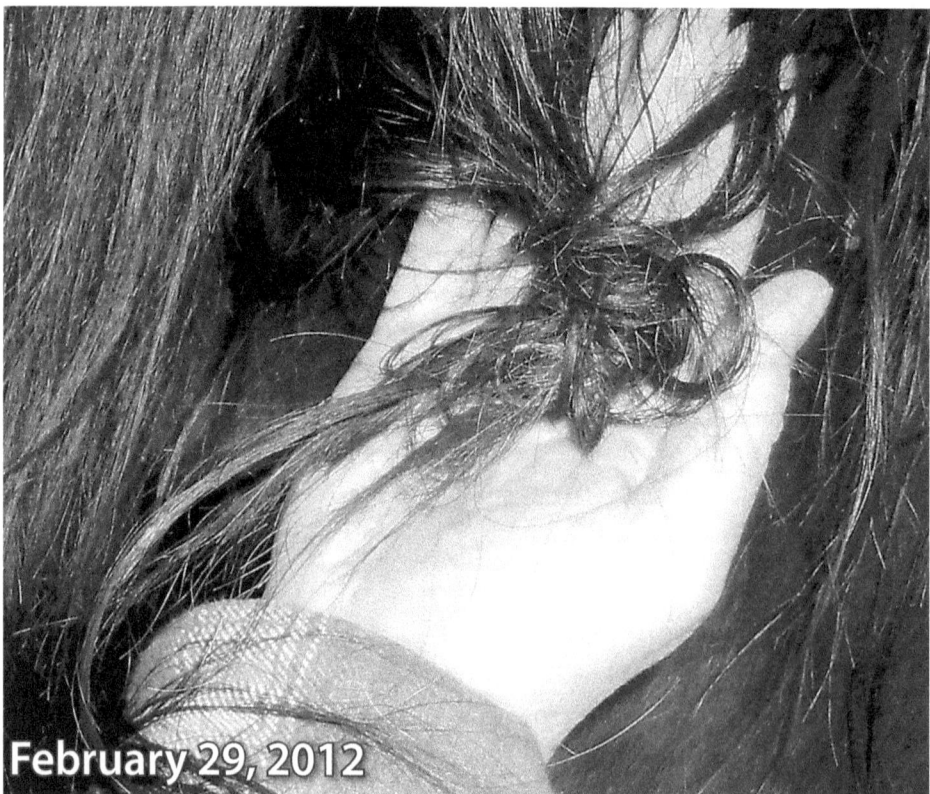

February 29, 2012

Weirder & Weirder

The strange goings-on in the woods around my home don't end with stick signs and mane braiding. Those phenomena are only the beginning. Almost from the start, other odd events have accompanied the two main phenomena. On separate occasions, I also discovered the carcasses of a rabbit and an armadillo. The bodies were mutilated with clean incisions and with no traces of blood anywhere in the vicinity. A stick sign lay a couple feet from the armadillo carcass. I recounted these incidents in my previous book, *Backyard Bigfoot*. Since the publication of that book, even weirder things have happened.

On Their Toes

On May 20, 2006, I noticed an odd mark gouged into my driveway, just outside the gate to my front yard. The mark looked like fingers or toes had dug into the gravel, exposing the dirt beneath. No other marks or tracks could be seen anywhere in the vicinity. The mark reminded me of something I'd found in Texas two years earlier.

In Texas, on the same morning I'd found a stick sign not twenty feet from my house, I also found (further away) scrape marks that seemed to terminate in finger- or toe-like impressions. The impressions were too

Figure 19.1: The toe-like impressions that turned up in my driveway in Michigan. May 20, 2006. Photo by Lisa A. Shiel.

Figure 19.2: The scrape marks with toe-like striations that I found in Texas. July 31, 2004. Photo by Lisa A. Shiel.

large to be dog feet, but too small to be human feet—and they looked nothing like horse hooves. Could the scrape marks have been made by fingers or toes? I asked myself the same question on May 20, 2006. In both cases, I can only guess.

For the Michigan mark, one possibility is that a bobcat left the impression by pawing with toes. We do have bobcats here, and one of my game cameras caught a single photo of one on the night of September 2, 2006. Bobcat tracks are about 2-2.5 inches wide, however, and the gouge mark measured nearly four inches across. Did the same type of creature make the marks in Michigan and in Texas? I'll never know the answer to that question.

Figure 19.3: A game camera image of a bobcat. September 2, 2006. Photo © Lisa A. Shiel.

Out-of-Place Objects

If I misplace my car keys and later find them in a strange place—say, the bathtub—I accept that I must've dropped them there. But when I find an object outdoors, in a place where it does not belong, I'm left with a mystery. How did the object get there? How far was it moved? Who or what moved it? Answers are not always evident, even possible. When the evidence leaves more questions than answers, the item is no longer a misplaced object, but an out-of-place object.

Magic Rocks

In September 2004, back in Texas, I began to find out-of-place rocks. They would turn up on my property, even though the nearest source for similar rocks lay half a mile away. The mystery of the magically appearing rocks only deepened after I moved to Michigan.

I've found them lying on top of green grass or smack in the middle of trails, with no evidence of where the rocks originated or how they got to their resting places. Many of these rocks resemble stone tools of types used by ancient hominids such as *Australopithecus*, *Homo habilis*, and *Homo erectus*.

A popular theory about Bigfoot identifies them as nothing more than very large, bipedal apes. Yet as I discussed in Part One of this book and in *Backyard Bigfoot*, the evidence suggests that Bigfoot has more in common with the ancient, pre-human hominids than with the great apes. The case for labeling Bigfoot a hominid rather than an ape strengthens when we consider the possibility that these creatures might use stone tools of a sophisticated type.

The rocks I've discovered show clear evidence of having chips flaked off them. Skeptics might argue the chipping occurred naturally, but the striking resemblance to ancient tools points to a different source. Besides, even if the chipping were natural, we're left with the question of how the rocks got to their final resting place. Skeptics might say birds carried the rocks there. This, however, seems unlikely given the size of the rocks in question. I often see ravens, yet I've never seen them picking up large rocks and depositing them in the fields—or along trails in the woods. And we must return again to the striking similarity between these rocks and ancient stone tools.

Figure 19.4: This rock turned up on green grass, in the middle of the horse pasture, in Michigan. August 2, 2006. Photo by Lisa A. Shiel.

Figure 19.5: This rock also showed up in the horse pasture, in Michigan, with no evidence of its origins. October 22, 2008. Photo by Lisa A. Shiel.

Figure 19.6
Bigfoot Tools

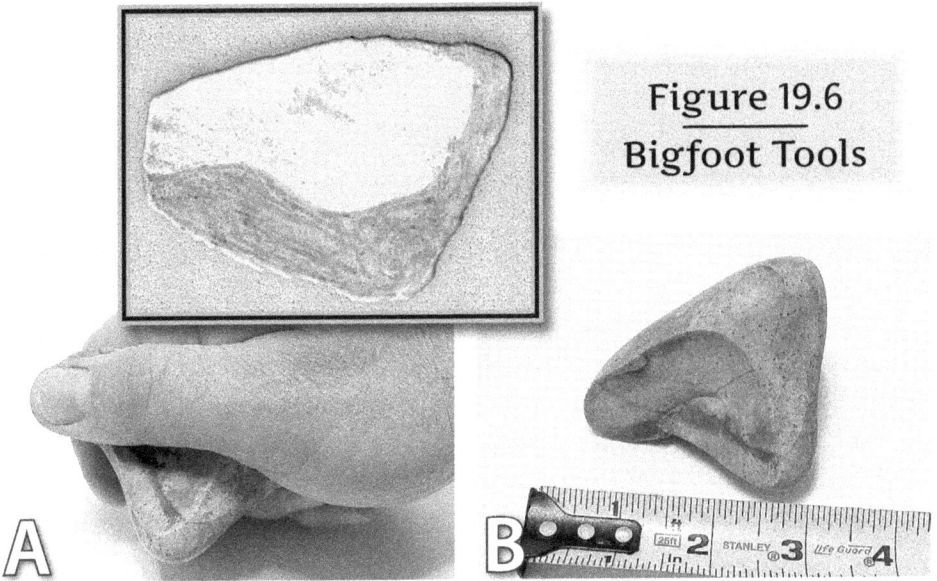

A triangular rock (B) that I found in Texas resembles a pebble tool (top inset) of the kind attributed to *Homo habilis*, a predecessor of *Homo erectus*.

Pebble tools were used by *Homo habilis* and possibly *Australopithecus*, hominids that died out over a million years ago. Early members of the species *Homo erectus* may have used pebble tools as well, but *erectus* died out around 200,000 years ago.

A close-up of the triangular rock (A) demonstrates how it fits in a man's hand.

An arrowhead-like rock (D), also from Texas, looks quite similar to an Acheulian hand ax (bottom inset). Acheulian hand axes are attributed to *Homo erectus*, a species that supposedly died out around 200,000 years ago. Though early modern humans made hand axes too, the type shown above was made only by *Homo erectus*.

A close-up of the arrowhead-like rock (C) demonstrates how it fits in a man's hand.

Photos by Lisa A. Shiel;
drawings by Kerrie Shiel

Could these rocks represent tools used by Bigfoot? That's a question without a definitive answer, a situation we encounter often when studying these creatures.

Branching Out

All of the evidence discussed so far has turned up on the ground or in a horse's mane. I've also discovered some odd things lodged in trees. On April 30, 2007, in a sapling adjacent to the horse shed a flash of blue caught my eye. On investigation, I realized the blue object was a length of twine that had somehow gotten wound around the sapling's branches. Where did the twine come from? How did it get wrapped around the sapling?

Then there are the apples. On several occasions, I've come across apples carefully balanced on thin branches. No tooth marks are evident, as would be the case if squirrels carried the apples to their resting places. I've watched a squirrel move an apple by carrying the fruit in its mouth. This leaves tiny teeth marks.

Figure 19.7

Mysteries in the Trees
photos by Lisa A. Shiel

April 30, 2007.: A length of twine draped over a sapling's branches (A & B).

November 20, 2007: Apples balanced in separate trees, several feet off the ground (C & D).

June 18, 2007: A shovel that mysteriously appeared in the fielvd (E).

October 12, 2008: A bone balanced in a tree in my front yard (G & H).

November 7, 2012: A stick carefully placed in a tree (F).

The year before the apples-in-trees mystery, I had a truly bizarre experience involving an apple. I'd set out from my house with the dogs for our morning walk. After passing through the farm gate, I turned east to head down one of the horse trails. As I approached a small ditch, preparing to jump it, I heard a crashing sound up in the trees. I glanced up at a large pine tree behind and to the left of me. Suddenly, an apple flew down from above and struck the ground near one of my dogs. The dog looked at the apple. Then both I and the dog looked around us to see from where the apple had fallen.

The nearest apple tree stood thirty feet away. The apple had fallen straight down, through some of the pine tree's branches. I tilted my head back to visually search the pine tree for any animals, but saw none. I searched the area for tracks of any kind, finding nothing. So far as I could tell, the apple had simply fallen from the sky—or it had been thrown. I will never know which was the case. I can, however, add the incident to a growing list of odd occurrences in the vicinity of my home.

On June 18, 2007, saplings played a role in another mystery. This time, rather than having apples balanced on their fragile branches, the saplings were bent down to the ground and held in place with an old shovel. The shovel had previously disappeared from the garage. How it wound up in the middle of the horse pasture, lying on top of saplings, defies explanation.

Apples aren't the only objects to wind up balanced in trees. On October 12, 2008, I noticed something odd perched in one of the large cedar trees in my front yard. The object turned out to be a dog bone (a soup bone bought in a grocery store and given to my dog). The bone was carefully balanced inside the crook where a branch connects with the tree's trunk. I'm certain the dog did not place the bone there. It's too large and heavy for a squirrel.

Then on November 7, 2012, I discovered a long stick carefully propped in the Y-shaped junction of a tree, where the two halves of its trunk split. The weather had not been windy or stormy, and the stick showed up there overnight. No large sticks had been lying on the ground in the tree's vicinity.

Did a human intruder sneak into my garage to steal the shovel and then, months later, return to deposit it in the field? Did squirrels figure out how to carry apples without leaving marks on the fruit, just so they could lob the apples at me or delicately balance them on tree limbs? Might an enterprising bear have balanced a stick in a tree? Well, sure, these things are in the wide realm of possibility. Are these notions probable? The fact is, no one can say for certain how these events occurred or what caused them.

Mysteries in the Grass

Most people have heard about crop circles, those strange designs that appear in fields of wheat or other crops. The phenomenon most famously occurs in England, where the circles appear most often and include the most elaborate designs. Though hoaxers have tried to claim responsibility for all crop circles, their claims fail to account for all the evidence. Many crop circles, found around the world, remain unexplained.

So imagine my surprise when a crop-circle-like formation appeared outside my house—not once, but twice.

On June 22, 2010, I noticed something strange in the tall grass and weeds across the road from my house. It looked like a classic crop circle. On June 19, 2011—almost a year to the day after the first formation appeared—I found another circle in the exact same spot.

Both formations appeared overnight. The first formation was vaguely fan shaped and measured six feet by nine feet; the second was more of a swirl shape, roughly circular, and eleven feet in diameter. In the area where the formations appeared, the grass had grown about three feet tall. The grass inside the formations was neatly bent over and swirled but not flattened down to the ground. The flattened grass hovered about six inches above the ground. I could find no tracks, animal or human, leading into or away from the formations, nor could I find any tracks inside the formations. With the first formation, rain the night before had left the ground muddy and capable of preserving tracks. In both cases, there had been virtually no wind and no thunderstorms. Interestingly, the grass at the center of the second formation had turned brown near the base of the stalks.

The window above my bed faces in the general direction of the area where the formations appeared. I heard no noises on either night. If humans created the formations, I'd expect to see tracks from either their feet or their vehicle. As I said, I found no tracks. I wondered if a bird

Figure 19.8

The Grass Circles
photos by Lisa A. Shiel

June 22, 2010: The first circle (A). A closer view (C) shows the flattening and fan-like pattern, and a close-up of the edge (E) reveals the flattened grass hovering above the ground.

June 19, 2011: The second circle (B). A close-up of the center shows the browning of the grass (D).

with a large wingspan could've swooped low, flattening the grass with its wings—but I would've expected a bird's wings to leave more of a butterfly pattern. I'm familiar with the squashed areas created when deer lay down to rest. These formations look nothing like that.

Skeptics might suggest that grasses can fall over on their own. Wind is generally a prerequisite for this to happen, however, and as I said no wind was involved. A sudden, concentrated wind that rotated enough to flatten the grass in a swirling motion would surely have caused other damage. The circles were the only visible signs that anything had happened.

Skeptics might dream up a lot of quasi-rational explanations, yet none stands up to the facts. Of course, I can't completely rule out the idea of hoaxing. A lot of people know about my interest in all things strange. So far, no one has claimed responsibility for creating the formations. If strangers had sneaked onto my property to make a crop circle, this would've created a ruckus and surely upset the horses.

They were not upset. I heard nothing. My dog heard nothing. No tracks were found.

The mystery lingers.

Enduring Enigmas

Debunkers often like to say that people who find strange things find them because they're looking for them. If someone wants to see paranormal phenomena in every shadow, then they will find such phenomena. Of course, this hypothesis assumes that the experiencer expected to find paranormal phenomena. Quite often, however, experiencers are not looking for and indeed did not wish to find the unexplained phenomena they encounter.

I did not set out to find stick signs, mane braiding, possible stone tools, out-of-place objects, or mysterious grass circles. I never expected to find these things, yet they turned up anyway—right in front of me, impossible to ignore, defying every attempt to assign a mundane explanation to the occurrences. When ordinary explanations fail, sometimes we're left with just one option.

The impossible.

Or, more accurately, the *seemingly* impossible.

Are all these phenomena related to Bigfoot? The answer is neither simple nor clear. Researchers who desperately want to classify Bigfoot as an undiscovered ape species will answer with an immediate and resounding no. But this is a knee-jerk reaction based more on personal preference than on a thorough investigation of all the evidence. For only by ignoring the seeming impossible, those phenomena deemed too implausible to consider, can those researchers proclaim that Bigfoot absolutely, positively has no relationship to other paranormal phenomena.

If we were studying deer, we would examine the surrounding ecosystem too, in order to understand the relationships between deer and other species, both plant and animal. We would explore the weather to see its possible influence on the deer. Indeed, if we wanted to gain a clear and complete understanding of deer, then we would have to examine everything that might affect the species.

When it comes to Bigfoot, however, we are apparently supposed to wear blinders so that we see nothing except the creature itself. Other, possibly related paranormal phenomena must be ignored. Rather than studying the creature and its ecosystem—which may include other paranormal phenomena—too many researchers want to study Bigfoot as if it exists in a vacuum.

When studying a creature science refuses to acknowledge might possibly exist, we must open ourselves up to the wider environment of the phenomenon.

20
Unidentified Freaky Objects

In both *Backyard Bigfoot* and Part One of this book, I discussed the possibility of a connection between UFOs and Bigfoot. Witnesses have reported seeing the two phenomena together, as well as separately but in the same area. When we think of UFOs, most of us think of large objects flying high above our heads. In *Backyard Bigfoot*, I discussed my sighting of six large lights and the twenty minutes of missing time I experienced. That was neither my first nor my last UFO experience.

A Personal Experience

On March 3, 2010, I witnessed something that remains unexplained to this day. I had not been asleep very long when I was awakened by a mechanical whining sound. The time was 11:19 PM. I sat up to look out the window above my bed, which faces north, expecting to see an airliner heading for the airport. The airliners normally come from the south, heading north. When I looked out the window, however, I saw a light coming from the west and moving approximately eastbound. The craft had one very bright, steady white light near its tail end and a flashing white light near its front end. The "plane" appeared, from my vantage point, to be just above the treetops.

Suddenly, the craft flipped ninety degrees downward, apparently diving straight for the ground. At the same time, the mechanical whining that had sounded similar to a jet engine abruptly changed to a high-pitched scream. The craft disappeared behind the tree line. I fully expected to hear an explosion as the "plane" crashed. Instead, the screaming stopped as suddenly as it had begun at about the same time that the craft sailed out of sight.

The next morning, I called the Houghton County Memorial Airport to ask if they knew of any aircraft in the vicinity at the time of my sighting. I spoke to a friendly lady who informed me that they knew of no aircraft in that area at that time of night. She also said that if a plane is out of contact for fifteen minutes, the FAA gets involved. This apparently did not happen. The airport official then told me that she knew a lot of people in the area claimed to have seen UFOs over the years. She did not ridicule the idea, but rather offered the information without making a judgment about it either way. Next, I called the Coast Guard station. The officer I spoke to reported that they had no aircraft in the vicinity at the time of my sighting.

What I saw is still unexplained.

I've spoken to other people in the local area who have seen strange lights they can't explain either. One man told me of his encounter with a forty-foot-wide glowing orb that passed over the highway near Baraga and then descended into Keweenaw Bay, an arm of Lake Superior. If I could fly like a bird, I'd need to travel just a dozen miles or so to reach Baraga from my home. Other people have seen black orbs, orange orbs, and white lights, all displaying traits that are difficult to explain away as conventional aircraft.

Here in my own literal backyard, I've seen evidence of bizarre lights—in the exact same areas where stick signs and possible Bigfoot tracks have turned up on other occasions.

Caught on Camera

I've seen glowing orbs with my naked eyes. They are not merely digital camera artifacts or dust particles reflecting light. My game cameras have, over the years, caught numerous instances of unexplained glowing orbs. For the past couple years, I've had the capability of taking videos with the game cameras. Those videos have shown strange lighted objects moving back and forth across the field of view. These lights appear on nights with no wind, meaning there's essentially zero chance the orbs are particles or objects being blown into the camera's view.

I present here some of the best orb images captured by the game cameras. Some show animals in the same frame as the orbs. If orbs flit about in the woods on a regular basis, as it would seem they do, then the animal life has clearly become accustomed to them. They pay little attention to the self-illuminated whatsits.

Figure 20.1: The weirdest of the many weird aerial objects my game cameras have captured over the years. This flying whatsit was self-propelled (no wind that night) and cast a shadow on the ground (inset). Two horses are visible, casually grazing, in the background above and to the left of the whatsit. A white salt block sits near the center of the frame. November 21, 2003.

Figure 20.2

An Assortment of Lights

Still photos from game cameras illustrate the wide variety of lighted phenomena. An elongated orb (A) on September 1, 2006; a "string of pearls" (B) on June 1, 2010; a luminous rope (C) hovering above a rabbit on June 11, 2009; a wispy orb (D) in front of a horse on November 14, 2010; and a larger string of pearls (E) near a deer on September 15, 2012. Photos © Lisa A. Shiel.

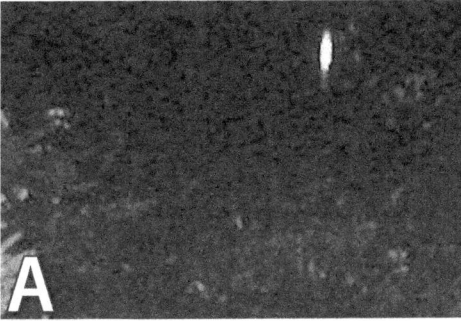

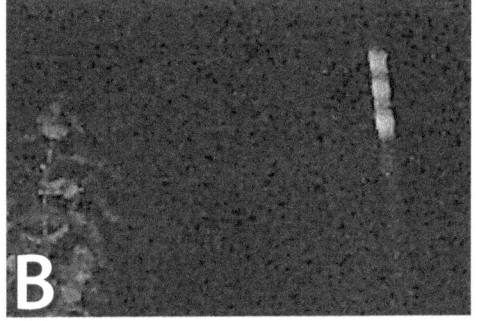

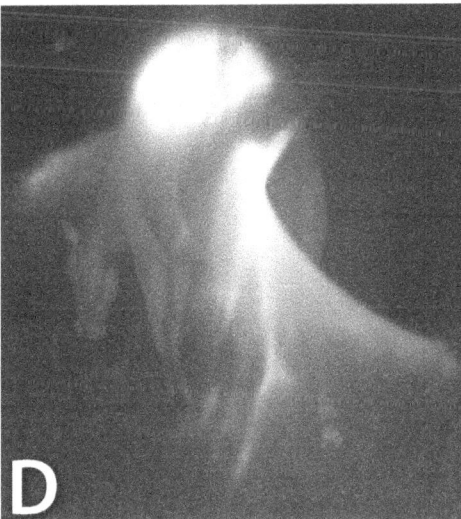

Figure 20.3
Orbs & Deer

Animals seem to either not notice or not care about orbs, since many photos show the two together—such as in these stills taken from game camera videos. First one deer (A) and then another (B) traipses past a hovering orb on June 17, 2011. A single deer moseys by (C) while an orb seems to follow along (D) on November 22, 2011. Photos © Lisa A. Shiel.

Figure 20.4
Orbs in Motion

On November 13, 2011, a game camera took a video of a "string of pearls" light moving from left to right, as if ducking behind a tree. The orb starts out to left of the tree (A), moves closer to it (B), floats higher (C), and finally ducks partway behind the tree again (D). Photos © Lisa A. Shiel.

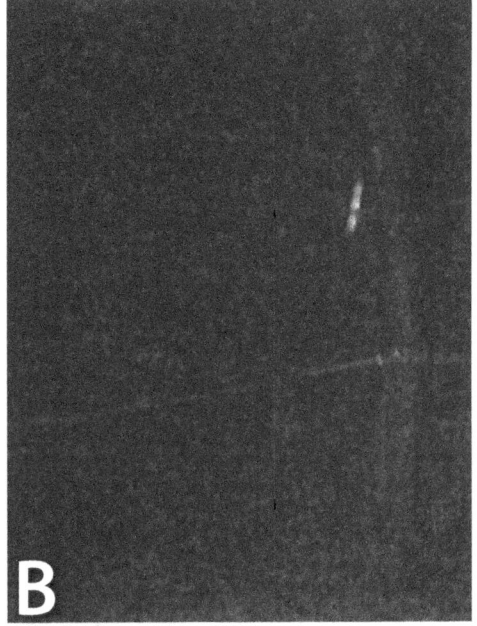

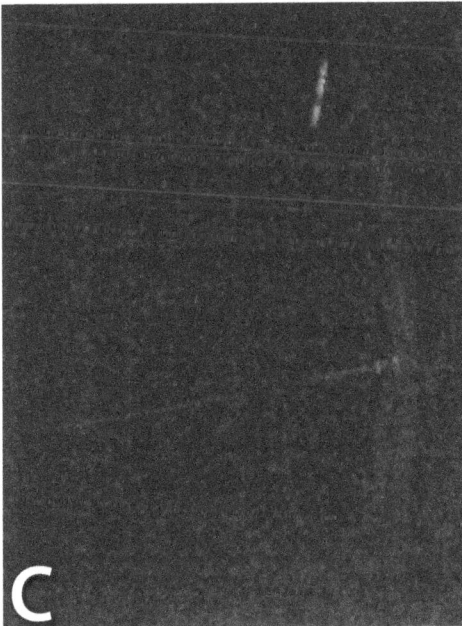

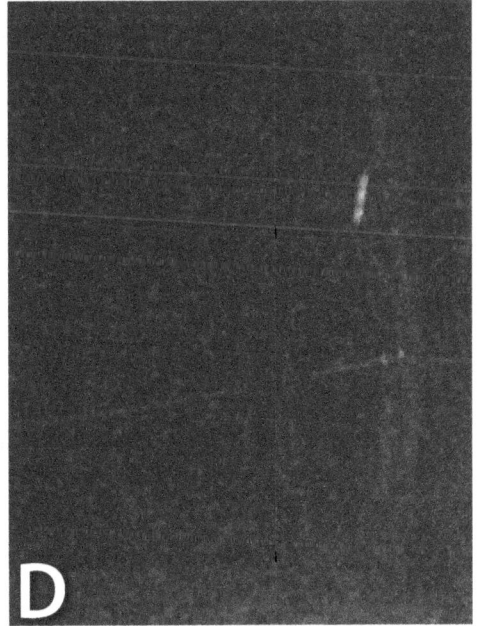

21
The Unending Quest

Researching a topic as controversial as Bigfoot can lead to many headaches, much frustration, and a distinct lack of conclusive evidence. A number of Bigfoot researchers seem to let the inconclusive nature of the phenomenon drive them to hotheaded behavior. They adopt a rigid mindset about what Bigfoot might be, a viewpoint that prevents them from treating the evidence in a rational manner, but instead forces them to discount everything that falls outside the narrow range of their vision. They can't see it because they refuse to see it.

Herein lies the hypocrisy. The Bigfoot researchers who ignore evidence that contradicts their ideas simultaneously proclaim that they are pursuing the Bigfoot mystery in the most scientific way possible. They dismiss those fruitcakes who think Bigfoot's not just an ape, calling them unscientific. But in fact, it is the self-proclaimed scientific Bigfoot researchers who breach the ethics of science.

Dumping data that you don't like is not scientific. Every accepted code of conduct for scientists lists evidence tampering as strictly verboten. This does not simply mean a scientist must not fabricate data. It also means that anyone wishing to pursue any line of research in a scientific manner *must not ignore data*. Yet a disturbing number of Bigfoot researchers say flat-out that they will not consider any sighting involving UFOs or other "paranormal" stuff, so don't bother reporting such sightings to them. These "paranormal" sightings don't appear on the websites of "scientific" Bigfoot researchers because those researchers refuse to accept the submissions or dump them in the virtual trash can immediately upon receipt of the reports.

Ignoring evidence is wholly unscientific.

Just because you can't explain a piece of evidence doesn't mean you get to toss it in the trash and pretend it never existed.

In this book, I've discussed various strange phenomena. Are they all connected to Bigfoot? Are any of them connected to Bigfoot? I don't know the answers. No one does. Thus far, the Bigfoot phenomenon has eluded all attempts to pin it down for scientific study. A phenomenon that cannot be captured cannot be rigorously tested, and testability is a prerequisite for science.

What should we conclude from all this?

The mystery that is Bigfoot shows no signs of finding a resolution anytime soon. Exploring the mystery in a scientific way means not ignoring evidence. The scientific community at large scoffs at any evidence related to Bigfoot. Discarding "paranormal" data will hardly garner approval from mainstream scientists, even if they think evidence tampering is okay. The

Figure 21.1: Just as the universe is filled with galaxies, Bigfoot research is full of possibilities we can only see by looking at the wider environment. Image courtesy of NASA, ESA, and the Hubble Heritage Team (STScI/AURA).

only truly scientific approach is to wade through all the evidence, piece by piece, rejecting old ideas as needed and proposing new ones. Whether Bigfoot proves to be an ape species or a robot from Saturn, one thing is certain.

We won't find the answers by ignoring evidence.

Answers spring from looking at the whole picture and daring to ask the questions raised by what we see. Some of the most treasured ideas in science began as wacko theories. Anybody remember the flat earth concept? At the time, it was the accepted model and its opposite, the notion of a round planet, was the lunatic fringe.

My how things change.

And yet stay the same.

The quest for the truth about Bigfoot unfolds around us every day. The idea of "paranormal" Bigfoot may be today's wacko extreme within the Bigfoot researcher community, but let's not forget that Bigfoot research itself is, to mainstream science, the lunatic fringe.

Once we accept this fact, we are free to explore all avenues of evidence, wherever they might lead us. What awaits in the wider world of Bigfoot research? We will only find out by looking. So take a deep breath, step across the threshold, and open your eyes.

References

Chapter 1

"2010 Census Results, United States and Puerto Rico: Thematic Maps." U.S. Census Bureau, accessed 28 May 2013. http://www.census.gov/geo/maps-data/maps/thematic.html

Knight-Jadczyk, Laura. *High Strangeness: Hyperdimensions and the Process of Alien Abduction.* Grand Prairie, AB: Red Hill Press, 2008.

"Paranormal Poll: Results." About.com Paranormal Phenomena, accessed 27 May 2011. http://paranormal.about.com/library/weekly/aa083099.htm

"State of Observed Species, Retro SOS 2000-2009: A Decade of Species Discovery in Review." International Institute for Species Exploration, Arizona State University. January 18, 2012. http://species.asu.edu/SOS

Chapter 2

Merriam-Webster's Collegiate Dictionary, 11th ed., s.v. "Bigfoot."

Chapter 3

Biello, David. " Stone Tools Push Back Human Occupation of Northern
    Europe by 200,000 Years." *Scientific American*, 15 December 2005. http://
    www.scientificamerican.com/article.cfm?id=stone-tools-push-back-hum
"Genetic Similarities: Wilson, Sarich, Sibley, and Ahlquist." Under-
    standing Evolution. University of California Museum of Paleon-
    tology, accessed 16 December 2011. http://evolution.berkeley.edu/
    evolibrary/article/history_26
"Lists of English Loanwords by Country or Language of Origin." Wikipedia,
    last modified 11 November 2011. https://secure.wikimedia.org/wikipedia/en/
    wiki/Lists_of_English_loanwords_by_country_or_language_of_origin
Merriam-Webster's Collegiate Dictionary, 11th ed., s.v. "Ape."
————., s.v. "Ape-man."
————, s.v. "Belief."
————, s.v. "Believe."
————, s.v. "Human."
————, s.v. "Paranormal."
————, s.v. "Pongidae."
————, s.v. "Supernatural."
Myers, P.Z., R. Espinosa, C. S. Parr, T. Jones, G. S. Hammond, and T. A.
    Dewey. "*Homo sapiens* (human)." Animal Diversity Web. University of
    Michigan Museum of Zoology, 2008. http://animaldiversity.ummz.
    umich.edu/site/accounts/information/Homo_sapiens.html
Pickrell, John. "Humans, Chimps Not as Closely Related as Thought?"
    National Geographic News, 24 September 2002. http://news.national
    geographic.com/news/2002/09/0924_020924_dnachimp.html
Stein, Philip L. "Hominin or Hominid? What's in a Name!" 2006.
    http://faculty.piercecollege.edu/steinp/docs/Paper%202.pdf
WordNet, s.v. "Human." http://wordnet.princeton.edu/perl/webwn?s= human

Chapter 4

Freeman, James S. "Theory, Law and Fact in Science." 2002. http://ola4.
    aacc.edu/jsfreeman/TheoryandLaw.htm
McComas, William F. "The Principal Elements of the Nature of Science:
    Dispelling the Myths." Project to Advance Science Education. http://

coehp.uark.edu/pase/TheMythsOfScience.pdf Adapted from *The Nature of Science in Science Education*. Dordrecht, Neth.: Kluwer Academic Publishers, 1998.

McLelland, Christine V. *The Nature of Science and the Scientific Method*. The Geological Society of America, accessed 7 July 2011. http://www.geosociety.org/educate/NatureScience.pdf

WordNet. s.v. "Scientific Fact." http://wordnetweb.princeton.edu/perl/webwn?s=scientific+fact

Chapter 5

Kanazawa, Satoshi. "Do Extraordinary Claims Require Extraordinary Evidence?" *Psychology Today* blog, 20 March 2011. http://www.psychologytoday.com/blog/the-scientific-fundamentalist/201103/do-extraordinary-claims-require-extraordinary-evidence

McComas, William F. "The Principal Elements of the Nature of Science: Dispelling the Myths." Project to Advance Science Education. http://coehp.uark.edu/pase/TheMythsOfScience.pdf Adapted from *The Nature of Science in Science Education*. Dordrecht, Neth.: Kluwer Academic Publishers, 1998.

McLelland, Christine V. *The Nature of Science and the Scientific Method*. The Geological Society of America, accessed 7 July 2011. http://www.geosociety.org/educate/NatureScience.pdf

Schwarz, Patricia. "So What is String Theory Then?" The Official String Theory Web Site, accessed 5 July 2011. http://superstringtheory.com/basics/basic4.html

Chapter 8

"1997 Humanoid Sighting Reports." Compiled by Albert Rosales. http://www.ufoinfo.com/humanoid/humanoid1977.shtml

Bord, Janet. *Fairies: Real Encounters with the Little People*. New York: Dell Publishing, 1997.

Bord, Janet, and Colin Bord. *The Bigfoot Casebook*. Harrisburg, PA: Stackpole Books, 1982.

"Eagle River Close Encounter (Man Given 'Pancakes' by UFO Occupants)." UFO Evidence: Scientific Study of the UFO Phenomenon and the

Search for Extraterrestrial Life, accessed 24 January 2012. http://www.ufoevidence.org/cases/case708.htm

Evans-Wentz, W.Y. *The Fairy-Faith in Celtic Countries*. London: Oxford University Press, 1911. Reprint, New York: Citadel Press, 1994.

Gustafson, Don, and Noreen Gustafson. "Burnt Bluff Caves and Pictographs." Central States Archaeological Societies, n.d. http://www.csasi.org/2000_october_journal/page_160_161.htm

Lewis, David. "Veridical Hallucinations and Prosthetic Vision." In *Vision and Mind: Selected Readings in the Philosophy of Perception*. Alva Noë, ed. Cambridge, Mass.: The MIT Press, 2002. p. 135-150.

Merriam-Webster's Collegiate Dictionary, 11th ed., s.v. "Veridical Hallucination."

Redfern, Nick. "Absurdities of the UFO Kind." Mysterious Universe, 19 March 2011. http://mysteriousuniverse.org/2011/03/absurdities-of-the-ufo-kind/

Retrieving Michigan's Buried Past: The Archaeology of the Great Lakes State. Ed. by John R. Halsey and Michael D. Stafford. Bloomfield Hills, MI: Cranbrook Institute of Science, 1999.

Sighting Report. National UFO Reporting Center website, 3 Apr. 2005. http://www.nuforc.org/webreports/015/S15938.html

"Telepathy as the Negation of Personal Survival after Death." Edward J. Wheeler, ed. In *Current Literature*, XLVI(1). The Current Literature Publishing Company: New York, January 1909. p. 208-210.

Vallee, Jacques. *Dimensions: A Casebook of Alien Contact*. New York: Ballantine Books, 1988.

Webster, Michael. "Tricksters." The World Mythology Course. Grand Valley State University, 2005. http://faculty.gvsu.edu/websterm/Tricksters.htm

Zubritsky, Elizabeth. "The Mysterious Roving Rocks of Racetrack Playa." NASA's Goddard Space Flight Center, 11 August 2010. http://www.nasa.gov/topics/earth/features/roving-rocks.html

Chapter 9

"Administrative Actions." The Office of Research Integrity (ORI), 7 March 2011. http://ori.dhhs.gov/administrative-actions

Fanelli, Daniele. "How Many Scientists Fabricate and Falsify Research? A Systematic Review and Meta-Analysis of Survey Data." *PLoS One*, 4(5): e5738. http://www.plosone.org/article/

info%3Adoi%2F10.1371%2Fjournal.pone.0005738

Fang, Ferris C., R. Grant Steen, and Arturo Casadevall. " Misconduct Accounts for the Majority of Retracted Scientific Publications." *Proceedings of the National Academy of Sciences*, 109(42):17028-17033. http://www.ncbi.nlm.nih.gov/pubmed/23027971

Powell, Thom. *The Locals: A Contemporary Investigation of the Bigfoot/ Sasquatch Phenomenon.* Blaine, WA: Hancock House, 2003.

Kelleher, Colm A., and George Knapp. *Hunt for the Skinwalker: Science Confronts the Unexplained at a Remote Ranch in Utah.* New York: Paraview Pocket Books, 2005.

"PHS Administrative Action Report." The Office of Research Integrity (ORI), 2 July 2013. http://ori.dhhs.gov/ORI_PHS_alert.html

Vallee, Jacques. *Dimensions: A Casebook of Alien Contact.* New York: Ballantine Books, 1988.

Chapter 10

"All-Day Symposium for Sasquatch Falcon Project Set June 22 in Portland." *Idaho State Journal*, 13 June 2013. http://www.idahostatejournal.com/ news/local/article_78b55ba8-d474-11e2-87b8-0019bb2963f4.html

"The Coelacanth: More Living than Fossil." Natural History Highlight. May 2003, Smithsonian Institution. http://www.mnh.si.edu/ highlight/coelacanth/

"Legendary Cryptids That Turned out to Be Absolutely Real." io9. http:// io9.com/5814976/cryptids-that-turned-out-be-absolutely-real

Merriam-Webster's Collegiate Dictionary, 11th ed., s.v. "Cryptozoology."

Merriam-Webster's Third New International Dictionary, Unabridged, s.v. "Crypto-."

"The Search Begins." The Falcon Project, n.d. Accessed 14 June 2013. http://the-falconproject.com/main_site/?p=492

Chapter 11

Angier, Natalie. "Scientists and Philosophers Find That 'Gene' Has a Multitude of Meanings." *New York Times*, 11 November 2008. http:// www.nytimes.com/2008/11/11/science/11angi.html

Berger, Eric. "I Had the 'Bigfoot DNA' Tested in a Highly Reputable Lab: Here's What I Found." *Houston Chronicle* SciGuy blog, 1 July 2013. http://blog.chron.com/sciguy/2013/07/i-had-the-bigfoot-dna-tested-in-a-highly-reputable-lab-heres-what-i-found/

Berger, Lee R., Darryl J. de Ruiter, Steven E. Churchill, Peter Schmid, Kristian J. Carlson, et al. "*Australopithecus sediba*: A New Species of *Homo*-like Australopith from South Africa." *Science*, 328(5975): 195-204.

"Bigfoot DNA Sequenced in Upcoming Genetics Study." DNA Diagnostics Inc., 24 November 2012. Accessed 21 February 2013. http://www.dnadiagnostics.com/press.html

Bolden, Kristen. "DNA Fabrication, a Wake-Up Call: The Need to Reevaluate the Admissibility and Reliability of DNA Evidence." *Georgia State University Law Review*, 27(2): 409-41.

Bower, Bruce. "Fossil Finds Give New Details on Ancient Relative: Species Proposed to Have Given Rise to First Humans." *Science News*, 180(9): 14.

Bradley, Robert D., and Robert J. Baker. "A Test of the Genetic Species Concept: Cytochrome-b Sequences and Mammals." *Journal of Mammology*. 82(4): 960-973.

"Case Summary—Luk Van Parijs." *Federal Register*, 74(14). http://ori.dhhs.gov/misconduct/cases/VanParijs.shtml

Ciochon, Russell L. "The Mystery Ape of Pleistocene Asia." *Nature*, 459(7249): 910-11.

———. "The Ape That Was: Asian Fossils Reveal Humanity's Giant Cousin." *Natural History*, November 1991. http://www.uiowa.edu/~bioanth/giganto.html

Cossins, Dan. "Bigfoot DNA Is Bunk." *The Scientist*, 15 February 2013. http://www.the-scientist.com/?articles.view/articleNo/34395/title/Bigfoot-DNA-is-Bunk/

Culotta, Elizabeth. "Spanish Fossil Sheds New Light on the Oldest Great Apes." *Science*, 306 (5700): 1273-1274.

Curry, Andrew. "Ancient Excrement: An unexpected Source of Human DNA Resets the Clock on the Settlement of the Americas." *Archaeology*, 61(4): 42-5.

Dalton, Rex. "Fossil Finger Points to New Human Species: DNA Analysis Reveals Lost Relative from 40,000 Years Ago." *Nature*, 464(7288): 472.

Darwin, Charles. *The Origin of Species by Means of Natural Selection.* 1859. Reprint of the 1st edition with an introduction and notes by George Levine. New York: Barnes & Noble, 2004.

Dewey, Tanya. "Classification: Reconciling Old & New Systems." Animal Diversity Web. University of Michigan Museum of Zoology, 2006. http://animaldiversity.ummz.umich.edu/site/animal_names/rank_inconsistency.html

"Evidence Collection and Preservation." In *What Every Law Enforcement Officer Should Know about DNA Evidence.* DNA Initiative/Department of Justice. http://www.dna.gov/audiences/investigators/know/collection/

"Finding Lucy" (Quicktime video file), 4 min., 33 sec.; from Evolution Library, WGBH Educational Foundation and Clear Blue Sky Productions, Inc., 2001. http://www.pbs.org/wgbh/evolution/library/07/1/l_071_01.html

Foley, Jim. "Fossil Hominids: Mitochondrial DNA." Fossil Hominids FAQ. TalkOrigins Archive, 22 May 2011. http://www.talkorigins.org/faqs/homs/mtDNA.html

———. "Hominid Species." Fossil Hominids FAQ. TalkOrigins Archive, 31 October 2004. http://www.talkorigins.org/faqs/homs/species.html

Geere, Duncan. "Oxford University to Probe 'Yeti' DNA." *Wired*, 22 May 2012. http://www.wired.co.uk/news/archive/2012-05/22/yeti-dna

"Genealogy Enthusiasts Mine DNA for Clues to Evolutionary History." Understanding Evolution. University of California Museum of Paleontology, November 2007. http://evolution.berkeley.edu/evolibrary/news/071101_genealogy

"German DNA Mix-Up Ends Search for Suspected Killer." *The Guardian*, 27 March 2009. http://www.guardian.co.uk/world/feedarticle/8425898

Gibbons, Ann. "Glasnost for Hominids." *Science*, 297 (5586): 1464-1460.

———. "In Search of the First Hominids." *Science*, 295 (5558): 1214.

Guynup, Sharon. "The Mating Game: Ligers, Zorses, Wholphins, and Other Hybrid Animals Raise a Beastly Science Question—What Is a Species?" *Science World*, 24 January 2003.

Harrell, Eben. "Scientists Discover an Ancient Human Relative." *Time*, 24 March 2010. http://www.time.com/time/health/article/0,8599,1974903,00.html

Himmelreich, Claudia. "Germany's Phantom Serial Killer: A DNA Blunder." *Time*, 27 March 2009. http://www.time.com/time/world/article/0,8599,1888126,00.html

Ishida, Yasuko, Yirmed Demeke, Peter J. van Coeverden de Groot, Nicholas J. Georgiadis, Keith E. A. Leggett, et al. "Distinguishing Forest and Savanna African Elephants Using Short Nuclear DNA Sequences." Journal of Heredity, 102(5), 610-616.

"ITIS Standard Report Page: *Homo sapiens*." Integrated Taxonomic Information System. Accessed 29 June 2013. http://www.itis.gov/servlet/SingleRpt/SingleRpt?search_topic=TSN&search_value=180092

Kerr, Kevin C. R., Mark Y. Stoeckle, Carla J. Dove, Lee A. Weight, Charles M. Francis, and Paul D. N. Herbert. "Comprehensive DNA Barcode Coverage of North American Birds." *Molecular Ecology Notes*, 7(4), 535-543.

Krause, Johannes, Qiaomei Fu, Jeffrey M. Good, Bence Viola, Michael V. Shunkov, et al. "The Complete Mitochondrial DNA Genome of an Unknown Hominin from Southern Siberia." *Nature*, 464(7290): 894-97.

Little, Emma. "Bigfoot: It's Yogi Not Yeti." *The Sun* (UK), 3 February 2013. http://www.thesun.co.uk/sol/homepage/news/4776098/Yeti-which-has-terrorised-Russians-for-3yrs-is-really-a-bear-from-the-US.html

Mallet, James. "A Species Definition for the Modern Synthesis." *Trends in Ecology and Evolution*. 10: 7 (294-299).

Malory, Marcia. "Bigfoot Genome Sequenced? There Are Skeptics." Phys.org, 19 February 2013. http://phys.org/news/2013-02-bigfoot-genome-sequenced-skeptics.html

Marks, Jonathan. "Phylogenetic Trees and Evolutionary Forests." *Evolutionary Anthropology*, 14(2):49-53.

Masters, J.C. "Primates and Paradigms: Problems with the Identification of Genetic Species." In *Species, Species Concepts, and Primate Evolution*, edited by William H. Kimbel and Lawrence B. Martin. New York: Plenum Press, 1993. p. 43-66.

Mattison, Ray H., and Robert A. Grom. Edited by Joanne W. Stockert. *History of Badlands National Monument and the White River (Big) Badlands of South Dakota*. Badlands Natural History Association, 1968. Reprinted at http://www.nps.gov/history/history/online_books/badl/index.htm

McKie, Robin. *Dawn of Man: The Story of Human Evolution*. New York: Dorling Kindersley, 2000.

"Melba Ketchum." Facebook page, accessed 2 July 2013. https://www.facebook.com/melba.ketchum

Merriam-Webster's Collegiate Dictionary, 11th ed., s.v. "Holotype."

————, 11th ed., s.v. "Type Specimen."

Myers, P.Z., R. Espinosa, C. S. Parr, T. Jones, G. S. Hammond, and T. A. Dewey. "*Homo sapiens*: Classification." Animal Diversity Web. University of Michigan Museum of Zoology, 2013. http://animaldiversity.ummz.umich.edu/accounts/Homo_sapiens/classification/#Homo_sapiens

Noor, Mohamed A.F., and Jeffrey L. Feder. "Speciation Genetics: Evolving Approaches." *Nature Reviews Genetics*, 7(11): 851-860.

Oxford Dictionaries, s.v. "Metazoa." http://oxforddictionaries.com/us/definition/american_english/Metazoa

"Phenotype." Glossary (Understanding Evolution). University Of California Museum of Paleontology, 2008. http://evolution.berkeley.edu/evolibrary/glossary/glossary.php?start=n&end=r

Pollack, Andrew. "DNA Evidence Can Be Fabricated, Scientists Show." *New York Times*, 17 August 2009. http://www.nytimes.com/2009/08/18/science/18dna.html

"Reproductive Isolation." Understanding Evolution. University of California Museum of Paleontology, 2008. http://evolution.berkeley.edu/evolibrary/article/evo_44

Schwartz, Jeffrey H., with response by Tim White. "Another Perspective on Hominid Diversity." *Science*, 301 (5634): 763 (2).

"Species and Subspecies." Centennial Museum/Department of Biological Sciences, University of Texas at El Paso, 18 January 2008. http://museum utep.edu/mammalogy/species.htm

Stringer, Christopher & Robin McKie. *African Exodus; The Origins of Modern Humanity*. New York: Owl Books, 1996.

Tattersall, Ian, and Jeffrey H. Schwartz. "Is Paleoanthropology Science? Naming New Fossils and Control of Access to Them." *The Anatomical Record*, 269: 239-241.

"Taxonomic Information for Human (*Homo sapiens*)." Encyclopedia of Life. Accessed 29 June 2013. http://eol.org/pages/327955/names

Trinkaus, Eric. "Denisova Cave, Peştera cu Oase, and Human Divergence in the Late Pleistocene." *PaleoAnthropology*, 2010: 196-200. http://www.paleoanthro.org/journal/content/PA20100196.pdf

"What Is a Gene?" Genetics Home Reference: Your Guide to Understanding Genetic Conditions. U.S. National Library of Medicine, 4 May 2009. http://ghr.nlm.nih.gov/handbook/basics/gene

White, Tim. "Early Hominids—Diversity Or Distortion?" *Science*, 299 (5615): 1994-1996.

Wilkins, John. "A List of 26 Species Concepts." Evolving Thoughts blog, 1 October 2006. http://scienceblogs.com/evolvingthoughts/2006/10/a_list_of_26_species_concepts.php

Windows to the Universe Team. "The Domain Eukaryota." Boulder, CO: National Earth Science Teachers Association, 27 October 2008. http://www.windows2universe.org/earth/Life/classification_eukaryota.html

Wright, Sylvia. "In Research: Surprise: Hybrid Salamander Species Thriving." *Dateline UC Davis*, 28 September 2007. http://www.dateline.ucdavis.edu/dl_detail.lasso?id=9743

Zamanskaya, Yulia. "Bigfoot Is Real, Claims Geneticist After Sequencing Genomes in DNA Study." *Albany Tribune* (Oregon), 2 March 2013. http://www.albanytribune.com/02032013-bigfoot-is-real-claims-geneticist-after-sequencing-genomes-in-dna-study/

Zorich, Zach. "Neanderthal Genome Decoded: Paleogenetics Shows Our Ancient Cousins Aren't So Extinct." *Archaeology*, 63(4): 36-7.

———. "Should We Clone Neanderthals? The Scientific, Legal, and Ethical Obstacles." *Archaeology*, 63(2): 34-41.

Chapter 12

Benton, Michael J. "Fossil Record: Quality." *eLS*. Wiley Online Library, 2005. http://onlinelibrary.wiley.com/doi/10.1038/npg.els.0004144/full

"The Bigfoot-Giganto Theory." Bigfoot Field Researchers Organization, 2005. http://www.bfro.net/ref/theories/mjm/whatrtha.asp

Bower, Bruce. "Red-Ape Stroll: Orangutans Step into the Evolutionary Fray over How We Became Upright." *Science News*, 172(5): 72-3.

ChangZu, Jin, Qin DaGong, Pan WenShi, Tang ZhiLu, Liu JinYi, et al. "Discovered Gigantopithecus Fauna from Sanhe Cave, Chongzuo, Guangxi, South China." *Chinese Science Bulletin*, 54(5): 788-97.

Christmas, Jane. "Giant Ape Lived Alongside Humans." *McMaster Daily News*, McMaster University, 7 November 2005. http://dailynews. mcmaster.ca/story.cfm?id=3637

Ciochon, Russell, John Olsen, and Jamie James. *Other Origins: The Search for the Giant Ape in Human Prehistory*. New York: Bantam Books, 1990.

Ciochon, Russell, Vu The Long, Roy Larick, Luis González, Rainer Grün, et al. "Dated Co-occurrence of *Homo Erectus* and *Gigantopithecus* from Tham Khuyen Cave, Vietnam." *Proceedings of the National Academy of Sciences*, 93(7): 3016-20.

Cowen, Richard. *History of Life*. Malden, MA: Blackwell Science, 2000.

Foley, Jim. "Hominid Species." Fossil Hominids FAQ. TalkOrigins Archive, 31 October 2004. http://www.talkorigins.org/faqs/homs/species.html

Gore, Pamela J.W. "Fossil Preservation Lab." 2006. Historical Geology Online Laboratory Manual. http://facstaff.gpc.edu/~pgore/geology/ historical_lab/2010Preservation.pdf

Krantz, Grover. *Bigfoot Sasquatch Evidence*. Blaine, WA: Hancock House, 1999.

Leggett, Mike. "Primatologist: If Bigfoot Exists, It's Not an Ape." *Austin Statesman*, 4 October 2009. http://www.statesman.com/sports/content/ sports/stories/outdoors/2009/10/04/1004bigfootside.html

Luoys, Julien, Darren Curnoe, and Haowen Tong. "Characteristics of Pleistocene Megafauna Extinctions in Southeast Asia." *Palaeogeography, Palaeoclimatology, Palaeoecology*, 243(2007): 152-73.

McKie, Robin. *Dawn of Man: The Story of Human Evolution*. New York: Dorling Kindersley, 2000.

Miller, Steven F., Jessica L. White, and Russell L. Ciochon. "Assessing Mandibular Shape Variation within *Gigantopithecus* Using a Geometric Morphometric Approach." *American Journal of Physical Anthropology*, 137(2): 201-12.

"Mountain Gorilla." African Wildlife Foundation. Accessed 14 December 2011. http://www.awf.org/content/wildlife/detail/mountaingorilla

O'Neil, Dennis. "The Primates: Apes." 2005. http://anthro.palomar. edu/primate/prim_7.htm

Pettifor, Eric. "From the Teeth of the Dragon: *Gigantopithecus blacki*." In *Selected Readings in Physical Anthropology*, ed. Peggy Scully.

Dubuque, IA: Kendall/Hunt Publishing, 2000. 143-49. http://www.wynja.com/arch/gigantopithecus.html

Treiman, Allan. "The Grand Canyon: The Great Unconformity." The Great Desert: Geology and Life on Mars and in the Southwest. Houston, TX: Lunar & Planetary Institute, 23 September 2003. http://www.lpi.usra.edu/science/treiman/greatdesert/workshop/greatunconf/index.html

Windows to the Universe Team. "What Is a Fossil?" Boulder, CO: National Earth Science Teachers Association, 11 June 2009. http://www.windows2universe.org/earth/geology/fossil_intro.html

Wayman, Erin. "Did Bigfoot Really Exist? How *Gigantopithecus* Became Extinct." *Smithsonian Magazine,* 9 January 2012. http://blogs.smithsonianmag.com/hominids/2012/01/did-bigfoot-really-exist-how-gigantopithecus-became-extinct/

Chapter 13

Bord, Janet, and Colin Bord. *The Bigfoot Casebook*. Harrisburg, PA: Stackpole Books, 1982.

Conley, C., and G. Kminek. "Introduction to Planetary Protection and Biological Contamination." EJSM Short Course on Planetary Protection, 29 July 2010. http://opfm.jpl.nasa.gov/files/audios/PP-EJSM-Short-Course_noAudio.pdf

Darling, David. "Earthlights." The Encyclopedia of Science. http://www.daviddarling.info/encyclopedia/E/earthlight.html

Drew, Amy. "The Wide Angle: Top 10 Eccentric Transgenic Animals." Discovery Tech, accessed 24 January 2012. http://dsc.discovery.com/technology/tech-10/genetic-engineering/10-transgenic-animals.html

Fort, Charles. *The Book of the Damned*. New York: Boni & Liveright, 1919.

Fountain, Henry. "Water Bears Triumph over Outer Space." *New York Times,* 11 September 2008. http://www.nytimes.com/2008/09/16/science/space/16obvacu.html

"Geographic Database of Bigfoot/Sasquatch Sightings and Reports." Bigfoot Field Researchers Organization. Accessed December 2, 2011. http://bfro.net/GDB/

Handwerk, Brian. "Ball Lightning: A Shocking Scientific Mystery." National Geographic News, 31 May 2006. http://news.national geographic.com/news/2006/05/060531-ball-lightning.html

Lindahl, Karen, and Susie Balser. "Tardigrades Facts." Species Distribution Project/Illinois Wesleyan University, 2 October 1999. http://www.iwu.edu/~tardisdp/tardigrade_facts.html

Muir, Hazel. "Could These Be the Right Balls of Fire?" *New Scientist*, 193(2586): 12.

"Population Estimates: State Totals, Vintage 2011." U.S. Census Bureau, accessed 23 January 2012. http://www.census.gov/popest/data/state/totals/2011/

"Report Index by State/Province." National UFO Reporting Center. Accessed December 2, 2011. http://www.nuforc.org/webreports/ndxloc.html

Salleh, Anna. "Ball Lightning Bamboozles Physicist." ABC News (Australia), 20 March 2008. http://www.abc.net.au/science/articles/2008/03/20/2194630.htm?site=science&topic=latest

"Voyager: The Interstellar Mission." NASA/JPL. http://voyager.jpl.nasa.gov/

"Western Bigfoot Society meeting report for October 1st, 2011." October 3, 2011. http://bigfootology.com/?p=918

Chapter 14

Bahn, Paul G., and Jean Vertut. *Journey Through the Ice Age*. London: Seven Dials, 1999.

Burenhalt, Goran (ed.). *The First Humans: Human Origins & History to 10,000 BC. (The Illustrated History of Humankind, Vol. 1)*. New York: Harper Collins, 1993.

"Cavetowns and Gorges of Cappadocia." Adventures Great and Small, accessed 25 January 2012. http://www.great-adventures.com/destinations/turkey/cappadocia.html

Creamer, Winifred, and Jonathan Haas. "Pueblo: Search for the Ancient Ones." *National Geographic*, October 1991: 84-99.

Cremo, Michael A., and Richard L. Thompson. *Forbidden Archeology: The Hidden History of the Human Race*. Los Angeles: Bhaktivedanta Book Publishing, 1998.

"Derinkuyu Underground City." Wikipedia, last modified 22 January 2012. https://en.wikipedia.org/wiki/Derinkuyu_Underground_City

Gathorne-Hardy, F.J., and W.E.H. Harcourt-Smith. "The Super-Eruption of Toba, Did It Cause a Human Bottleneck?" *Journal of Human Evolution*, 45(2003): 227-230.

"Giants in the Mountains: The Search for Sasquatch." Washington State Historical Society, accessed 25 January 2012. http://www.wshs.org/wshm/featuredexhibits/giantsinthemountains.aspx

Hancock, Graham. *Fingerprints of the Gods: The Evidence of Earth's Lost Civilization*. New York: Three Rivers Press, 1995.

———. *Underworld: The Mysterious Origins of Civilization*. New York: Crown Publishers, 2002.

"Is Still at Large: Crystal Falls Wild Man Escapes Capture by Searching Party." *The Sault News-Record*, 15 October 1901.

"Magnitude 9.1—Off the West Coast of Northern Sumatra." U.S. Geological Survey, accessed 7 February 2012. http://earthquake.usgs.gov/earthquakes/eqinthenews/2004/us2004slav/

Marshack, Alexander. "An Ice Age Ancestor?" *National Geographic*, Oct. 1998: 478-481.

Noble, David Grant. *Ancient Ruins of the Southwest: An Archaeological Guide*. Flagstaff, AZ: Northland Publishing, 2000.

Roberts, David. "The Old Ones of the Southwest." *National Geographic*, April 1996: 86-109.

"Story of the Deer River Wild Man." *The Sault News-Record*, 17 December 1901.

"The Alleged Wildman Discovered by Crystal Falls Hunters." *The Sault News-Record*, 11 October 1901.

"Wild Man Near Crystal Falls." *The Ironwood News Record*, 12 October 1901.

"Wild Man Near Crystal Falls." *The Sault News-Record*, 10 October 1901.

Chapter 18

Bayanov, Dmitri. *In The Footsteps of the Russian Snowman*. Moscow: Crypto-Logos Publishers, 1996.

Dorson, Richard M. *Bloodstoppers & Bearwalkers: Folk Traditions of the Upper Peninsula*. Cambridge: Harvard University Press, 1952.

Dowie, Mark. "Pony Destroyed after Incidents." *The Montrose Review*, 4 February 2010. http://www.montrosereview.co.uk/news/local-headlines/pony-destroyed-after-incidents-1-342792

Evans-Wentz, W.Y. *The Fairy-Faith in Celtic Countries*. London: Oxford University Press, 1911. Reprint, New York: Citadel Press, 1994.

Grimm, Jacob. *Teutonic Mythology*, 4th ed. Translated by James Steven Stallybrass. London: George Bell & Sons, 1888.

Harpur, Patrick. "Straight from the Horse's Mane." *Fortean Times*, March 2010. http://www.forteantimes.com/features/articles/3016/straight_from_the_horses_mane.html

Morris, Steven. "Animal Magic as Warlock Reveals Mystery Behind Plaits Found in Horses' Manes." *The Guardian*, 7 December 2009. http://www.guardian.co.uk/world/2009/dec/07/horse-mane-plaits-magic-ritual

"Mr. John Pomroy, Who Resides on a Farm A Few Miles from Here." *The Copper Country Evening News*, 19 December 1896.

"Police Warn Horse Owners over Blidworth Mystery Mane Plaits." *The Nottingham Post*, 21 July 2012. http://www.thisisnottingham.co.uk/Police-warn-horse-owners-Blidworth-mystery-mane/story-16573880-detail/story.html

Williams, Rob. " Bigfoot on the loose? Residents report an eight-foot hairy apeman with demonic red eyes stalking Tunbridge Wells." *The Independent*, 22 November 2012. http://www.independent.co.uk/news/uk/home-news/bigfoot-on-the-loose-residents-report-an-eightfoot-hairy-apeman-with-demonic-red-eyes-stalking-tunbridge-wells-8344020.html

Redfern, Nick. "Bigfoot in Britain?" Cryptomundo blog, 1 September 2012. http://www.cryptomundo.com/bigfoot/bigfoot-in-britain/

Chapter 19

O'Neil, Dennis. "Hand Ax." Glossary of Terms. Accessed 30 January 2013. http://anthro.palomar.edu/homo2/glossary.htm#hand_ax

———. "Oldowan Tool Tradition." Glossary of Terms. Accessed 30 January 2013. http://anthro.palomar.edu/homo2/glossary.htm#Oldowan_Tool_Tradition

————. "Hominin Biological and Cultural Evolution." Accessed 30 January 2013. http://anthro.palomar.edu/homo2/table_of_hominin_evolution.htm

Chapter 21

"Participants in Science Behave Scientifically." What Is Science? Understanding Science. University of California Museum of Paleontology, accessed 23 January 2013. http://undsci.berkeley.edu/article/0_0_0/whatisscience_09

Index

Page numbers in **bold italics** refer to images.

A

abductions 60, 69
Acheulian hand axes 233
adaptive radiation 123
advice for researching Bigfoot 101–102,
    181, 217–218
Afar region (Ethiopia) 120, *121*
Aine (fairy goddess) 67
Air Force 70
airships (UFOs) 62
Algonquian Indians 68
aliens. *See* UFOs
almasty 224
Altman, Eric
  biography xxi
  quotes 6, 11, 16, 18, 19, 37, 39–40,
      43, 45, 47, 51
American Bigfoot Society. *See* Hovey,
    Melissa
American Samoa *168*
Anasazi
  cliff dwellings 172, *173*, 174

Anasazi, cont.
  disappearance of 172, 174
  evidence of warfare 172–173
  watchtowers *173*, 174
Ancient Aliens (TV series) 166
ancient astronaut theory 167
ancient depictions of Bigfoot 68–69,
    161–163, 174
animals
  surviving outer space 157
  transgenic 158
Antarctic ice cores 168
apes
  defined 22
  fossils 120–121, 124–125, 134–139
  vs. ape-men 22–23
apples balanced in trees 234–236
apple thrown from above 236
Archaeology magazine 105, 119
Ardipithecus 120, 123
artificial DNA 109

tracks of Bigfoot. *See* footprints
transgenics 158–160
trees, out-of-place objects in 234–237
tricksters, defined 69
tsunamis 169
Turkey, ancient cultures of 175–176
twine lodged in tree 234
type specimen
    defined 104
    as proof of Bigfoot 125–126

U

UFOs. *See also* sightings: Bigfoot-UFO
        sightings; glowing orbs; sightings:
        UFO sightings
    affinity for water 67
    as paranormal 73–74
    ball lightning as 151
    behavior, hypothetical 157
    flying paper plate *244*
    food gifts 70
    genetic research 157–160
    ignoring evidence 56–57
    the Invisible World and 62
    mass extinctions, possible role in 158
    scientists' involvement 84
unconformities 131–132
underground cities, ancient 175–176
Underworld (book) 168
unethical practices. *See* Bigfoot
        research: unethical practices;
        scientists: misconduct
unidentified submersible objects (USOs) 67
uninhabited land 4–5
University of California, Berkeley 108, 120
University of Edinburgh 79
"unknown primate" designation 104, 125, 133
Unzelman, Steven 67

V

Vallee, Jacques 76
veridical hallucinations 63–64

Vietnam, map of *138*
visions 62–63
vocalizations 78, 164, 192, 218
volcanic eruptions 167–168

W

Wallace, Alfred Russel 183
warfare
    between Bigfoot and humans 180
    evidence of ancient 172, 174
Washington State History Museum 161
watchtowers, ancient *173*, 174
water bears 157
Weidenreich, Franz 134
White, Tim 122
whooping calls 192
wild men
    described 164
    German wild man *56*
    historical accounts 164, 223
    Kwakiutl costume *164*
    in traveling sideshows 164
Willerslev, Eske 119
Wiltshire (England) *165*
Winchell, Alexander 170
wisdom, imparting of 60, 62, 64
witnesses. *See* sightings
wood knocking 65, 78
Wookies 145

Z

zoologist, defined 95

Lisa A. Shiel researches and writes about everything strange, from Bigfoot and UFOs to alternative history and science. She has a master's degree in library science and previously served as president of the Upper Peninsula Publishers & Authors Association. As a fiction writer, Lisa blends her paranormal interests with sci-fi and romance elements to create her own brand of adventure stories. Her fiction works include short story collections as well as the other novels in the Human Origins Series —including *The Hunt for Bigfoot*, *Lord of the Dead*, and *Relic of the Ancient Ones*. Lisa's non-fiction books explore topics as diverse as Bigfoot, evolution, and Michigan's quirky history.

www.LisaShiel.com

www.ingramcontent.com/pod-product-compliance
Lightning Source LLC
Chambersburg PA
CBHW031827090426
42741CB00005B/157